Manual of Public Relations

Manual of Public Relations

PAT BOWMAN *and* NIGEL ELLIS

Forewords by

HERBERT LLOYD, *President*
The Institute of Public Relations

and

JOHN DODGE, *Director*
National Council for the Training of Journalists

HEINEMANN : LONDON

William Heinemann Ltd

LONDON MELBOURNE TORONTO
JOHANNESBURG AUCKLAND

Printed in Great Britain by C. Tinling & Co. Ltd
London and Prescot

Forewords

The literature of public relations is growing rapidly. This is excellent, since a man can only learn his job by practising it and reading about it.

This particular contribution by two highly experienced public relations men fills one outstanding need. It gives the student a comprehensive range of entirely practical advice on the workings of the craft he is entering. Anyone, whether in public relations or still outside it, who reads it and makes proper use of it cannot fail to become better at his job and better equipped to pass The Institute of Public Relations examinations.

Public relations is now a significant part of our daily life and the IPR is achieving the standing for the profession that it deserves. The service rendered by practitioners is of the highest quality. Organized, skilful, and well-devised programmes of public relations activity have an undeniable place in modern society.

This book will help newcomers to operate more efficiently. I am glad to commend it.

HERBERT LLOYD, FIPR
*President, The Institute of
Public Relations*

Journalists and public relations men, now inextricably part of each other's world, are often at loggerheads. This book should help mutual understanding in two ways. It explains simply and cogently the scope of public relations and sets out basic standards of good practice. This makes it a textbook which will be of value to trainee journalists and PR students alike.

JOHN DODGE
*Director, National Council for
the Training of Journalists*

Why this book was written

There are a number of sound British books on public relations, but most of them are intended for the practising professional and are only of partial value to the student. There has long been a need for a book designed specifically for the beginner and for the student taking the examinations of The Institute of Public Relations. This book is just that, and its content is closely related to the IPR educational syllabus.

The book gives detailed advice on many aspects of the intricate craft of public relations. It also offers the student an outline introduction to subjects of which he needs some knowledge, but in which he may not become deeply involved. On some topics it is necessarily simplified, for reasons of length as well as of assimilation by the student with limited experience. It does not attempt to answer all his questions, not only because no one can be expert in every aspect of public relations, but also because it is a business in which solutions usually have to be tailored to particular problems.

With this book, the student should be able to make the most of his own imagination and initiative. Practice and experience will do the rest.

We would like to thank the many people who over the years have made it possible for us to collect the experience that has gone into this book. Some of our colleagues and friends in public relations have given useful advice. In particular, Mrs. Amanda Barry, chairman of the IPR education committee, contributed to the chapter on entry and training; and Roy Brewer, editor of *British Printer*, and Richard Millett, senior marketing executive of Astral Marketing Ltd., advised on the chapters on print and research respectively.

PAT BOWMAN, FIPR, MAIE

NIGEL ELLIS, FIPR

London

Contents

I

The Principles and Place of Public Relations

I.I DEFINITIONS

WHEN A PUBLIC RELATIONS MAN was once asked by a young, pretty girl to define his job he is alleged to have said: 'If I tell you I am handsome and exciting, that is advertising. If somebody else tells you I am handsome and exciting, that is sales promotion. If you come and tell me you have heard I am handsome and exciting, that is public relations'.

The public relations profession, craft or trade has long been cursed by both the need and the desire for a more exact definition of its scope. The attempts to arrive at a simple, brief, and accurate form of words are countless. The description above was a fair attempt to summarize in a few easily understood words the objective of what the man was doing in his job. It had the merit of being directly related to the world of the questioner. At the same time, it avoided saying precisely how the objective was to be reached.

Clearly, however, it would not do for anyone other than a young, pretty girl.

The more serious attempts at definition range from the brief, if sinister: 'Arranging the truth so that people will like you', through the classic from Edward L. Bernays: ' . . . the attempt by information, persuasion and adjustment to engineer public support for an activity, cause, movement, or institution', to the wordy exercise in *Communication and Public Relations* by Professor Edward J. Robinson of Boston University (published Merrill, 1966):

'Public relations as an applied social and behavioral science is that function which:

1. measures, evaluates, and interprets the attitudes of various relevant publics;

I

2. assists management in defining objectives for increasing public understanding and acceptance of the organization's products, plans, policies, and personnel;

3. equates these objectives with the interests, needs, and goals of the various relevant publics; and

4. develops, executes, and evaluates a programme to earn public understanding and acceptance.'

Against No. 1 the author starred the world 'publics' and in a footnote added this: 'The word *public* is used throughout this volume to refer to any group of people who share a common interest. The employees of a company are an example of a public—good pay, the company's stability and future, and the opportunity for advancement are a few of the common interests of members of a company. Some publics, such as employees, are part of an organization; these are called *internal* publics. In contrast, customers are an example of an *external* public. Other examples of external publics of a typical manufacturing company are suppliers, the community and retail dealers. The internal and external publics will differ from one kind of organization to another.'

The basic problem is quickly seen in these three examples. They all cross the barrier between *what* is public relations and *how* it is done.

Most definitions are a description of the practice of public relations, or its function, rather than descriptions of its objectives.

Thus Sam Black, in *Practical Public Relations* (Pitman, 1962), said: 'The fundamental purpose of public relations practice is to establish a two-way flow of mutual understanding based on truth, knowledge and full information.' He was nearer the mark than the cynic who summed up the function as ' . . . the truth, nothing but the truth, but never the whole truth.'

Paul I. Slee Smith, in *Industrial Public Relations* (Business Publications, 1967), maintained: 'Broadly speaking, it can be said that the main function of industrial public relations is to create a healthy climate for the company so that all its operations benefit from it.'

In his comprehensive book *The Nature of Public Relations* (McGraw-Hill, 1963), John E. Marston, Assistant Dean in the College of Communication Arts, Michigan State University, listed a series of definitions to illustrate the steps along the path from the general to the specific. Having said, rightly, that 'public relations is as hard to define as religion or education,' he started with: 'Public relations is planned, persuasive communication designed to influence significant publics.' He ended with a definition taken from *Public Relations News*, to which he added a brief but worthwhile contribution. It then read: 'Public relations is the management function which evaluates public attitudes, identifies the policies and procedures of an organization with the public interest, and executes a programme of action to earn public understanding and acceptance,'

Once again, it will be seen that these are all definitions of the practice of public relations: what it does more than what it it is setting out to do. They are accurate, although they tend to be long.

Trying to arrive at a concise definition engaged the close attention of many pioneer members of The Institute of Public Relations. The result of these attentions was the Institute's present agreed formula: *Public relations practice is defined . . . as the deliberate, planned, and sustained effort to establish and maintain mutual understanding between an organization and its public*. It is this definition which is most generally accepted in Britain.

The search has always been for a reasonably small number of words which will contain the agreed elements of public relations work in action and which will be readily understood by anyone.

To describe fully how a public relations practitioner exercises his calling takes a book. It is impossible to crystallize it in two or three lines. Acceptable definitions at least achieve the results of clarifying it and simplifying the practitioner's task of expanding and explaining it.

In the process of clarification, the vital six words in the IPR definition are 'deliberate', 'planned,' 'sustained,' 'understanding,' 'organization', and 'public'.

Deliberate—because public relations practitioners try to make it clear that the success of their job depends on the premise that nothing should happen by accident. They must start with a set of carefully created objectives. They must then ensure that whatever they do afterwards will take them accurately and inevitably towards those objectives.

Planned—because a public relations man must always remain

in control of what he is doing. The job is too important to take chances and he must thus work to a plan and on a planned basis. The thought is sufficiently vital for it to demand the double emphasis of 'deliberate' and 'planned'.

Sustained—because a public relations man is always trying to implant a thought or an idea that will remain with the person at whom it has been aimed. The pressure must therefore be maintained. Human memories are short. There are many things for people to try to absorb. Sporadic attacks on their consciousness and awareness merely mean that they will forget too easily.

Understanding—because of the difficulty of bridging the awful gap in any process of communication between what the sender means and what the receiver thinks he means. They are not necessarily the same thing. In section 1.6 some of the problems of the nature of communication are considered.

Organization—because no man can work in a vacuum. Everybody works for somebody. A public relations man works for an organization, whether it is a government, a charity, a commercial company or any other. To put it at its most simple, it is his job to see that the organization is understood and appreciated.

Public—because the organization for which the public relations man works wants to be understood and appreciated by the people around it who affect what it does or are affected by what it does. There is clearly no such thing as the general public—as Professor Robinson explains in his definition of public relations practice. Imagine the organization as the hub of a wheel. The rim is made up of special groups who are attached willy-nilly to the hub by the spokes. They can include customers, shareholders, suppliers, wholesalers, retailers, national or local government departments, the communities in which the organization has factories or branch offices, the press, employees, opinion-formers of all kinds (for example, consumer councils, careers advisory officers or investment analysts), children (the employees and customers of the future), and so on. The spokes are the lines of communication between the hub and the rim.

The six words govern what the public relations man is trying to do in his job. Possibly the most important of all of them is *understanding,* since without that he can achieve nothing.

At the same time, it is a mistake to try to learn them parrot-fashion. It is best to try to find alternative words to explain them, to make the meaning clear to the person reading or hearing the definition. Words mean different things to different people. The six key words in the IPR definition are a good example. To an antagonist of public relations it is easy to regard the words as baleful and sinister. A protagonist will regard them as sharp and packed with meaning.

Attempts to achieve public relations purposes have been going on since the dawn of time. The channelling of these attempts into an organized craft is more modern, dating from the last quarter of the nineteenth century. A great deal of twentieth century thought has been focused on techniques—the 'how' of life—and public relations is no exception. Since it is, and always will be, an imprecise science it is bound to thrash around rather more than the exact sciences. It is only important to understand that there is no evil intent in the verbal acrobatics.

It is not difficult to describe public relations as opposed to the practice of public relations, although it is equally difficult to sum it up in a few words. There is no doubt that many of the problems of the public relations craft (including its own public relations) have been caused by the two words themselves.

In the end, public relations means what it says: relations with a public.

Again there have been many attempts to explain this. One practitioner, when he appeared in a television interview, carefully pointed out that relationships exist in any situation. They may be active. They may be passive. They may be good or they may be bad. They are nonetheless there—to be accepted, ignored or altered as desired. As already pointed out, the key to all this is seeing clearly that there is no such thing as one public. There are many publics, or groups of people.

Here is one attempt at an explanation. The world is divided into three sets of people. There are those who know you and like you; those who know you and do not like you; and those who neither know you nor care. The third are usually the large majority. The aim is to reach a position where those who know you and like you stay that way; where those who know you and do not like you change their opinion; and where those who neither know you nor care wish they could meet you and do business with you. Then you are enjoying good public relations.

A crisper definition of the same thing is: 'Public relations is the effect of our actions upon our reputation'.

Neither of these is wholly accurate or easy to use. They go some way towards helping to draw the distinction between what a public relations man actually does for a living and what he is hoping to achieve by doing it. An organization exists in a state of public relations whether it does anything about it or not. It is sensible that organizations of all kinds should wish to do something to ensure that the relationships which they have with others are well maintained, or even improved. Putting that wish into effect is the reason for the growth of public relations practice throughout the world.

1.2 NEED FOR PR IN MODERN SOCIETY

When Ralph Waldo Emerson produced his aphorism about the world beating a path to your door if you made a better mousetrap, he was demonstrably correct in terms of a society where deliberate communication was virtually limited to religion, politics, education, and current affairs. For most people the media of communication were newspapers, pamphlets and books, speeches and lectures, and—most powerful of all—individual word-of-mouth report and comment.

The fame of a better mousetrap might lead to newspaper reports, read by a far smaller public than today's mass circulations provide, but for the most part the mousetrap maker's reputation would be built and sustained by those who talked favourably about him. Small businesses operating in small communities where there was little demand upon people's mental time and receptive powers did not need to use the skills of the professional communicator for their messages to be acceptable and understandable.

Now there is rapid transport over any distance and instant communication around the world. The small businesses have taken their place as parts of large industries and the small communities are seen as part of one vast industrialized society. Television commercials assault the eye and ear in Bangkok as much as in Birmingham. Coloured magazine advertisements tempt readers in Helsinki and Hawaii, offering the same brands through the same selling techniques. The latest news from the remotest areas is seen and read everywhere within hours and may be watched as it happens via telecommunications satellite.

The demands of every form of communication upon the time and receptive capacities of men and women in the advanced nations has increased enormously over the past twenty years, and is increasing still. At the same time, the media of communication have grown in number and complexity. Communication itself has become a twentieth century skill, or rather a group of skills, with the attendant need for professionalism and the resolution of ethical problems.

This does not mean, however, that public relations is a new phenomenon. The first man who had a product to barter, the first leader with an idea to convey had an involvement in public relations: they needed to find their audiences and get their messages across effectively.

The tavern keeper who started the tradition of hanging a bush outside his door to indicate that he sold drink was engaged in advertising. The later tavern keeper who devised the phrase 'good wine needs no bush' was alert to public relations, because he realized that, in his business, reputation was more important than merely making an announcement.

The demagogues of the past, from Tamburlaine to Hitler, crudely practised some of the techniques of public relations. They knew their audiences and what they cared about, whether it was loot or nationalism, and they fired their imaginations by conveying to them dramatic concepts couched in colourful words. Their effectiveness derived much, of course, from the ruthlessness of their approach, careless of the effect on others, and the single-minded directness of their propaganda. They were not troubled over the morality of their actions; for them the end justified the means.

Today, society having learned something from the past, the terms of reference of communication have largely changed. The audience is better educated and more people are equipped and willing to make objective judgments on the messages they receive. At the same time, the forelock-touching meekness of previous centuries has long been left behind by the average

7

western man and there is everywhere an impassioned belief in the right to be told what is going on and why. The objectives of those who communicate are constantly and rightly questioned; there is much healthy scepticism and the mealy-mouthed can expect no mercy.

The checks and balances of what is known as civilized society have brought about a situation in which it is rash to contemplate a course of action without at the same time weighing its effects on others and its acceptability to them as groups or as individuals.

Communications is a current catchword, both as a problem and as a solution. It is worried over by managers and trade union leaders as much as by priests and politicians—and with reason. Failure of communication can be identified as part of the cause of many industrial, commercial, and social troubles. But only as part of the cause.

Public relations is by no means a universal specific for every situation, but it is at least a concept of analysis, action, and communication which can do a great deal to help.

Public relations as it is known in Britain today first began to be generally recognized in the nineteen-thirties, although the phrase had been used long before in the United States and a few pioneers were operating many years earlier on both sides of the Atlantic. Not surprisingly, the thought that relations with the public mattered tended to mature first in those organizations where a major sector of the general public could be identified as of commercial importance. Service corporations like London Transport and national promotional bodies like the Empire Marketing Board were, understandably, among the first to adopt public relations thinking and practices in Britain.

The functions of what would today be known as propaganda and psychological warfare were, of course, in use during the 1914–18 war and there developed the planned presentation of information, much of it ruthlessly doctored to meet the government's needs. After that war, the first information posts in ministries and government departments appeared.

The 1939–45 war suddenly enlarged the official need to inform more people in greater detail than ever, to relate the objectives and progress of the nation's battle. For plain information and—as we now know—for far-from-plain propaganda, the government developed machinery for issuing news, background information, and ideas through the press and radio, posters and pamphlets, films and lecture tours, such as had never previously been known or needed. The informative and emotive powers of radio were fully exploited for the first time during the war and the British-American public's devotion to spot-news coverage has continued more strongly still with television.

After the war, both in central and in local government, the information concept remained. Many of today's successful public relations men learned their craft in government departments or the larger local authorities, most of them having previously been newspapermen. From this point the realization of the potential values of public relations began to spread slowly into industry and commerce.

At first staff appointments were less common than the use of the services of a consultancy or advertising agency department, of which only a pioneering few had existed before the war. Now these developed at a mushroom rate, many of them with an inadequate appreciation of the nature and techniques of public relations and sometimes with little motive other than to provide a fashionable service to clients. The poor reputation of public relations people among journalists and businessmen that persists in some quarters today can be traced back to this period of uncontrolled and unthinking growth. A few charlatans and more than a few old-time publicists contributed during the late 'forties and the 'fifties to the confused reputation of public relations from which skilled and honest operators suffered and, to some extent, suffer still.

Changing social attitudes have since forced a new responsiveness and sense of responsibility in official and commercial life. The average man's belief that he is entitled to be told is gradually becoming matched by a sense of accountability that was largely missing from life and affairs as little as thirty years ago.

Governments are felt to be more directly accountable to the electorate, and MPs to their constituents. Boards of directors can no longer dispose the ordinary shareholders' money without adequate explanation. Local authorities are unlocking the doors of their committees to press and public. Industrial concerns can expect a bitter reaction if they offend in some way against the communities around them. Each part of society is felt to be accountable to the rest for its policies and actions.

It is in this social climate that an appreciation of public relations as a management and advisory function has slowly been won, not by words but by the deeds of the professional communicators who have proved the value of their work in all walks of life. They have managed to make it plain (although the work of increasing the understanding of the place of public relations will probably never cease) that planned communication, ethically conducted from the base of a soundly considered policy, is a worthy and valuable activity.

Almost forgotten now are the extravagant claims of those who spoke of public relations in the terminology of a new way of life, a philosophy, almost a religion. The merits of ensuring that mutual understanding is achieved by the skilled analysis of attitudes, the planning of programmes of action, and the carrying through of deliberate communication by a great variety of techniques, have won recognition in their own right. Almost.

1.3 PLACE OF CONSULTANTS AND STAFF

The growth of awareness of public relations and the increase in the number of practitioners has been phenomenal over the past twenty years. The recognition of the need for organized public relations activity has been equally remarkable.

No era of rapid growth is without its problems. Public relations practice has been no exception. It has been one of the major difficulties of practitioners to carve out their place in business life and society. Their own difficulty has been matched by that of the users of public relations services in trying to work out where the PR people fit in the structure of management.

In the process there have been many misunderstandings and misconceptions on both sides. Some of them still linger. In the early 'twenties of this century, when the first public relations consultancy (even though it was not called such) was formed, it concentrated on publicity. Over the years the allied functions of promotion, publicity, and organized public relations practice grew at uneven rates. If the growth were illustrated on a graph it would show a fairly recognizable pattern. The different jobs met and parted steadily. They diverged wildly, overlapped frequently. Slowly they came closer and closer together and began to run along parallel lines. Most public relations men are now agreed on where each part fits, even though they may disagree on matters of emphasis or method.

If another graph were prepared to show the recognition of public relations practice by users, it would demonstrate the same jerky steps. Laid under the first graph it would show a few points in time when both sides were thinking the same way.

Since all public relations is concerned with human beings it is not surprising that the development of its practice has been overshadowed by human beings. Clever men, stupid men, sharp men, honest men, dishonest men—and women—have all appeared on the public relations scene. Some have been larger than life. Some have crashed in a spectacular fashion. With the development of exposé and in-depth journalism, the spotlight has been turned more than once on pressure groups. Inevitably this has sometimes included public relations men.

It is in the nature of public relations that it is difficult to explain exactly where it fits. This has left the door wide open for the fast talkers. At the same time, the techniques of communication and the need for it are constantly changing. Nobody who was in public relations practice twenty years ago is doing the job the same way now as he did it then.

The first operators have had the twin tasks of learning the job while they did it and trying to create the conditions in which they could do it properly. They have had to work out for themselves what relationship they should have or need to have with others in management on whose work they impinge. They have also had to present their needs in such a way that they could not be accused of merely seeking status. They have often not succeeded. Equally, when they have succeeded it has not always been for the right reasons. A man may have been able to walk his proper path along the corridors of power because he had luck, or because he married his employer's daughter, or because he chose his staff well. His ability to exercise judgment, to achieve the right public relations results for his employer by his sheer efficiency or professionalism, may never have entered into it.

Basically speaking, any organization—commercial or industrial undertaking, government, voluntary body, and so on—should consider the public relations consequences of any action it proposes to take. It does not matter whether those consequences are immediately beneficial or harmful, short-term or long-term, major or minor. It should always remember that there will be an effect of some sort on some part of its state of public relations. Any organization must retain the right to decide to ignore the consequences, provided it is clearly understood that ignoring them does not make them go away. If that premise is acceptable—and it must be—then it is also the duty of the organization to have available the best public relations advice it can afford. It goes without saying that, having got it, it should use it.

There are two aspects of public relations advice in this context. One concerns the principles involved, the other the methods. It is in this dichotomy that public relations people have found one of their biggest problems.

Public relations men do not have the sole prerogative of ideas or ability to gauge human reactions. Many of them have believed that they do indeed have this prerogative and have become hidebound. They have also become presumptuous. For example, in the floating of a new issue of shares, a stockbroker is just as capable of knowing likely reactions as a PRO; in most instances he will probably know much better. The public relations man can claim—rightly and fairly—that his particular knowledge and skills entitle him to a place at the decision-making table, but once there he is no more than a man among his peers. It is because too many people in the past have tried to insist that theirs should be the sole deciding counsel that public relations has been exposed to many of the attacks upon it.

Once a decision has been taken the public relations man comes into his own. It becomes his job—often, but not always, alone—to communicate the decision, to interpret it, to maximize or minimize its impact. This is what he must be trained to do.

It is from this second part that the attitude of many public relations people has arisen. They are fond of explaining carefully that they are advocates. They add that it is their duty to communicate facts, opinions, and decisions whether they agree with them or not. In this they are right. Of course, it is always open to them to resign if they disagree fundamentally with a decision.

Once the need to communicate has arisen, the public relations practitioner can begin to work with other people. And in so doing he must understand the ways they work and the rules by which they work. This is an area of human relationship which he must study carefully if he is to succeed. There are many simple examples of this. They have to do with the method chosen for communication.

If advertising is the method then he needs to understand how advertising works and how advertising men work. He may feel that the advertising schedule (the publications where the advertising will appear) should include a magazine he knows is read by the chairman's wife because this will please her. He must listen when the advertising man carefully explains that by doing this the public relations man firstly will not reach the people he wishes to influence and secondly will have to miss out a publication which is vital. The advertising man knows what he is talking about. The PRO may at the end of it all decide for a variety of reasons that the magazine must be included, but at least his decision will have been reached after hearing the facts.

If the communication is to shareholders, the public relations man must listen to the company secretary, who will explain the rules of the Stock Exchange. However wrong either may think those rules, they must be observed.

The closing of a factory is a further example of the two-headed problem that is at the root of many of the difficulties both sides— users and practitioners—experience in setting the right place for public relations in management structure. The decision to close a factory is hard to make. It is dictated by many factors and can only be taken by the directors of a company after long, serious thought. Some of its effects will be obvious; some will not be seen until later. The directors most closely concerned in the reaching of the final decision will probably be the managing director, the financial director, and the production director. The views of the sales director or marketing director will be sought. At some point, the views of the public relations expert—be he director or not— should also be sought. It is not an essential prerequisite that he should be a member of the board. It is only essential that he should be brought in as early as possible.

There are many reasons why public relations people are not

called in as early as they would like. Their professionalism could have been higher in the past. The readiness of directors to hear public relations advice could have come more quickly.

If the senior representative of public relations in a company is not a director, then he must work to one. If it is true that public relations is a management function then he must report to the chief executive, whether that is the chairman, the managing director, or another senior director. In practice, he will also almost certainly work with other directors. There are many facets of a company's operations which involve public relations techniques and need public relations advice but which do not involve board decisions. It is a matter of debate what position the public relations man needs if he is to exercise his function properly and not become a slave to be pushed around by anybody and everybody. It is impossible to generalize on this question since it can only be related to the particular structure of the company in which he works.

A further consideration is that just as the function of public relations is to pass information both inwards and outwards, so the public relations man himself must be a bridge between the different islands that comprise a company. He must be equally acceptable—and for good reasons—to the directors and to the personnel on the factory floor or at the sales point. He must be impartial. He must never grind the axe of one side against another.

It has become acceptable in many companies that the public relations officer has the same standing as the advertising manager and that both work to the marketing or sales director. There are dangers in this, and there are countless variations on the theme.

To say that advertising is a tool of public relations is correct. To say that therefore the advertising manager should be subservient to the public relations manager is not correct. The same applies when the public relations officer or manager is on the same level as the marketing manager. They are all servants of the company in the same way as the directors are the servants of the owners. The argument is not affected even if the owners are also the working directors.

It is a common practise for one man to combine the jobs of public relations and advertising, with staff below him to carry out the day-to-day functions. Clearly there is nothing wrong in this, provided that the man in the job is properly qualified.

To understand all this it is necessary to consider briefly the structure of a normal commercial organization, whether it actually manufactures goods or provides a service.

The running of the company is in the hands of management, usually a board of directors. Not all board members necessarily work full-time in the company, but some will. The chairman may be chairman of many companies, but in each he will fulfil the same function of overall direction and of ultimate responsibility to the shareholders. The broad day-to-day control of the company will be in the hands of a managing director. Around him will be specialist full-time directors covering finance, production, marketing, sales, export, research and development, personnel, and so on. They will draw the information which allows them to do their jobs from what is often called 'middle management'— departmental heads who should be the directors of the future. These will include the public relations man, the advertising man, and a host of others.

This is not the place to argue whether the marketing director is more important in the scheme of things than the finance director, or the sales director, or the production director. It is important to record that the public relations officer (whatever title he is given) faces one special difficulty. He becomes involved with all the directors, since every activity the company undertakes produces a public relations reaction. Thus the more senior he is the easier it is for him to put his point of view with some hope of success. What he has to do is to earn whatever standing he gains.

Once again, it is almost impossible to make sensible generalizations. In a company making motor-cars and having a bad record of labour relations the most vital function of the public relations man for some years may be to concentrate on that aspect of the business. If that is so he will work extremely closely with the personnel director, but much less with the marketing director. In another company making, say, plastic toys the important job may be to earn the goodwill of children. This will bring the public relations man into close contact with the marketing or sales director. It is merely a question of setting the right priorities and then adhering to them.

The outside public relations practitioner—consultant or agent —faces slightly different problems. If he is retained as a consultant or adviser he must work at the highest possible level in the company. He is probably called in to deal with the company's fundamental problems, short-term or long-term, and can only really understand them if he is dealing with the senior executives of the company. He will have to be a man of outstanding ability, if only because he will be viewed with suspicion by many people inside the company. They will resent any outsider being brought in to advise in areas which they consider to be their own. This may be even more true if the company has a staff public relations man. It is argued, with some justification, that the outside man has strength as an adviser because he is not involved in day-to-day problems and company politics. He may thus be more impartial. He can also draw on experience gained away from the company and continuously refreshed by other contacts.

He can work at many levels. In any event, he should establish a working relationship with the most senior executives of the company in order that he may know the way they are thinking and the directions in which they are aiming. Day to day, he may deal with marketing men, sales men, advertising men, production men and others. The exact ways he deals with them and the level at which he works must vary with each organization by whom he is retained and the job he is being retained to undertake.

The problems of working are slightly different for the public relations man in an advertising agency. He is normally retained as a doer, and the jobs he is normally called upon to do are often in support of advertising campaigns (which may in turn be in support of marketing campaigns).

Up to now, the comments have been dealing with what can properly be termed the 'creative' public relations practitioners. This means those who conceive programmes of activity, even if they may sometimes also implement them. However, there are many people in the whole field of public relations who hold down what may be termed 'passive' jobs. This will include press officers, information officers, house magazine editors, assistant executives in public relations consultancies or agencies, and others.

The distinction between 'creative' and 'passive' is not intended to cast a slur on the latter. A press officer is called upon to exercise his initiative and ingenuity in the implementation of a programme. He is expected to contribute as much as he can to the creation of that programme. In certain circumstances more of his time may go into answering press queries (as in government departments) than in trying to generate press interest in a subject (as in product publicity agencies). He is not given the responsibility for the total programme, but only for part of it. He is therefore working to general direction.

The organization and structure of a public relations department must be settled at the beginning. Its size is dictated by the scope of the job it is trying to undertake. The public relations needs and duties of a small company making cricket bats are clearly not comparable to those of a major civil engineering contractor. The cricket-bat manufacturer would probably need only one man, or part of an executive in a consultancy. The contractor may need a number of specialists—mostly on the staff, but possibly also outside consultants—and someone to co-ordinate their work. This can lead to the growth of a large department.

Basically, there are three jobs to be done. One is the creation of a programme of activity, which carries with it the responsibility of ensuring that the programme is undertaken properly. This is followed by the job of disseminating information, as for the press or for internal use. The third job is the handling of print and other techniques.

As the practice of public relations becomes more professional, and the definition of its tasks more exact, it becomes less and less possible for a one-man department to do a proper job. An organization of any size should employ specialists and may well expect to have at least three people in its public relations department, who in turn will need a minimum of two secretaries. From that base the department will grow to whatever size is needed. In the process, one of the main tasks of the manager will be to see that the growth does not get out of hand.

1.4 COSTING

It is vital that a public relations man should understand the principles, contents, and elements of costing a programme of public relations activity. Although his involvement in the setting and final control of the budget may be minimal, he can make a vital contribution to its success by remembering the need for financial commonsense.

A public relations campaign devised with no heed to the money available is bound to fail. This is a principle which must not be forgotten at any stage.

For example, a company which has consistently returned profits of £50,000 a year cannot consider a full public relations programme which would cost £75,000 a year. Equally, in an organization which has regularly made profits of £5,000,000 a year, it would be unwise to conduct a public relations programme which cost only £2,000 a year. In both instances the budgeting would be unrealistic for either the likely results or the likely needs.

The difference between the apparent cost of any item in a public relations programme and its true cost must be remembered. For instance, a press release sent to 100 newspapers will apparently cost just over £2—that is, the cost of the stamps. The true figure will be much higher. It must take account of the cost and upkeep of the typewriter on which the press release was cut as a stencil; the cost of the desk on which the typewriter was placed; the cost of the chair on which the typist sat; a proportion of the cost of cleaning, lighting, and heating the office where the typist sat; the cost of the stencil; the costs involved in buying and maintaining the duplicator on which the stencil was produced; the cost of the paper and envelopes and a proportion of the costs of the stationery store; and the incidental equipment which all offices must carry, such as erasers, pencils, ball-pens, and a host of other things. Above all, the true cost of the release will include the time of the executive who wrote it and checked it; the time of the girl who typed it; the time of the girl who ran it off (even if it was the same girl doing both jobs); the time of the office girl who stamped or franked the letters; the time of the messenger who took it to the post; and the time of the management and supervisory staffs who exist in all offices (directors, secretarial supervisors, office managers, and so on).

Any money spent, however little, is only well spent if it makes a direct contribution to the achievement of the public relations objectives. Success does not necessarily come only to the big spenders. The really important point is that however much is spent none of it must be wasted. It is the PR man's duty to himself and his employer, whether a company or a public relations agency, to make sure that he does not waste money. There are many ways in which this rule can be proved. The public relations man should be ready to look for ways in which he can do a job for less money. He is, after all, spending somebody else's cash. He would like to feel that they would not waste his money, so he must not waste theirs. If it has been a practice to send out 12 x 10 in. photographs to publications, he should find out whether 10 x 8 in. would not be equally acceptable. If he telephones somebody and finds they are not there he should not wait. He should call back; it costs money to hang on.

This is not a doctrine of penny-pinching. It is advice based on the fact that it is the easiest thing in the world to spend money and one of the most difficult to spend it wisely.

The general rules by which a budget is created, whether in a commercial company, a non-profitmaking organization, or a public relations agency are the same. There are only two basic elements: time and operating costs.

A company employing a public relations officer or department costs time in one way, and will often not cost it completely. As an approximate rule the total cost of the department is double the actual salaries paid. Thus if a public relations officer is paid £3,000 a year, the actual cost to the company will be about £6,000 a year. The difference between the salary and the total is made up by a proportion of normal overheads (rent, rates, light, heat, cleaning, and so on), pension and insurance costs, car or car allowance, equipment (desks, curtains, decoration of offices, carpets, typewriters, stationery, and so on), and share of services (messengers, telephones, and so on). The items included in this breakdown vary slightly from company to company. Naturally, the overhead recovery necessary for a public relations officer working in a 20 ft by 20 ft modern office in a block at a basic rent of £5 a square foot is much higher than for the man working in a smaller office in a provincial factory at a rent of less than £1 a square foot.

A public relations agency must make the same calculations in arriving at a fee for its professional services, with the all-important addition of a margin for profit. A fairly standard procedure is to treble the total of staff costs. This will usually produce a profit of 10 per cent before tax, or 4 to 5 per cent after tax.

Once again, the three-times rules is a dangerous generalization. An agency with offices in central London and considerable resources for the provision of extra facilities or services (say, full-time television monitoring or a staff photographer) must charge more than a one-man organization operating from an office in the provinces.

The point is made only to show how fees are calculated, and does not suggest that a staff public relations man is better than a consultancy, or that the mammoth London organization can necessarily do a better job than the solitary man in Birmingham.

The operating costs of a public relations programme will be much the same whether it is controlled from within a company or by an outside agency. The Institute of Public Relations has published a guidance paper on the subject entitled *Fees and Methods of Charging* (1966). It makes the point, sometimes forgotten, that fees are the income of a consultant (equivalent, as explained, to the salary of a staff practitioner or department) and expenditure is the cost of implementing an agreed programme. The latter is usually mainly a debit and credit transaction.

It is normal practice, although there are no definite rules on this, to charge operating expenses monthly in arrears. They will tend to fall into major and minor categories. The former can include research, market analyses, and similar surveys; advertising, exhibitions, displays, and visual aids; the design, production, and distribution of printed materials, including house magazines; films and filmstrips; direct mail; the organization of speakers' programmes; and special events. Minor costs can include travelling; entertainment, including press contact; toll and trunk calls and telegrams; press-cutting and monitoring services; photocopying or duplicating; and special stationery.

The detailed items of major expenses are usually charged according to the customs of the particular trade, while minor expenses are charged at cost. For instance, advertising budgets include agency commissions, and printed material often includes a commission element.

If anything extra is added to an invoice to a client, especially when it is commission, the client should know and be able to see clearly how much has been put on.

At the same time, it is the responsibility of the public relations man, whether on the staff or outside, to supervise all work done and check the expenditure and invoices. This remains true even if a client has agreed to pay major invoices direct, such as for advertising.

It is normal practice for the agreed budget for a programme to be placed into categories, so that all involved can see how money is being spent and can maintain a regular check on the rate of expenditure. A fairly common list for predominantly minor expenses, with explanatory clauses, could read like this:

1. *Travelling.* Travel within London (or consultancy's head-quarters city) is not normally charged. Out-of-town travelling is charged, including subsistence and hotel accommodation.

2. *Press contact.* When an account—the consultancy's term for a client—calls for regular meetings with the press (for example meals or other hospitality) the bills are charged.

3. *Press releases.* When releases are regularly issued to a long list of papers in Britain, the postage, paper, envelopes, and handling are charged. The cost of special envelopes and postage for photographs is also charged.

4. *Photography.* The cost of photographs and photographic sessions is charged, including the purchase or hire of special equipment or props, model fees, and any fees paid to specialist consultants.

5. *Press-cuttings.* The cost of duplicate sets of cuttings is charged, including the provision of extra copies of publications.

6. *Special events.* When special functions (lunches, dinners, press conferences, and the like) are needed, the costs are charged.

7. *Special stationery.* If it is decided that special stationery is needed, this is charged, subject to commission arrangements (normally 15 per cent).

8. *Temporary services.* It is sometimes necessary to call in temporary help—executive, secretarial or other—to deal with particular jobs. Costs incurred are charged.

9. *Demonstrations.* Some accounts call for demonstrations and lectures. The costs incurred (including fees and expenses) are charged.

10. *Specialist consultants.* Routine advice from outside specialists is not charged, but for extensive work a special fee is calculated and agreed in advance.

11. *Print.* The normal 15 per cent commission is added to all print bills.

12. *Films and exhibitions.* Such work may be subject to a special additional fee.

13. *Direct mail.* A commission may be charged in certain circumstances, subject to prior agreement.

14. *Toll and trunk telephone calls and telegrams.* If an account needs constant use of long-distance telephone calls or telegrams, these are charged.

15. *Overseas assignments.* These may be subject to an additional fee, and out-of-pocket expenses are charged in all instances.

A public relations man asked to cost out items in a programme before it is submitted for board or client approval should take care that his costing is as accurate as it can be and includes all the elements in the price of an activity. For instance, it is necessary to remember that producing a good photographic record of what a company or client does entails more than just the cost of the photographer. He may have to travel some distance to take pictures on location and have to stay overnight. Thus the costing would include his travel, accommodation, and subsistence. There may be constant use for prints from his photographs for which allowance must be made. There will certainly be need for a reference index or album of the pictures. Certain aspects of a company's or client's activities may need to be brought up to date frequently, so that the photographer has to make recurring trips to take new pictures. All these, and others, must be remembered when a total budget for the year is proposed.

Another simple example is press-cuttings. Whether papers are cut or a cuttings service is used, the public relations man may be required to circulate copies within his organization or to his client. The papers are relatively inexpensive in themselves, but added together over twelve months they can represent a sizeable chunk of the budget.

The point behind this—one which must always be kept in mind—is that he must always clearly be seen to be in control of the spending. Nothing so erodes the confidence of an employer—whether in a company or in a consultancy—than to hear: 'I am sorry, but I forgot that X would cost money'. All it needs is care when making estimates to see that they include everything that is reasonably likely to happen.

Naturally, a budget cannot cover every eventuality. It is for that reason that it should contain a reserve. However, this must be a reserve for unforeseen contingencies and not an excuse for sloppy, uncontrolled forecasting.

Once the budget has been set it dictates the broad scope of work for twelve months. It should not be allowed completely to control the PR man, otherwise he will lose the initiative that is a part of his stock-in-trade.

Another task is to keep a running check on expenditure. It is easy to do this, either with a small notebook or a chart. The categories in which money is to be spent are listed and the accounts department provides up-to-date figures each month (or at a greater frequency if need be). There are two essential items of information: what specific jobs are in hand and what suppliers' invoices (photographers, printers, and so on) or petty cash have been paid or are due to be paid.

Naturally, it is never possible to tie up all the loose ends between the time a job is commissioned or handled and the time invoices either come in or are paid out. With a good (thus simple) system it should be possible to produce quickly adequate accurate figures at a moment's notice.

There are two further points. Hieroglyphics that only one person can understand should never be used; somebody else may need to refer to the figures. Secondly, many companies work on general financial systems of running estimates, quarterly estimates, annual estimates, five-year projections, and the like. The chart or book should show what is available in the budget and what has been spent up to any given point, plus expenditure that has been incurred even if not actually yet met. In this way the figures will be genuinely useful as a guide.

Many young people are afraid of figure work. They think it may turn them from being in public relations to being in accountancy. This is not so. It is the job of the accounts department to monitor or collect the money passing through an agency or department. It is the executive's job to see that he can explain why money has been spent and to ensure that, when it is his responsibility, it is not spent wildly. This is not accountancy or book-keeping; it is merely commercial commonsense.

1.5 ETHICS

Public relations, like most other forms of human activity, can be measured in moral terms. Indeed, it is highly desirable that it should be, since all communicators by the nature of their work are capable of influencing others and therefore have a responsibility to society to maintain decent ethical standards.

The ethical considerations of public relations are not easily decided. As the business is young in comparison with the established professions, there is as yet no universally acknowledged code of conduct and the case law that has accumulated is relatively slight.

Similarly, since public relations is not a fully organized or controlled business, and it is still possible for anyone to endeavour to set up in practice, there is no disciplinary control outside the provisions of the law, apart from that covering members of The Institute of Public Relations, the National Union of Journalists, and the Institute of Journalists. Even the codes of these organizations and their disciplinary powers are far removed from the strictly regulated and enforced standards of, for example, the legal or medical professions.

In effect, of course, there are other indirect controls which have a bearing on public relations practice. The rules and regulations governing advertising, the case law being built up by the Press Council, the pressures of the consumer organizations, the watchfulness of hundreds of groups representing particular interests, and, of course, the opinion of his colleagues and contacts in the communication business, all have their effect on the public relations man's attitudes and actions.

Endless ethical questions can be raised in an ordinary week's work in public relations, but most of them fall into four categories: social responsibility; relationship with the client or employer;

relationship with the media of communication; and relationship with fellow public relations people.

Social responsibility, in addition to basic commercial honesty and fair dealing, is very much a matter of not engaging in practices which are contrary to the general good, and of not supporting or condoning such practices on the part of a client or employer.

For instance, if a process is to be installed in a factory and it becomes apparent that the noise level will be harmful to employees and constitute a major nuisance to the community, it would clearly be contrary to the public interest to deny or discount the hazard. The public relations man would be failing in his duty if he did not draw the attention of the management to the social and human problems involved, encourage preventive and remedial measures, and do his best to explain to employees and others the necessity for the process and the mitigating action taken.

Responsibility for the process and its hazards lies with the management; responsibility for honest assessment of the problems created and for frank communication with those concerned lies with the public relations man.

A negative, but equally important, form of social responsibility is to avoid and prevent misrepresentation. This is far more complicated than not making exaggerated claims for products or services.

The choice of what type of product to make or service to offer, what to charge, and how to sell is a management responsibility, although the public relations man can contribute to the marketing thinking preceding the decision. It is a public relations responsibility, often a matter of personal conscience, to be sure that the presentation of the product or service is honest and that no direct or indirect deception of the audience takes place. This does not mean that it is only possible to work for a Rolls Royce type of organization; there is nothing wrong in promoting a cheap ballpoint pen for what it is, although there would be in presenting it as a luxury product.

Misrepresentation can also take the form of suggesting incorrect or only partially true reasons for an organization's policies or deeds. For example, it would be unethical to suggest that a price reduction had been brought about by increased efficiency in production if it had been forced upon the manufacturer by failure to compete in the market place.

One of the most insidious forms of misrepresentation is the creation of 'front organisations'. For example, an organization might purport to be a research trust when in fact it promotes a medical product or appear to be a study group when in reality its purpose is political propaganda. Even when this type of organization is set up with good intentions, its operation must involve deception and half-truths, if not worse.

Anything less than complete honesty in public relations work is bound to harm all those involved. In the communication business, falsehoods and deceptions seldom remain unrecognized for long and when they are discovered the trust which is essential among those who convey messages is damaged.

This trust is just as important in the public relations man's dealings with his client or employer. Confidence based upon frankness and honesty is necessary if a relationship is to be built up within which the full benefits of inward and outward communication can be enjoyed.

The public relations man must be happy that the client's or employer's affairs are decent, honest, and useful—or, at the very least, harmless and innocent. On the other side, the public relations man must be trusted as a person of integrity. The client or employer must be sure that his affairs are regarded as matters of confidence and be secure in the knowledge that no detail of his business or item of information is transmitted without explicit agreement.

Another aspect of confidence is that of loyalty. It is clearly not ethical to accept payment from or engage in work on behalf of any competing or potentially competing organization without the consent of one's client or employer. Consultation among all parties when such an issue arises is the only fair way to determine any conflict of loyalties.

Although a few people in public relations do not agree, it is generally held to be unethical and unprofessional to work on the basis that reward shall be related to specific achievement: for example, a fee of £X for Y column-inches of editorial coverage, or a fixed percentage of a sum to be raised for charity.

The public relations man's dealings with the various media of communication are usually critical, in more than one sense. He generally needs their help more than they need his, and he therefore has to understand and play by their rules. At the same time, his activities are frequently regarded with scepticism and the man who offends against the unwritten laws is not readily forgiven.

The cynicism of the press, radio, and television towards those who wish to give them information is a healthy safeguard which protects the public from deception and dishonesty; it should be welcomed rather than resented, even when it acts against the acceptance of entirely worthy approaches.

Corruption of the media of communication by misinformation, by the withholding of relevant information which can reasonably be held to be in the public interest, or by attempting to influence editorial judgment on the use or rejection of information is one of the most distasteful and damaging forms of unethical behaviour.

Immediately, however, problems of ethical judgment are raised. What is the dividing line between information that is in the public interest and facts which, by normal commercial prudence, should be confidential? Is telling a journalist some additional background to a story over a friendly drink an attempt to influence his editorial judgment? Is a lunch for his news editor on a getting-to-know-you basis an endeavour to undermine his independence or merely an attempt to establish personal confidence. Is placing a series of advertisements in a trade paper to be interpreted as liable to affect the editor's view on the news value of stories about the advertiser?

The answers to questions like these mostly lie in the realm of commonsense. It is barely possible to lay down hard and fast rules, but the development of an objective approach and a sensitivity to the attitudes of others can, with the growth of experience in communication and the help of mature advice, keep the public relations man on the straight and narrow path of unimpeachable behaviour.

In his relations with his colleagues, his competitors, and his employers, he is on surer ground. It is accepted that it is unethical to injure the reputation or practice of a fellow public relations man, to endeavour to supplant him with his client or employer, or to encroach upon his business in any way. This includes the soliciting of work by unfair means, such as misrepresenting another's ability or reputation, or implying that his work could be performed better or cheaper.

The common practice of agency and consultancy executives leaving their employer and taking with them certain accounts so that they may set up a business of their own may be ethically dubious, although when agreement has been reached among all parties this procedure is quite proper.

On the other hand, for a client to engage on a staff basis a consultancy executive who has served him well is, far from being unethical, often a logical development even if it means a loss of business to the consultancy.

The Institute of Public Relations has a code of professional conduct covering most of these points (*see* Appendix). The National Union of Journalists and the Institute of Journalists have codes, too (now being rewritten as the two organizations approach a merger), which contain basic ethical principles applicable to public relations as much as to journalism. The Advertising Standards Authority and other advertising and sales promotion bodies have also laid down standards of good practice, many of them concerned, as are the film and television codes, with the ill-defined area of good taste.

There will always remain issues that cannot be decided by rule nor even by generally accepted practice. These must be a matter for the social, moral, and professional conscience of the individual. The responsibility of the public relations man is to remain alert at all times to the ethical aspects of his work, to act honestly and decently, to guard his loyalties and to respect the integrity of others. When all else fails, and his attitudes, advice, and opinions are not respected, his ultimate action must be to resign from the job or the account.

1.6 THE NATURE OF COMMUNICATION

Communication is easy; everyone does it all the time. Effective communication is difficult. It involves attracting attention, compelling interest, and conveying information with impact, accuracy, and lack of ambiguity. It also requires that the audience should be clearly defined and that means of reaching that audience should be identified and skilfully used, which involves understanding and operating a variety of techniques.

As if this were not problem enough, there are also the physiological and psychological barriers of the selective and subjective mechanisms of every individual member of the audience to be appreciated and overcome.

For example, it is usually accepted that colour is a subject of infinite difficulty to talk and write about without misunderstanding. Apart from those who are wholly or partially colour-blind, colours are seen differently by different people. Some shades of blue to one are green to another, and so on.

In other words, the physical apparatus of the eye and the nervous mechanism for transmitting its messages to the brain are unique to every individual and what one person sees is never seen as precisely the same by any other person.

What is seen is also selected by a variety of factors: alertness, experience, frame of mind, prejudices, physical surroundings, and many more. The choice of facing fractionally one way instead of another immediately makes what is seen unique to the individual. No other person can be looking with the same eyes and attitudes at the same subject from exactly the same place at the same time.

A street scene containing all kinds of activity will be seen by different people in different ways. A nervous old lady will see a frightening rush of vehicles and people. A man who is late for an appointment will see the big clock outside an office. A housewife will see a supermarket sign. A youth will see only a pretty girl walking by.

The validity of these subjective factors has been amply demonstrated. Examine any two eye-witness accounts of a street accident; ask any two people to carry a verbal message and check on its delivery. The 1914-18 war joke about the message, 'Send reinforcements; we're going to advance' being passed from man to man along the trench until it arrived as, 'Send three-and-fourpence; we're going to a dance' has a sound basis in observable reality.

The spoken word has its own hazards and its peculiar differences from the written word are often overlooked. Any shorthand-writing reporter will confirm that he transcribes what the speaker meant to say, for if he wrote what he actually said it would often be gibberish. This is true of almost any unscripted speech, apart from that of the gifted few who are able to compose sentences to speak as others compose them to write.

Read any transcript of a radio or television unscripted discussion just as it comes from the monitoring organization and it becomes apparent that what sounds plain enough at the time is often confused, broken, and jumbled when seen in written form.

Facial expression, inflection and tone, the interplay between speaker and audience, the visual context of the occasion—all contribute to enhancing the meaning of the spoken word and none can be conveyed adequately in a written report. Only in rare cases, such as Sir Winston Churchill's speeches, is the mastery of language such that the words are equally acceptable and effective whether read or spoken. Yet, however precise the words, there remains the obstacle of subjective reaction and interpretation to overcome.

At its most macabre, it is possible to postulate that each separate member of an audience thinks he hears what the communicator thinks he is saying, and the fear begins to develop that clear communication is not possible. It is possible, but it is not certain. As long as everyone whose work it is to convey messages remembers that uncertainty and guards against it, there is hope for effective communication.

Most communication is by word, spoken or written, or by some form of pictorial or visual presentation. That words are liable to be ambiguous, however carefully used, is obvious, but visuals can be equally ambiguous if their effect on the chosen audience is not the intended one.

A non-representational work of art may convey a variety of emotional 'meanings' to those who view it; it may also convey to some a representational meaning far removed from what the artist had in mind. The question 'what does it mean?' can produce many answers, according to the subjective interpretations put upon it by those who look at it. The question 'what did you mean?', addressed to the artist, may produce only one answer.

The differing interpretations put upon the words of a politician by professional commentators, who may or may not have been present to hear them, instantly illustrate both the potential ambiguity of even cunningly conceived speech and the selective acceptance of a message by those who filter it into their minds through fixed attitudes.

Subjective thinking is often ᴵa matter of believing that some things are 'right' and others are 'wrong' without necessarily defining at any time what those moral terms may mean. Even if it is not possible to establish what someone else means by his subjective reaction, it is vital in public relations to recognise that it exists, that it is, in fact, a part of the make-up of every human being.

To take a simple example, the steel-engraved company letter-heading with a vignette of the bearded founder looks just as right to the elderly manufacturer as it looks wrong to the graphically alert young manager. Either might in theory be correct in believing that his personal choice of what is right is also right for the company's audience. The only way to try to find out is to seek the advice of those who are trained in the visual disciplines involved and of those who are trained in the techniques of measuring attitudes.

In other words, subjective public relations judgment is dangerous—for all the value of flair and hunch—and the scientific approach of using available, proven techniques is more likely to produce useful answers to problems. Allied to this, there is a permanent need for the public relations man to retain a cold objectivity about his work.

This does not mean any lack of loyalty to client or employer, nor any lack of enthusiasm for a cause or a company. It does mean the ability to see and hear through the eyes and ears of the audience as well as those of the concern he serves. Loss of objectivity, lack of the scepticism which motivates the best in journalism, of criticism and social analysis, can be mortally damaging to a public relations man's effectiveness. To believe coolly and calmly in what, after study, he propounds is one thing; to believe unthinkingly in what his masters wish the world to believe is quite another.

With as objective an attitude as he can retain (and it can be cultivated and fostered, particularly by those with a journalistic upbringing), mastery of a number of skills and an understanding of several more, the public relations man is still faced with the lack of ôbjectivity of every member of his audience and almost certainly of his client or employer as well. Apart from the occasions when that lack of objectivity is on his side (preaching to the converted is easy if unrewarding) he has to overcome a barrier which he cannot touch, for it is within the minds of his public.

In these circumstances he has to persuade, he has to engineer consent, to convey information that may not be wanted or welcome.

His task is made easier by the developed techniques of analysis and communication which now exist, and by the specialized advice and help which is available to him. Many of the skills he must acquire for himself, although no man can be master of all the many methods of communicating which come within public relations.

He must learn to understand the attitude and reactions of his public as well as identify its location and habits. He must discover which techniques to use and when, in order to reach the minds of his audience. He must plan and he must work to a policy.

Technical skill alone will not carry his message all the way unless he has also retained his objectivity, unless he is able to put himself in the other man's shoes and to listen to the other man's point of view. If he cannot identify himself with other people and with what they believe is right for them and for society, he will have little hope of overcoming the barrier of subjectivity which is in every man's mind.

2

Planning and Investigation

2.1 ESTABLISHING POLICY, DEFINING ACTION, AND BUILDING PROGRAMMES

THERE WAS A TIME when a good publicist was a man who could dream up newsworthy stunts and invent new angles to attract attention to otherwise worn-out stories. Around the same time, a good pilot was the man who flew an aircraft by the seat of his pants, relying on instinct, experience, and personal reaction rather than on instruments and ground control. To be successful, both required the indefinable element called flair.

Flair is a desirable ingredient in public relations still, as it is in most jobs that involve a sensitive appreciation of techniques and the feelings of other people. An ability to see a new aspect of an old story or to invest a routine occurrence with a fresh significance is always valuable. But, just as the modern airline pilot must be meticulously trained, constantly refreshed, and assisted by a variety of complex mechanical aids, the public relations man of today must work within a discipline, using methods he has been taught and assessing scientifically gathered information to guide his actions. The world in which each of them works has become too complex for the instinctive approach to be reliable in every circumstance.

If a public relations programme is to be effective, then it is vital that its objectives be defined; that means of achieving them be determined; that a timetable and a budget within which the means should achieve the ends should be laid down; and that progress, success, and failure should be reviewed. This is the difficult and time-consuming process of establishing policy, defining action, building programmes, budgeting, and assessing results.

Is it necessary to do this? Does not one flash of inspiration (or luck) that produces an apparently major effect do more than plodding away at a detailed plan of campaign? If a company's urgent need is to demonstrate to its distributors that its past bad record of unreliable delivery is no longer justified, a two-page spread in a business magazine about the chairman's home life is an irrelevant achievement, however much it pleases him. Getting a top executive into a major television programme to discuss sound labour relations may impress the board, but will weigh little with them when their ultimate judgment on the contribution of public relations is how far it has assisted in the launching of a series of new products.

Either of these two achievements might be valuable in their own right to any client or employer, but if they absorb time and funds that would otherwise have been applied to the continuation of a programme aimed at specific, consistent, and agreed objectives, then they would be a diversion of effort and a divergence from a disciplined plan.

It is sometimes considered easy to lay down objectives for a public relations campaign, whether short-term or for a long period. Basic textbook phrases about 'creating greater awareness of reputation' and 'developing an overall identity' and 'attracting high-level recruits' can be written into any programme. These are about as useful compared with a properly assessed and structured programme as a patent medicine is compared with a skilfully prescribed drug.

A public relations programme can only be built after study and discussion and, frequently, some form of research. Responsible top executives—the higher the better—in the employing or client organization must be involved in the consideration of the organization's own aims and problems. Their view of what they believe public relations could do for them must be sought, although it will not necessarily be informed or even relevant.

The time within which given problems are hoped to be solved must be established. The motivating forces of the organization must be understood by the public relations man and its 'feel' be communicated to him so that he can begin to understand what actions and policies would be logical for it to follow. (This aspect of intimate appreciation of what is right for an employer or client grows only slowly with association and experience.)

Then, applying his professional objectivity and his knowledge of techniques and media, the public relations man can try to propose a programme of action to achieve what he believes needs to be done, just as a doctor questions, tests, and investigates before making a diagnosis and prescribing a treatment. And, like any doctor, the PR man may be partially or wholly wrong in either diagnosis or prescription.

In some instances, a programme may be little more than a checklist of activities formulated as an organized routine, but this occurs only in the most elementary circumstances.

Far more often a programme includes a variety of activities—simultaneous or consecutive, independent or interlinked—set out as a phased plan. In such cases, it is almost essential to agree a central theme which can be used as a touchstone by everyone concerned at all stages of the operation.

A theme is similar to the copy platform concept used in advertising campaigns: it is an idea that ties together various activities and relates them all to the central intention. The theme grows from the objectives of the programme.

For example, if a large and old-fashioned engineering group has applied modern management methods and brought itself up to date commercially and technically to make the best use of its broadly based resources, its public relations objectives might be to convey the group's new look to customers and potential customers. A theme for a public relations programme to do this might be: the technologically advanced group which is changing British engineering. Every proposal and every achievement could be measured against this theme.

In a consumer goods promotion, the programme theme might be close to, or even identical with, the advertising copy platform. If a new household aid is claimed to save four hours' house work each week, the theme might be: a half-day holiday for every housewife.

A theme must never be just a bright idea dreamed up by the public relations man. Always it must be a crystallization of the needs of the client or employer in the given circumstances surrounding the campaign, and always it must arise logically from the nature of the concern, its policies, and its audience as the PR man has assessed them after study and discussion.

A planned programme, once the objectives and theme have been agreed, is therefore more than a list of actions to be taken. It almost always requires these actions to be organized so that they may be controlled, timed, and analysed, and this is done in the form of what are usually called projects. A programme may include few or many projects.

If publicity to distributors is one means of achieving the objectives, a project might be to ensure a steady flow of information to the trade press every week of the year, while another—which might take a year—could be to organize a symposium attended by all the top executives of the major distribution companies.

If establishment of a new corporate identity is the problem, a long-term project could be a total redesign of every facet of the company's visual presentation, while a short-term project could be to ensure that financial editors understood the company structure and its commercial significance.

Within the total timetable of the programme, each project may have its own timetable. This serves not only to control the application of executive time in the most fruitful way, but to permit an accurate assessment to be made of the progress of the campaign. Measurement of results at regular intervals is the natural partner of planned activity.

Progress reports and meetings are a simple means of keeping all those concerned adequately informed of what is happening. Review meetings are more basic occasions when progress is assessed against the objectives and theme, success in terms of tangible results or reactions (perhaps as measured by some form of research) is assessed, and adaptations of the programme are considered. Obviously, it is desirable to ask not only 'how are we getting on?' but also 'having come this far, should we go on, change direction, try harder or give up?'.

Only when a programme is broken down into its component parts is it possible to budget successfully for the best use of available funds. A certain sum may be all that can be afforded for the PR programme; analysis of the programme will determine which projects should take priority, which could be brought into play if they do not involve too much expense, and which must be deferred until it becomes clear that remaining funds would be adequate for them.

Occasionally, enough money can be made available to meet a need. In this rare and desirable circumstance, only a detailed programme, logically constructed around objectives and theme, and set out as a series of phased projects can demonstrate accurately how much money would be required, for what precise purposes, and how it is justified.

With money allocated to specific projects, each with its place in a timetable, it is practicable to control the flow of expenditure, to forecast where and when major items of cost will arise, and to assess the value of projects in relation to the proportion of their cost to the cost of the whole programme.

A budget also provides another form of discipline that is necessary to avoid dissipation of effort and diversion from the main objectives. Always opportunities will arise or be seen which might make a contribution to a campaign. It is easy to overestimate the value of such welcome opportunities, particularly when they are enthusiastically propounded, and to misjudge their relevance to the theme. Because an opportunity arises, it does not follow that it should be taken. First it must be assessed, and the most practical way to do this is to consider if it justifies the diversion of effort and funds from previously agreed projects. If it does not, then it should be put into the deep-freeze of good ideas that might be used another time.

The public relations man's maturity of judgment often shows at its best when he has learned to say 'no' to a bright idea which could make a pleasing marginal contribution to the campaign but which would involve unjustifiable effort and cost.

This does not mean that an agreed programme must slavishly be followed. Apart from changes brought about by reviews of policy and progress there must also be sufficient flexibility for a programme to be adapted, a project dropped or deferred, if a truly worthwhile opportunity is seen.

If a new magazine starts up with readership covering the main public for the campaign, it would probably be worth diverting effort to try to organize a big feature in the first issue. If sponsorship of a popular sporting event becomes available, it would be worth considering carefully if the time and money involved should be spared from the agreed allocations. If a sculptor asks for help with materials for a work in a widely publicized show, it may be worth a contribution from the contingency item (if there is one) in the budget or paring down some minor project to find the cash.

Each judgment of this kind has to be made on its merits. A properly organized programme based on the logic of the organization, with a theme, carefully prepared projects, a detailed timetable, and a budget breakdown will usually provide the guidance that leads to the right decision.

If adoption of opportunist projects that have no relation to a theme, or insufficient relevance or potential impact to make them worthwhile, is an ever-present hazard, so is over-planning. To write a plan that attempts to forecast exactly what will happen throughout each phase of a long-term programme is clearly unrealistic. To create a programme that proposes more projects than the available time, manpower, and money can encompass is equally impracticable. It may impress management or client that the public relations man can think of so many ways of tackling the problem, but it is essentially his professional duty to select the best ways of doing the job in order of priority.

2.2 RESEARCH

The abuse and misuse of words abounds in public relations practice. This is especially true of research (often called market research, and equally often wrongly so called). It is important that the public relations man should know the value, potential, and limitations of research, just as it is important that he should not pretend to be an expert in it. He needs to know what the jargon of the craft means (up to a point) so that he can avoid recommending or even using wrong methods.

Basically, the purposes of research are either to find out something that is not known, or to confirm something that is suspected. For instance, a company may want to know exactly what its shareholders think of its performance over the past year. Properly used, research can discover it. Equally, the company may suspect that the shareholders are not at all impressed with its performance. Research can confirm the suspicion, or prove it unfounded.

Research can deal in facts and figures. It can also deal in human attitudes. The public relations man can become involved in both.

Whichever applies, there are two fundamental principles he must remember.

Whatever information is being sought, the person questioned must not know what it is. Otherwise he will give the answer he thinks is wanted rather than an impartial one.

Research is not the be-all and end-all of life. It is a guide to aid companies in making a decision or a set of decisions. In the end action will be taken or avoided as a result of the interpretation put upon the research findings, and not as a result of the findings themselves.

It is most important to remember these two points. It is plain folly to believe that research can be a substitute for correctly calculated management decisions.

It is essential to ensure the impartiality of the person interviewed. For example, if it were desired to know what shareholders thought of a particular company the first step might be to select the home addresses of 100 shareholders. They would be visited by research workers carrying out 'a survey into public companies'. The approach could be: 'I am going to ask you about ten companies. Can you tell me what your image is of each one? For example, is the company progressive/static; expanding/contracting; increasing profits/decreasing profits?' The company seeking the information would be included with nine others.

Another question might be: 'Do you hold shares in any of these companies? If so, do you consider that this has been a good investment? Are you satisfied with current management', and so on. By concealing the direct interest it is possible to obtain an accurate reading of the shareholders' interest and views.

Most surveys of this type are carried out with a preprinted questionnaire so that the interviewer merely has to tick the answers. It is also normal practice to include a section of basic information, such as sex, age category, social class, marital status, children, and the like.

Of course, if a company is to obtain genuinely useful answers to questions, it has to accept that the answers are not necessarily going to be those it wants or expects. They can only be useful if they truly reflect the attitudes or statistics of the particular public in which the company is interested.

It costs a great deal of money to launch a new product. No

company will invest many thousands of pounds without a reasonable prospect of success. Fifty years ago the basis of a launch would probably have been the intuition or experience of a managing director or sales director. Today's risks are too great to work that way.

This can be illustrated by a simple example. A company is to launch a new toilet soap and wants to sell it to women. The first piece of information needed is the range, price, and availability of other toilet soaps. The second is the money spent to promote them by all means. The third is whether sales of existing brands are rising, falling or remaining static. The fourth is the possible outlets for distribution: chemists, supermarkets, department stores, and so on. All this information is relatively easy to discover. Some of it will come from specialist research organizations which analyse information on the sales patterns of toiletries.

However, there is a gap in the picture created by this information. Do women want to buy yet another toilet soap? If they do, what is lacking in the range from which they already buy? Can they be attracted by a new colour, or a new perfume, or a new shape? Are they dissatisfied with the lather they get from existing soaps? What claims that would capture their imagination could be made and substantiated for a new brand?

This is an immediate opportunity for research. A well-constructed questionnaire will provide many, if not all, the answers to these questions. One questionnaire could be used to test reactions or attitudes on the part of chemists and other sales points; another would test women's reactions.

Ideally, the questionnaires would go to all possible retail outlets and all housewives, but this is obviously impracticable. Research thus employs the technique of sampling. It works on the fact that if you want to know what one million people of a certain type think of any given idea you do not need to ask all of them. A sample of 10,000 will give you the answers, provided they are carefully chosen to represent in miniature the characteristics of the total.

The Market Research Society sums up what research is all about in a brief booklet *About Market Research* (1967). This says: 'Market research started when more than a century ago a manufacturer took an objective look at his sales figures and took action to find out why one product was selling very well and another similar product was ailing. In the early days, the means of investigating the market were limited, and research probably ended at a handful of his wholesale customers. For one thing it was thought that to canvass accurately the opinions of customers in the shops one would have had to seek out all of them in order that every opinion could be properly represented. The expense of doing this was prohibitive.

'At the start of this century the techniques of population sampling were developed, and accurate sample surveys among the whole population became possible. One could now interview a few people whose views represented within reason the views of a much larger number. Sampling has, of course, been used by cooks since cooking began. A single spoonful of a well-stirred pot gives a good idea of the taste of the whole, and a small plateful gives a good idea of the sustaining qualities of the whole. Sampling is also as old as examinations, where a student answers a few questions which have been carefully chosen to represent the whole of the knowledge he should have acquired.

'With the development of sampling came developments in framing questions, in interviewing, in tabulating the answers and in interpreting them.

'Market research can be defined as any activity that gathers knowledge about a market by interviewing people and by sifting existing facts. A market in this sense is the actual or potential demand for a product. As an example, if the potential market for shaving equipment is all adult men (it is not entirely, of course) the actual market will depend on the rate of beard growth, the fashion for beards, sideboards and moustaches, and the habit of barber shaving. Within this the market for electric shavers will depend on electricity supply, the attitudes to mechanical shaving, and general purchasing power to afford the higher initial outlay. Market research can provide this kind of information in detail, both for consumer products, or those bought and used by the public at large, and for industrial products, or those bought and used by industry and commerce.

'Market research plays its vital part in the consumer revolution by enabling a manufacturer to find out which products will really satisfy the needs of his potential customers, and which will not, before a production line starts to turn. To do this market research uses many of the methods developed by statisticians, sociologists, and psychologists. In its turn, market research has evolved methods of its own which it feeds back to people who practise those disciplines.'

The public relations man does not need to be an expert on research. Indeed it is one of those crafts where a little learning is a dangerous thing. He does need to know its uses and its limitations, so that he can advise his client or employer when research should be brought into use. It is said with considerable justification that it is probably not possible to mount a correctly balanced programme of public relations activity without some form of research. There is almost certainly a need for periodic research to review progress.

Research is not cheap. The cost is, of course, relative; nothing that produces a required result should be labelled cheap or expensive without thought. A full-scale national survey may cost more than £5,000, but if it leads a manufacturer to an investment which makes him a profit of £500,000 or helps him to avoid losing £500,000, it cannot be called costly.

Once it has been decided to conduct a research survey, it should be allowed time to operate properly. It is not possible to construct a questionnaire, conduct interviews, analyse the results, and produce conclusions in a matter of a few days. It may take two or three months or even longer. An attempt to force it through more quickly may well produce answers which are wholly or partly untrue. Then the survey will have been costly, whatever amount is actually involved.

As pointed out earlier, research can delve into human attitudes, or it can make statistical, quantitative analyses. It has its own language and jargon. The public relations man should not reel off any of the jargon without being sure what it means. Some words and phrases in common use are:

Fieldwork—the completing of questionnaires away from the research worker's head office.

Desk research—work done without leaving the office, usually either by studying published material, or extensive telephoning.

Sample size—the total number of people interviewed with one questionnaire.

Product definition research—finding out and making recommendations about a possible new product or service, covering such considerations as flavour, texture, colour, size, shape, packaging, name, and so on. Often carried out by 'blind' tests, where the new product is packed with no identification.

Market definition research—seeking to discover the actual or potential demand for a product. A 'profile' is created of users against relevant characteristics such as social class (A, AB, B, C, CD, D, E), age, area of residence, sex, and so on. Sometimes it may be necessary to use a continuous consumer panel, in which the same group of people keep a running check on their purchases.

Motivation research—tries to find people's real attitudes or those of which they are not consciously aware, rather than those to which they will admit.

Recall—people's spontaneous or prompted memory of an advertisement.

Campaign effectiveness studies, or *brand and corporate image studies*—aiming to discover people's true attitudes to a product or the company making it.

Retail audit and distribution research—finding out the actual or possible distribution of a product by analysing its sales through a panel of retail outlets. Each shop in the sample provides figures of deliveries and stocks of competing products so that the sales can be calculated. Some companies specialize in this work.

Sociological research and public opinion polls—more often concerned with non-commercial affairs, like forecasting election results.

Qualitative investigations—dealing with human attitudes and providing new material which may be useful but will not have statistical validity.

Quantitative investigations—always have statistical validity.

It has long been accepted that public relations programmes and campaigns based on generalizations stand a 50:50 chance of failing. That ratio can be changed markedly by tailoring the mixture of techniques to the particular problem to be solved. Research can be an invaluable extra shot in the public relations man's locker. He should review his programme regularly, and if he believes that professionally conducted reserach can make a contribution, he should not hesitate to advocate its use forcefully.

3

Personal Communication

CHAPTERS 3 TO 7 deal with reaching the audience, through communication that is personal, printed, visual, audio or specialized.

Personal communication, from one human being to one or more others, is the strongest and most persuasive means of putting across a message, despite all the natural hazards described in an earlier chapter. The message is aided by the force of the personality of the communicator, who can instantly adapt both matter and manner to the reactions of his audience. The listener has the full benefit of minute changes of inflection and expression, and these subtleties contribute to the accurate acceptance of the message. No contrived medium of communication, not even live television, can match the power of direct human communication.

Every politician knows that he has a far better chance of getting a few ideas over to a few lively minds during a tub-thumping tour than he has by a serious article in a weekly review. Every manager has to face the fact that his carefully composed noticeboard announcement stands little chance against the instant acceptability of the latest rumour.

The power and the limitations, the advantages and the risks of direct personal communication need to be understood by the public relations man so that he may know not only how to use it, but, perhaps more important, when to use it.

There are three basic considerations: the ability to communicate effectively in speech; the need for others to pass that communication onwards; and the likelihood of any reporting or recording of spoken words for further use.

Words to be spoken are different from words to be read. Only rarely does one man write words that read well aloud and also make speeches that read well silently. Lesser beings need to practise and to try their drafts aloud before being sure that they have written a speech and not an essay.

Probably the nearest to verbatim reporting of spoken speech is to be found in law reports and in *Hansard*. Even there a little discreet smoothing out of verbal infelicities is done. Yet, with all the speaking skill of the advocate or the professional politician, the words as they are spoken take a widely different form from that which would be required to convey the message adequately in writing. It is worth studying a Commons debate and then, as an exercise, trying to express the thoughts of the speakers as they might have been put over in writing.

The mental processes of balance, adjustment, and correction, with no fear of pausing for assessment, which are at the heart of writing, are totally different from those imposed by the overriding need for fluency, variety, and impact in speech-making.

With the spoken word is it possible to be informal, even in formal circumstances, and to disregard many of the rules of grammar and syntax. Nevertheless, it is still vital to create a logical flow of concepts and to group sentences into the verbal equivalent of cohesive paragraphs. And clichés are an even bigger danger than in written English. The temptation to use the stock phrase, the latest jargon, is very great.

Some people have the gift of coherent speech; most people can learn to speak reasonably clearly; a few can never manage it, usually because they are unable to discipline their thought processes. Nervousness in public is too easy an excuse for most poor speakers. The very best speakers are nervous and they would not be able to perform successfully if they were not: nervousness sharpens sensitivity, both to one's own performance and to the audience's reactions.

It helps to remember that it is perfectly possible to communicate verbally in words and phrases that would look trite, elementary or even confused if written down. As in any other form of communication it is necessary to know what you wish to say, to understand the nature of the audience, and to organize an effective means of putting the message over. This applies whether one is writing an after-dinner speech or preparing a ten-minute talk for a works committee.

To write text or notes for other people's speeches, is, of course, more difficult. It is necessary to appreciate the speaker's attitude of mind, his ability to speak and memorize, his approach to the subject and the audience, and, preferably, his style of speech. All this is in addition to one's own need to know the subject.

Clearly, the style and content of speeches and talks must be adapted for different audiences. The popular author on a lecture tour of women's clubs in America might be able to get away for months on end with one text containing the same jokes, but a trade union official visiting branches all over the country to put across a policy change has to think carefully about such things as regional attitudes, local sensitivities and the previously recorded views of each particular audience. His speech might change drastically, even though the intention and the basic message would remain the same.

Frequently the object of speaking to an audience is not merely to inform, but to encourage action, and the action may be to carry the message on to other audiences. In this case it is vital to be sure of the capacity of the audience to grasp the essentials of the message and to convey them accurately to others. To send an audience away with a false or incomplete idea that they then pass on is clearly dangerous and may be disastrous.

The politician making a theme speech at the party's annual conference enumerates a number of black and white concepts in the trust that he is speaking to the converted who will relay his thoughts to other equally willing believers. On the other hand, a university lecturer moves slowly and carefully through a narrative of subtle or complex issues. These he knows must form part of a chain of communication extending over years, and must be both acceptable and challenging to a knowledgeable audience of alert and sceptical young people who may use his thoughts in a great variety of ways. His task is vastly more difficult.

When the spoken word is to be reported or recorded, other factors come into play. The further audience beyond, which will read the spoken word, has to be considered. So have the techniques of the medium being used.

If a speech is to be reported in the press and this in itself is to be a means of conveying the message further, then the spoken words must obviously include ideas and phrases that are newsworthy and appealing within the context of the occasion and the subject. If the proceedings of a conference are to be published, the spoken words must contain ideas or information of sufficient merit to sustain a wider audience's interest over a period of time, if only as reference material.

If the proceedings of a conference are to be broadcast or televised, it is essential that at some predetermined point words will be spoken which crystallize the basic meaning of the occasion, so that within the desperately narrow time limits of the medium the vital concept may be put across in simple, comprehensible terms.

More than in any other form of communication, it is desirable with the spoken word to consider the aim in relation to the circumstances in which the communication takes place. To take an elementary example, the speech replying to the toast to the guests at a dinner is no occasion to announce policy changes. Similarly, if a conference is dealing with techniques and the audience consists of specialists, it is unlikely to be sensible to present a paper consisting of broad generalizations.

Likewise, if the basic requirement is to start a chain of thought and activities in the minds of the audience, it is obviously as well to keep the main idea brief and simple and to enumerate only those developments which will not tend to stimulate argument over details.

It is a mistake to try to attempt too much within the limitations of speech. Basically, one or two concepts, plus their logical corollaries, are as much as should be tried. The limitations are, apart from the audience's general capacity to comprehend and the speaker's ability to convey, largely a matter of intellectual acceptance of complex or detailed concepts at a single hearing. Repetition will ram almost any idea home, however complicated, but in personal communication there is seldom the opportunity —other than by slogans—to make points over and over again.

The need to hold the attention of the audience, to offer interest, excitement, entertainment or whatever is appropriate, applies to spoken communication as much as to any other form. At least, in direct personal communication, the speaker has the chance to assess any failure to communicate instantly and to try to adapt his approach accordingly.

In addition, the physical circumstances in which the communication takes place have an effect on understanding and acceptability. Possibly as many seductions have been started on the top of crowded buses as over the traditional candle-lit dinner for two, but certainly fewer lecturers get their points home when the slides are upside down, the telephone interrupts from the next room, and there are no ashtrays in the front row. Attending to such mundane detail is always worthwhile.

As in most aspects of public relations, a combination of organisation and a sense of showmanship is a vital ingredient of successful personal communication. Even in a simple lecture, adequate chairmanship, sound timing, reasonable comfort for the audience, audibility, lack of distraction, a courteous atmosphere, and ample additional information for people to carry away can make all the difference between success and failure.

There are, of course, occasions when the physical circumstances are beyond the control of the public relations man. If he has to provide a speaker for someone else's conference, it is his responsibility to try to ensure that the arrangements are adequate. In more formal cases, such as for a witness giving evidence at a public enquiry, he can at least survey the ground in advance, get the atmosphere of the event if there is time, brief his man thoroughly, and provide the press with background information.

Sometimes circumstances may be such that there is no possibility of rehearsal or any way of controlling the audience or the surroundings. The factory-gate press conference during a labour dispute or the public figure obliged to appear on a doorstep to meet demonstrators or petitioners are two of the more striking possibilities. Here there is no substitute for having earlier foreseen the likelihood of such circumstances arising and defining firmly for all who might be involved the line to be taken in any statement or in answer to questions. The rest has to be ad-libbed to the speaker's best ability.

The strength of personal communication—the bringing of communicator and audience face to face and the opportunity this provides for questions and discussions—applies also to visits and tours. Taking the audience to see for themselves is as effective as putting the man who knows before them in person. The same criteria apply as for spoken communication: a clear idea of the message to be conveyed, a person or persons able to convey it, and an understanding of the audience's power to accept and pass it on (if that is appropriate).

Finally, it is dangerous to pay too little attention to presentation, which in many circumstances means showmanship, in personal communication.

The immediate acceptability of the message is as likely to be inhibited by the fact that a speaker keeps nervously putting his hand to his mouth as it is by a basically unimaginative approach lacking in the ingredients that will enable it to capture and hold the audience's attention. In other words, the tiny practical details matter in even the simplest form of person-to-person communication just as much as the inspired dramatization which puts life into a presentation to a mass audience.

4

Printed Communication

4.1 DIRECT MAIL

DIRECT MAIL can be one of the most important jobs undertaken by the public relations man. It is often considered as an advertising function, but in fact has much wider uses, both commercial and non-commercial.

It means what its title says: material distributed through the post to selected people. When used for advertising purposes it may be restricted to once-only operations, such as a premium offer. In a public relations context it more often means continuing operations, such as material sent regularly to people with mutual interests, like a news bulletin or house magazine.

The material sent may be printed. It may be stencilled or otherwise duplicated. The mailing method may be wrappers or covers or envelopes. The selection of the recipients may be random or closely controlled. Whichever applies, the essence of this means of communication is that there is no barrier (other than understanding) between the sender and the receiver. The sender puts his message right in front of the recipient without any intervention, such as by a newspaper sub-editor.

Using direct mail involves four things: an objective; a list of names and addresses; the content and its presentation; and an understanding of postal rules and regulations.

As in all public relations programmes, the objective of a direct mail campaign must be clearly stated and understood before the work begins. Although direct mail is undoubtedly effective, it can also be relatively costly. It is therefore necessary to decide at the outset whether direct mail is the best method. Normally, even if somewhat obviously, the reason for using it is that nothing else will do the job as well. Certainly, no other method achieves the same impact. The direct mail shot arrives at the recipient's house or place of business. It stands a good chance of being opened.

Once opened, and provided it has been well conceived and presented, it should find the recipient in a receptive atmosphere. It is difficult to ignore completely an envelope which comes through one's own letter-box. Everybody is aware of the unsolicited letters that arrive at their homes, and everybody can remember good (meaning effective) examples and bad ones.

In most businesses, it is the customers who come back who represent real success and profit. It is repeat orders that many companies are striving to create and maintain by their public relations activities, advertising programmes, and sales promotion efforts. A part of all this effort is necessary because people's memories are short and they must be reminded constantly that they have bought a good product or enjoyed a useful service. This may be a regrettable aspect of human nature, but it is nevertheless a fact. Having given satisfaction to someone, a manufacturer or provider of a service wants to keep in touch with them. He can do this by many means, but direct mail is one of the most obvious, especially when he has customers totalling thousands of people.

In effect, when he sends something—a catalogue, for instance —to a regular or former customer he is saying: 'Remember me? I gave you what you wanted or needed before. Give me the chance to do it again'. Of course, he can also do it by advertising, which has the added benefit of attracting new customers. Sensibly, he will consider combining the two.

There is also a faint quality of snobbishness attached to mail received at home. The recipient, however foolishly, can feel that the letter, catalogue or sample was addressed to him alone. It thus flatters him. This is particularly marked in charity appeals. Lastly, there is the certainty of hitting the target, even if not of registering a bulls-eye each time. If, for example, a company makes products designed for sale by ironmongers, it is possible to mail information about it to all ironmongers and only to ironmongers. There is thus no wastage, and the demands of cost and profit can be met.

The second main implication of a decision to use direct mail is the existence of a list of names and addresses. This can be compiled in several ways, but generally speaking a list will come from one of two sources. Either it is bought from a list broker or it is built up by the sender himself.

List brokers, or direct mail houses, publish booklets showing the lists they hold. These cover almost any category that can be conceived. Cabinet makers, supermarkets, bank managers, personnel officers, companies employing more than 5,000 people or fewer than 50, members of football supporters' clubs, housewives living in a particular district—the list of lists they can provide is endless. It is compiled from a study of reference books, telephone directories, electoral rolls, and a host of other sources.

The lists are constantly brought up to date, although it is fair to point out that every list broker will admit that any list can contain a notable percentage of errors at any one time. It will probably, indeed, contain even more errors than they will admit. People die or move their jobs or homes more quickly than printed lists can be changed. If a list is bought, it is wise for the public relations man to check constantly on the rate of mail returned. This is one of the most worrying aspects of direct mail, if for no other reason than the wasted cost and the factor of irritation.

It is normally the duty of the sender to provide to the mailing house enough copies of the material he wants to send; they then wrap it or put it in envelopes and post it. They charge for the use of the list—in some circumstances they will actually provide the names and addresses either on envelopes or on labels—and make further charges for wrapping or enveloping or otherwise handling. It is normal practice for the stamps to be paid for in advance, since postal regulations do not allow stamps to be bought on credit.

For many jobs, the use of a list purchased from a specialist company is sufficient. In others, it can be better to build up a list of one's own. Most often the decision is dictated by the frequency with which the list is needed, and the relationship between the sender and the receiver. A simple example of this could be the sending of a staff magazine to all employees, especially those of a company with plants or branches in many parts of the country. Here, the compilation of a list is simple enough, and the mechanics of keeping it up to date are equally simple. The same would apply in the instance of shareholders, where the operations of a company are such that a quarterly report is found to be a sensible instrument of communication.

However, many companies send material by direct mail to

people who are not on their staff, but with whom they need to maintain constant contact. Petrol companies, for example, issue material regularly to their dealers throughout the country; tobacco companies do the same to retailers. In instances such as these—where it can be within the competence of the public relations man to recommend that such activity is undertaken—building up and maintaining the list presents some problems.

Any company will have the country divided into marketing or sales areas, with sub-divisions related to its particular pattern of distribution. All the areas will be in the charge of salesmen of one rank or another (area managers, divisional managers, field sales managers—the titles vary). It is from them and from the company's central accounts and records departments that the original list will be created. It is also from these sources that the changes in names, addresses or descriptions will come.

The manner and frequency with which alterations are advised will be different in all companies, but it is not difficult to devise a system. The key requirement is simplicity. Depending on the size of the list, it is usually best to run off copies of all the names and addresses at prescribed intervals, send them to the salesmen in areas, and ask that changes should be made on the actual lists. The copies are then returned to the issuing point and checked against a master list.

Another method—which seldom works very efficiently—is to ask the actual recipient to advise any changes. Long experience has taught most companies that this so seldom happens that it is hardly worth making the effort. If this method is used, it should be implemented by sending a prepaid card asking three questions: Is the address correct? Do you still want to receive (this publication)? Should someone else be receiving it? If there is no response after sending the card, say, three times, then the name should be automatically taken off the list.

All this can work easily when the company knows to whom it wishes to send material. However, it may decide to create a list, as in the instance of a new company sending out an introductory offer or its first catalogue. One standard method of building up such a list is by the use of coupon advertising. Readers fill in their names and addresses on the coupon, occasionally adding some other information, such as their occupation, or their particular interest if the advertisement is offering more than one thing. The coupons are returned to a central distribution point. The request having been met, the coupons are then kept and the names and addresses turned into a mailing list. In future years, offers, catalogues, and the like—whether advertised or not—are sent direct to the names on the list.

The alternative is the use of the same sources as list brokers—reference books, electoral rolls, telephone books, and so on. This is clearly time-consuming so that the effort is probably only justified in exceptional circumstances or if the list is relatively short.

It is also worth recording that some organizations deliberately do not publish lists of members, to make it as difficult as possible for a would-be direct mail user to get at them.

Making up a mailing list and maintaining it presents no great problems when one is dealing with a few hundred names and addresses. But when the total runs into several thousands, with perhaps 500 changes each month, the job is beyond the reach of anything but the most sophisticated organization.

The most common way of keeping addresses is on metal printing plates stored in cabinets, and fed through simple machines. The amount of space used to store, say, 10,000 such plates, and the equipment and staff needed to transfer the addresses to envelopes or wrappers and keep them in order, requires a larger investment than most companies will wish, or even need, to make. Of course, glaring exceptions to this rule are the mail order or department stores with hundreds of account customers, to whom invoices and goods must be sent each month. However, these are a special instance.

This situation, added to the growth of the use of direct mail, has led to the formation of some companies who specialize in distributing material through the mail. They differ from list brokers in that they only hold their customers' lists, acting as the distribution agents. They do not build up their own lists, neither do they make the lists they hold available to other people.

As an example of the scope of their operations, it is worth noting that one such company in Britain alone sends out more than 70 million items each year. It has storage space exceeding 50,000 sq ft.

The public relations man who is faced with the need to be

distributing material regularly to a long list of addresses is well advised to investigate the possibilities of contracting-out the work to such a company. Their services go beyond merely issuing the material. For example, if the original list has been built up from couponed advertisements, each one will have been keyed to show the paper in which it appeared. The mailing house will analyse the returns to show the pulling power of each paper. The wrappers or envelopes in which material is sent will carry an address to which the material is returned if it cannot be delivered. The mailing house handles this, allowing for a quicker check on the proportion of 'dead' letters, a crucial point.

In some highly organized operations where material is provided from a central company to dealers who actually buy it (for window display, or for re-issue as individual items to local customers) the mailing house will handle the whole exercise. They will issue the material, collect the money and pass it on to their client, maintain records, and keep their lists up to date. Naturally, this is only a viable proposition when the operation is one demanding an investment of several thousands of pounds a year.

One of their great advantages is that they can ensure a rapid response to requests from customers. Few things are more likely to dampen the enthusiasm of a person who has asked for a catalogue than not to receive it until three weeks later. An efficient mailing house can process a request speedily enough to make sure that the enquirer gets the item within 48 hours.

Having established the value of direct mail, and the problems involved in building and maintaining a list, the next consideration must be the content. What is to be sent?

Obviously, the list of possible contents is lengthy, but usually for public relations men it will mean printed material of one kind or another. External magazines, staff magazines, members' newsletters, catalogues, sales leaflets, renewed membership cards, books, gramophone records—all these are common examples.

The need to sell successfully on a big scale in some areas of commerce has forced direct mail into the forefront of activity. When many people are shouting in the market place success comes to the one who shouts loudest, or most subtly, or employs two or three people to shout with him.

For the direct mail business, this has caused one complicating factor—the measure of anger, irritation, or rejection of direct mail shots by recipients. An outstanding example of this is the pharmaceutical industry, which has acquired an unwanted reputation with doctors, especially general practitioners. All the immediacy of impact and the removal of barriers between sender and receiver are nullified if the direct mail shot is instantly thrown away, probably unopened.

This should not, however, necessarily deter the public relations man from using a novelty mailing, provided he is satisfied it will achieve his objective. Thus he might decide to mark a Scottish occasion by mailing a miniature haggis, or a gardening event by sending a dozen red roses to everybody on his list.

The public relations man who is wanting to send material to a group known to be sensitive must study this aspect closely and carefully. A great deal of direct mail is wasted or issued unwisely. When this is true, it is often because not enough time has been put into thinking clearly about the content. There is nothing more useless than an unopened direct mail shot. This all means that the public relations man may wish to conduct some small-scale research in advance. He will certainly need to find out what competitors are doing, or what other material his audience is already receiving regularly (whether competitive or not).

In a national operation or, indeed, in any operation larger than the local dry-cleaners advising a few hundred housewives of this week's free offer, the standard of design and presentation must be high. Even if the content is as simple as a letter telling people something they really want to know, it must look good, and it must be well written. There can be no excuse for letters badly printed or duplicated. If envelopes or wrappers are overprinted, it must be well done. If the item being sent is bulky—like a mail order catalogue—it is false economy to use envelopes that tear at the corners before they reach their destination.

With anything that is being sent regularly, the public relations man must include himself on the distribution list, at his home address. In this way, he can see whether material turns up on time, whether it looks good after handling, and can at least gauge in a small way its acceptability.

It is the content that governs the enclosing method used—

57

either an envelope or a wrapper or a carton. This in turn has to be decided with an eye to postal regulations, all of which are easily ascertained. As more and more countries adopt international paper and envelope sizes, the problems of deciding the method of enclosing will become easier. However, it is wise to study postal regulations closely—and when necessary to consult the postal authorities—before taking any final decisions.

It may be wished to issue a twelve-page newspaper monthly to 10,000 addresses, but if reducing the number of pages to eight markedly cuts the postage bill then this could be a wise move. A paper may look most impressive in a particular page size, but if that size puts it into a higher postage category it is—at the least—sensible to experiment with a smaller size and save money.

More countries are adopting two-tier postage and here again it is likely that the second class post, usually taking a day or so longer to arrive, will be good enough for a publication or sales leaflet. The only imposition it makes on the public relations man is proper advance planning, which he should be doing anyway.

The important point to remember is that the material must arrive at the time when it will be most effective, and it must look interesting. The public relations man who takes steps to see that he meets these two conditions is a long way towards ensuring that he is using direct mail to its utmost value.

When a direct mail campaign is intended to contribute in a straightforward manner to sales—as with a mail order catalogue —it is important that the procedures which the recipient has to follow are made as simple as possible. If instructions are being given on how to order a product, they must be easy to read. If money is to be sent, or not sent, this fact must be made clear, for example. The rule to follow is to aim the instructions at the lowest common denominator (even if that is itself fairly high because the people being mailed are thought to be of above-average intelligence). If the material incorporates a call to action of any sort, this must stand out.

Up to now, the procedures dealt with have all been for commercial (selling) ends. However, the public relations man is likely to find himself handling non-commercial operations. This is very much in the area of community relations. A company establishing a major factory in an area where it is unknown may want to write to residents explaining what will happen while the factory is being built. It may want to follow up with progress letters. A company seeking to recruit married women as part-time labour may think the best results will come by writing to local women direct.

For the public relations man there are three considerations. One is whether direct mail will do the trick. Another is making up the list of recipients. This will be done best from the electoral roll, although some local advice from an agent, dealer, or local government office may be solicited. The third consideration is the wording of a letter. The electoral lists will show that Mrs. A. Blank lives at a particular address. It does not show that she is 85 years old. She is hardly likely to be interested in the offer of part-time work! The content of the letter must take such factors into account.

Direct mail is international in its scope. Companies become more internationally minded all the time. A house magazine can be sent anywhere through the post, as indeed can any give-away. When a public relations man becomes involved in this, he needs only to make sure that he is not contravening an overseas postal regulation. It becomes slightly different if the direct mail shot requires people to do something—particularly if they have to send money. In that instance, international monetary exchange controls must be studied, but it is not difficult to obtain advice on this.

There are few fully rounded public relations programmes in which direct mail does not or cannot play a part. It presents interestingly different problems to a public relations man. When he has solved them, he should be doing a better job.

4.2 BOOKS AND PAMPHLETS

Despite the attractions of other means of communication, the book still remains one of the most effective and permanent ways of getting a point of view or a complex piece of information home to an audience. For all the rising prices of bound books and the diminishing number of booksellers, more and more books are published each year in Britain, both fiction and non-fiction. It is frequently the non-fiction works which reach the best-selling lists and create the widest interest.

As intruments of organized public relations, books and pamphlets are surprisingly under-used, although they have been employed for persuasion and propaganda ever since the invention of movable type.

Basically, books fall into two groups: on the one hand those which the public relations man writes, edits or commissions himself, publishes or has published privately, and distributes non-commercially; and on the other hand those which are independently written or edited or merely stimulated by the public relations man, produced by an established publishing house, and distributed for profit through the normal wholesale and retail channels.

To some extent, it is possible to choose whether to follow the private or the commercial publishing route, but this choice is obviously governed by the judgment of the marketability of any book. This is a specialized decision and the person to make it is probably a literary agent who knows which publishers are potentially interested in which types of book and what the commercial possibilities are of books on various subjects. Without a literary agent, most authors and those promoting them are liable to get lost in the idiosyncratic world of commercial publishing.

How is the decision reached that a pamphlet, booklet, book or series of books is a desirable method to use in a public relations context? As with any other choice of a medium of communication, knowledge of the nature of the audience and of the message is the vital starting point. For instance, if the audience consists of engineers and the message concerns the outcome of a lengthy technical research operation, then a book might well be a sound way to present the information and to leave it with them for reference. The book might be specially written, or it might be an edited version of papers presented to technical meetings or of articles in the trade press.

Similarly, if the objective is to increase the use of household foil, the audience consists largely of housewives and a cookbook is an obvious way to put the message across acceptably and usefully. Likewise, if the long-term intention is to redevelop interest in cycling and the selected audience is the twelves to twenties, a lively booklet presenting fashion, pop music, and other teenage interests related to cycling as a sport and a recreation might be a valuable addition to a campaign.

Each of these three examples might be written or edited, published, and distributed in more than one way.

The results of research need not necessarily be written about by the man or men who have done the work, although this would be the likely choice. Sometimes, if the results have been published in a company document or a paper to a learned society, there is merit in commissioning an outside expert to interpret them for a wider technical audience. Usually, particularly if more than one specialist has worked on the text, editing is necessary to ensure readability and a consistent style.

A company or a research organization can perfectly well publish such a work for itself, but the means of distribution should be considered first. Is the book to be sold or given away? Is the audience homogeneous and accessible through one factor, such as membership of a technical institution? Would the book be more acceptable if it were published under the aegis of a learned society or an established technical publisher?

If the book consists of reprinted talks or press articles, the choice might be for the organization sponsoring the lectures or the journal which originally published the articles to produce and distribute the book. In addition to practical convenience, this would give it the authoritative endorsement of a respected third party. Nevertheless, if the content were sufficiently basic to have a wide audience, by textbook standards, a commercial publisher could well be interested in incorporating it into his lists, particularly if it fitted into an existing series.

A cookbook intended to promote the use of aluminium foil in the home could be published and used in a variety of ways. There are many cookbooks produced every year, from lavish and expensive volumes written (at least nominally) by the big-name cookery experts, to give-away leaflets included with women's magazines or merchandised in grocery shops as part of branded food promotions. The market needs to be assessed, once again the decision on method of distribution being a cardinal factor.

Such a cookbook could be a blatantly branded leaflet, unlikely to be acceptable to the book trade but potentially effective as a promotional offer to stimulate sales of the product. It might, on the other hand, be a cookery volume of the highest order, soft-selling the use of foil in the most discreet way and, therefore, if blessed with a big-name author or editor, a commercial proposition to a publisher and the retail book trade.

A foil cookbook could be compiled from the work of the foil manufacturer's own home economics consultant, or that of his advertising agency, or it might be commissioned expensively from a cookery expert known to be enthusiastic about foil. Or the two methods could be combined to give a book with much of the manufacturer's standard material leavened with 'star' recipes from an outside expert.

Such a company book or booklet might be produced by the PR department itself, through an advertising agency or by one of the growing number of graphic design and print production units specializing in sponsored book production.

Sponsored publications are often not acceptable to the book trade, although they may be if the commercial element of the content and presentation is discreet. Sometimes the bookstall end of the trade is more flexible than the hard-cover bookshops over accepting commercially backed publications. The buyers for the bookstall chains are usually prepared to give an opinion on any publishing proposition. If their judgment is unfavourable, it is unlikely that any major retail distribution can be achieved through the conventional bookselling channels. However, nowadays a far wider range of shops sell paperback books and it is possible to organize the sale of suitable titles through other retail outlets.

A teenage booklet with a gentle selling message about the delights of cycling as a sport and recreation, included amidst general interest material, might also be produced by the established method of commissioning an editor or author, finding a commercial publisher, and distributing through the trade. On the other hand, it could be published in co-operation with a youth or sporting organization and distributed primarily to members; or it could be geared to a marketing promotion of cycles and fitted into a consumer contest; or it could be no more than a give-away available to any youngster responding to a cycle publicity campaign.

The permutations on authorship, editorship, sponsorship, private or commercial publishing, trade or specialized distribution, and so on are endless. The choice is determined—as is the case with any other medium of communication—by the nature of the message and of the audience. Unless successful distribution can be arranged, the message will not reach the audience.

This is the weakness of the pamphlet, historically a favourite means of putting across religious or political views. Today, no one reads this rather forbidding form of publication except the dedicated few, and there is no satisfactory means of commercial distribution other than direct mail. If the message is brief enough to be contained in the few pages of a pamphlet and has any intrinsic interest, it is probably more effective to try to have it published in a relevant periodical or newspaper and then to obtain reprints for reference and further distribution to the selected audience.

Admittedly, it is artificial to define the pamphlet as a persuasive instrument to distinguish it from the leaflet as a promotional or informational publication, but the terms are loosely used as interchangeable when in fact the purposes may be very different.

The leaflet—which may be no more than a single sheet — is an endlessly useful form with a great variety of purposes. At its most elementary, it may be intended for give-away or 'help yourself' distribution to the general public to announce an event or inform about some local occurrence, for example, a temporary change in the traffic flow or the cutting-off for a day of the water supply.

In essence, it is the simplest and often the most effective means of answering an enquiry. The tourist who calls at the factory gate and asks: 'What goes on here?' is easily served without waste of employee time by the issue of a leaflet. There are limitless instances of simple information simply given by leaflets, from directions for new out-patients at a hospital to callers at the town hall asking about jobs at a new factory to be built in the town.

If the contents are succinct, accurate, and immediately comprehensible, a leaflet can be valuable in conveying information out of all proportion to its modest cost. On the other hand, there are occasions when a more elaborate form of leaflet is desirable, as for answering public enquiries about consumer products or services, or providing facts and figures for school children preparing projects.

Planned series of information leaflets can be distributed to schools, women's organizations, first aid groups, domestic science students, gardeners, and any other grouping of individuals with a common interest. Alternatively distribution, with a strong third-party endorsement effect, can be bought by loose or stitched-in inserts in magazines read by the chosen audience. This is particularly popular with food and cookery subjects, where the women's magazines usually organize the whole exercise, but can also be applied to do-it-yourself, motoring, sailing, and other specialized popular interests.

The public information leaflet supplied on request, often stimulated by advertising or pack announcements, such as laundry facts from a washing powder manufacturer or gardening hints from a seed distributor, is basically sales promotional in intention and verges upon the area of the catalogue. Strictly, catalogues are part of advertising and direct selling, but as an immediate point of contact with the ultimate customer, whether individual or collective, the public relations man cannot afford to ignore them. Where catalogues include guarantee cards, terms of sale, and similar commitments to a commercial attitude, the PR man must exercise a guiding hand.

Other forms of public relations through published works include the commemorative volume, the major commissioned study, the book stimulated by some event or cause, and the ghosted book.

The commemorative volume, most frequently the history or anniversary book, is seldom a success. That it serves a reference purpose is undeniable, but as a form of communication, even if well done, it rarely has sufficient inherent interest in its content to hold the attention of any audience other than those already directly concerned with the subject. Much time and money is wasted in companies and other organizations over the production of tomes that no one wants to read and that end up as autographed presentations suitable to be given with long-service gold watches.

The commissioned study of a subject, almost inevitably given to a writer of authority, is an uncommon public relations activity, but can be an extremely effective one. If the client is a charity engaged in famine relief overseas, an independent-minded book written by an international expert or a journalist of world renown may—always provided it reaches the right quality—turn into a big seller that attracts publicity and discussion in its own right and thus advances the charity's cause.

This is, of course, frequently an expensive method, but it can sometimes be justified. For example, a definitive, lavishly illustrated book on the architecture of Britain's cathedrals might be an international best-seller as well as make a major contribution to fund raising for the cause of preservation.

Time is a critical consideration. To determine what a book should cover, find and brief the right author, extract the manuscript from him, organize the illustrations, and have the finished work designed, printed, and issued is a matter of months, not of weeks, even for a relatively slim volume.

Planning is vital if a timetable is to be maintained. Time must be allowed for discussion of the content, research into facts and illustrations, checking of the text by experts, reading and approval by any relevant authority or someone writing a foreword, rewriting and editing, proof correction, discussion of cover or jacket design, and long enough for the printer to produce work of the required quality. Books can be got out in a matter of weeks to meet an urgent need or a topical opportunity, but these are exceptional (and probably expensive) cases. Generally speaking, there is no substitute for ample forward planning time.

On rare occasions a writer is moved to tackle a subject outside his customary range because he believes it to be of importance. A great novelist may turn to non-fiction to write about some form of social injustice. A noted expert in one field of human endeavour may decide to give his attention to some pressing cause, as, for example, a great violinist may give much of his time to the plight of refugees, or a film star may turn aside from his career to help the under-privileged. A book by such a person carries weight and promises public attention from the outset. There is nothing wrong in the public relations man endeavouring to stimulate the idea of authorship to aid a chosen cause.

Those who are eminent in their own world are often sadly inept at written expression and this is where the ghost writer has his uses. From the low level of the 'as told to' reminiscences of the professional footballer to the skilful interpretation of another man's ideas is a long journey. In between, there are many possibilities for sound, useful books.

The ghost writer is often derided, but he has his justification in the many successful and worthwhile books that would not have been written but for his skill, even if it is not his name on the cover that attracts the audience.

4.3 THE PRESS

4.31 *Principles of press relations*

It has often been said that press relations is only a part of public relations. This is, of course, entirely true. However, it is a comment which has become distorted over the years to the point where there is almost a sense of shame on the part of a public relations man whose main preoccupation is dealing with the press. Clearly this is ridiculous. Press relations (or editorial publicity) is a vital part of almost any public relations campaign. It may be a minute part of the programme of activity; it may be the largest part. That is irrelevant. It is certain to enter the life of a public relations man at many points and he must be a master of its techniques.

Strictly speaking, it can be argued that the most effective way of selling or explaining something is good personal communication backed by understanding, but the pace of modern society makes it impossible to conduct business this way. As society has become more and more complex, and the level of education has risen, there has been a growing need and a growing demand for more information. People may misuse the information, they may misinterpret it, but that does not mean that they should not have it. It is the role of the press to provide the information.

At the same time, the press has other duties, which have been encapsulated in many aphorisms, definitions, and statements of principle. They can be most easily summed up by saying that the press exists to inform, educate, and entertain. The press is one of the media of mass communication. A news story in one national daily paper may be read by almost five million people. It will be read by those five million within hours of the happening it describes. Nothing can match the speed of the mass media in transmitting information, education, and entertainment and, despite television and radio, nothing can quite equal the power of the written word.

The public relations man exists to establish and maintain relationships between his organization and the groups around it who are important to it. To do his job he needs to receive information and to issue information. Since he is dealing more than anything else with human attitudes, he must pay close attention to the forces which create and influence those attitudes. If he wants to know what people are thinking or saying about any given subject he must read and interpret the press (although he must also read books, pamphlets, and typescripts, watch films and television, and listen to the radio). If he wants to tell people what his employer or client is thinking, he must use the media of mass communication, in which the press is a major element.

The public relations man must have an absolutely clear understanding of where press relations fits in his job. Without this understanding he cannot hope to be successful and cannot hope to play his proper role in the confused and confusing network of communication that surrounds him.

It does not matter if his dealings with the press are remote or infrequent; he must still understand what the press is all about. This is particularly true in the United Kingdom, which has the greatest number of newspaper readers in proportion to its population of any country in the world.

One illustration is the man in a public relations department whose sole concern is handling queries or complaints from members of the public, as in, say, a transport undertaking. He will probably never answer press questions or issue press releases and may thus wonder why he should know anything about the press. The reason is simple. Almost without exception, the members of the public with whom he deals will be readers of newspapers or publications of one sort or another. They will have all the normal human being's prejudices and attitudes, and many of these will be created or fed by the press. To do his job fully, the customer relations officer, as he might be titled, should know the source of the prejudices and attitudes. He himself must also be an informed person, not only in the narrow sphere of his daily duties but on a wider front. He can only become so by participating, which will include studying the press.

Finally, the public relations man is a communicator. He communicates with words and pictures, since these are the only tools he can use. The words may be written or spoken; the pictures may be still or moving. They may never be intended for publication in a newspaper or periodical. But the public relations man owes it to himself and to those he serves to be the master of words and not their slave. To arrive at the stage where he can claim that he uses words well and effectively, he will find that a constant diet of the press is invaluable and irreplaceable.

4.32 *Structure of the press*

The pattern of the press in Britain is matched nowhere in the world. The combination of national morning and Sunday newspapers covering all parts of the country, and popular and specialized periodicals serving every commercial, technical, and personal interest is not found in any other country, even in the similar industrialized societies of North America and western Europe.

The reason is largely geographical. Britain is a sufficiently small country for it to be possible for morning newspapers published in London and printed in various centres to be delivered within hours to all but the most inaccessible areas. This is not so in much larger countries where distance and the economics of distribution have inhibited the development of truly national daily papers.

An industrial society has so many facets that a great variety of publications can exist profitably by serving specialized interests, but only if there is sufficient population to make publishing economically viable. This is the case in Britain, but not always so in other advanced societies like, for example, the Scandinavian countries where potential specialist readers are much fewer.

In fact, there are newspapers covering the interests of people living in every corner of Britain and magazines dealing with every subject from accountancy to Zen Buddhism. The extent and variety of the press in Britain is so great that no public relations man can hope to acquire a detailed knowledge of all parts of it. He must, however, acquaint himself closely with those sections of the press immediately relevant to his current work and understand the nature and structure of the press as a whole.

At the time of writing there were 10 national morning news-papers; 7 national Sunday papers; 22 provincial morning news-papers; 6 provincial Sunday papers; 81 evening newspapers, including the two in London; almost 1,200 weekly newspapers; nearly 2,000 general magazines; and more than 2,100 trade and technical periodicals.

The national dailies and Sundays all base their main editorial staffs and printing operations in London. *The Guardian, Daily Mirror, Daily Telegraph, Daily Express, Daily Mail,* and *Sun* also print northern editions in Manchester, and the *Express* and the *Mirror* produce complete Scottish editions in Glasgow, called the *Scottish Daily Express* and the *Daily Record.* The *Mirror* also prints in Belfast by facsimile transmission from Manchester, using the web-offset process including colour pictures.

The provincial morning newspapers serve both the cities in which they are published and regions of varying size. For ex-ample, the Cardiff-based *Western Mail* is the only morning news-paper for the whole of Wales, while the Sheffield-based *Morning Telegraph* serves a much smaller area and competes not only with the national dailies but with the Leeds-based *Yorkshire Post*.

The major provincial dailies provide their readers with news and features of regional interest in addition to national and inter-national news. Because they tend to concentrate their smaller staffs in their own areas they have to rely mainly upon the news agencies and tie-ups with other papers for material from farther afield although the larger papers have editorial staff in London.

There is no easy comparison among provincial mornings be-cause of the diverse nature of the papers themselves. Study of the papers and their coverage quickly reveals the balance of content. Day-to-day dealing with regional newspapers provides the PR man with the opportunity to learn how their operations are organized in the places in which he is interested. If he has a Highlands story, for example, he needs to know which dailies have editorial offices in Inverness, which have free-lance corres-pondents in the area, and which rely upon staff men in Glasgow.

The provincial evening papers are more narrowly concerned than the mornings with news about their own areas, although they carry in varying degrees national and international news of major importance. Most provincial evenings publish stories of the strictly local character to be found in the weekly press in addition to items of much wider concern. The physical limitations on rapid distribution during a few hours of the day restrict their circulation areas, in comparison with morning papers which can be distributed throughout the night.

All the provincial morning papers have associated evenings, sharing administrative and advertisement staffs and production facilities. As a generalization, the evening papers tend to be more profitable than the mornings. The editorial staffs usually work separately, although extensive co-operation is, of course, arranged to make the most of facilities.

Many of the provincial morning and evening papers are organized into groups, some of which are also linked with national papers and magazines. The four largest provincial paper groups are the Thomson Organisation, Westminster Press Group, Associated Newspapers, and United Newspapers. These and others maintain London editorial offices serving all their papers.

The weekly press is incapable of general definition beyond the statement that there is a closer emotional relationship between the papers and the readers than in any other section of the press. There are weekly newspapers which in writing, comprehensive coverage, and visual presentation can match national paper standards, have circulations of scores of thousands and which flourish on national advertising and closely read local classified advertisements. There are others which are put together by a man and a boy, perhaps tackling some of the printing themselves, in a style left over from the last century and which survive on tiny circulations and a few goodwill advertisements from local tradesmen. Once again, there is no substitute for studying the papers themselves and getting to know the staffs and the way they work.

Many weekly newspapers are part of groups, sharing executive and advertisement overheads and usually production facilities too. A long list of weekly titles in a group may represent in fact the same basic newspaper with limited editorial changes for different areas. Others may be totally different papers except for the classified advertisement pages and perhaps some feature articles. Editorially these groups are organized through a head office and a series of district offices, which are sometimes wholly responsible for local editions.

The vast magazine and trade and technical press field is also dominated by groups, of which by far the most powerful are International Publishing Corporation (linked with the *Daily Mirror* and with extensive printing and book interests), the largest periodical publishing house in the world, and the Thomson Group (linked with *The Times* and *Sunday Times*). There are a number of other smaller magazines and specialized publishing houses and a great variety of concerns producing one or two publications.

Many magazines of specialized appeal are published by or for organizations of people with common interests, from those as general as the Women's Institute to those as restricted as matchbox label collectors.

Apart from the women's press, general magazine publishing has decreased in recent years, but every area of specialized publishing has continued to flourish. As with weekly newspapers, it is impossible to generalize about the character of the magazine and technical press; the variations in content, appeal and presentation are too wide.

A magazine such as *Woman*, with the largest circulation of any periodical in the world, is a highly polished example of journalism directed to a closely defined purpose, exhibiting brilliant professionalism in every aspect of its writing and design. How can it be compared with a weekly like *Engineering*, which with equivalent brilliance and journalistic skill covers a broad spectrum of technical subjects and presents them in a manner suitable for both specialized and general management?

A quarterly serving the interests of, say, railway enthusiasts may be produced part-time by a railway enthusiast who may or may not be a journalist, or by a journalist who may or may not be a railway enthusiast. A trade weekly for ironmongers may be staffed by men from the trade who have learned to be journalists, or by journalists who have learned about the trade, or by both. A tabloid newspaper for the medical profession is likely to have a writing staff with specialist knowledge and a production staff with the journalistic skills of presentation.

The variation in the number and nature of staff, the style of writing and design, the extent to which information offered by public relations people is accepted, the degree to which the editor is open to ideas, and so on, defies description. Know your papers and your journalists is the only general advice that can be given.

Collecting and distributing news to the papers at home and abroad are the news agencies, or wire services. The main internal news agency is the Press Association, which is a co-operative owned by provincial newspapers. The PA has correspondents everywhere, many of them free-lances or on the staff of local papers, and distributes news around the clock to subscribers by teleprinter ('the tape', since it used to print out in tape form). The general service of the PA is concerned solely with hard news and has a high reputation for speed, accuracy, and reliability.

In addition, there are PA sports and law report services and the Exchange Telegraph company operates a commercial and sporting wire service. The PA also has a special reporting service which can be commissioned by any publication to cover a story for which it cannot provide its own staff. This service is available to commercial subscribers, too, so that, for instance, a company in London interested in a rapid verbatim or edited report of a planning hearing in Lancashire can order this in advance and receive the text within hours.

Reuters is the principal British news agency collecting news from abroad and distributing it over here and at the same time collecting UK news and sending it overseas. It also operates a financial service. There are a number of foreign news agencies also operating in London sending material to their own and other countries.

Of particular interest to the public relations man is Universal News Services, a news agency which distributes PR stories to newspapers and a wide range of periodicals in precisely the form to which journalists are accustomed to receiving them from the commercial wire services. The difference is that the PR clients pay the agency and the papers have teleprinter machines installed free of charge, instead of paying the agency for the service they take.

In London there are other news and feature agencies, which often specialize in certain types of work, such as court reporting, sport, distribution of feature material to the provincial press or the exploitation at home and abroad of the writings of prominent personalities (known as syndication).

There are also photographic agencies which handle photo news coverage for publications without their own photographers, take pictures on their own initiative and sell them to the papers, and accept assignments from public relations people to take and distribute photographs. The photo agencies all maintain extensive libraries from which can be obtained pictorial coverage of a vast variety of subjects.

In the main news centres outside London there are free-lance news agencies of varying sizes. Many of these specialize, particularly on sports coverage, and many of them are accredited representatives of provincial and national papers or have established connections with the trade press.

Both in London and around the country there are thousands of individual free-lance journalists earning their living in a great variety of ways. In London they tend to be specialist writers, since general news coverage is almost totally organized by the press itself, but in the provinces the news free-lance functions as an extension of newspapers' own reporting staff.

4.33 *How the press works*

There is a pattern of editorial operation that is common to all publications, from the largest national daily to the smallest quarterly. Each has to gather and sift information, write description and comment, process material and select illustrations, plan whole issues and design single pages before the complete paper is printed and distributed. This procedure may be carried out by a team of scores of journalists, each with his own responsibilities and specialized skills, or the whole operation may be in the hands of one man: the editor.

Whether he leads a team or works alone, the editor has the same basic function. He represents and interprets the policies of the proprietor (in weekly newspapers and the specialized press he may, indeed, be the proprietor). He carries the legal responsibility for the content, although this is nominally shared with the publisher and printer. And he directs all the editorial activities which create a paper that will inform, stimulate, amuse, educate— and sell. He may impress his own personality on every facet of the paper to give it a character of its own.

From the largest to the smallest publication there are three basic sections to the editorial operation: administration, obtaining and creating material, and processing words and pictures into print.

No two papers, even of comparable size and type, have exactly the same editorial structure and the titles given to various functions are liable to have differing definitions. The same basic activities have to be carried out within the editorial context of any paper whether it has a staff of three, thirty or three hundred. Here is a broad outline of the departments and staffing of a daily newspaper.

Immediately responsible to the editor are one or more deputy and assistant editors. Frequently they are administrative heads of departments: news, features, and so on. They participate in editorial planning and the management of the newspaper's day-to-day operation. During the evening and early morning when the paper is in production, the night editor is in charge.

Kingpin in the organization of the news content of the paper is the news editor. On a large daily paper there are a home news editor and a foreign news editor; on an evening paper the news flow is channelled through only one news desk.

The home news editor probably has a deputy and certainly a chief reporter to assist him in directing a staff of reporters and specialist writers who go out on stories, develop information that comes in, and follow leads or items of potential interest. He builds up a schedule of the items expected, being pursued or in hand, that he judges the paper might include.

The foreign desk is the link with the paper's overseas correspondents and also handles the overseas copy that comes in from news agencies.

The sports editor heads a department that generally stands alone, with its own reporters, specialist writers, columnists, cartoonists, and possibly photographers. He has a self-contained section of the paper to fill and, apart from an occasional overlap into the news pages, the sports department is a world of its own. However, on an evening paper, particularly on a Saturday, sports news may be the main news.

The women's page editor also tends to work within prescribed limits and her team is more often concerned with feature material than with hard news.

The picture editor, or art editor, deals with all the illustrations in the paper (except perhaps in the sports pages): photographs, cartoons, decorative drawings, and so on. He has a team of photographers who work in conjunction with the news editor's team of reporters. He assesses pictures coming in from outside sources. He culls past illustrations from his own files and the picture libraries.

The financial, business or City editor also has a department of his own, often operating from a separate office in the City itself. He will have a small staff of specialist reporters and financial analysts and his own sub-editors skilled in the ways of commerce, banking, stock markets, and currency.

The leader writers produce leading articles expressing the paper's views on the issues of the day and the editor will probably be more concerned with this part of the content of the paper than any other.

The diary or gossip column editors tend to operate on their own, although they may clash with the news staff over the part of the paper in which an item should appear. A columnist may lose his lead story to the front page on a night when hard news is scarce.

The specialist writers—industrial, motoring, air, local government, medical or what you will—also often work on their own, pursuing their own lines of enquiry, but ultimately subject to the control of the news editor. The political and diplomatic correspondents will frequently be involved with higher editorial management and with leader writers because their stories create problems of interpretation.

The features editor has a staff of writers who research, devise, and create feature articles on topical or general interest subjects. He may finish his day's work earlier than his news counterpart, since the feature pages tend to change less through varying editions, while news pages are changed to accommodate fresh material edition by edition. The features editor needs to plan well ahead, since articles written in depth require time for preparation. For example, an article on the fiftieth anniversary of the end of the 1914–1918 war would not be written on the day before publication, but might be prepared a week in advance. On topical subjects, however, features may be prepared at great speed to back up news coverage.

The process of assessing stories for inclusion in the paper is known as copy-tasting. In a large newspaper there is more than one copy-taster and these men with a highly developed news sense make an initial selection of material they believe is suited to the particular needs of the paper. They examine all copy and submit their selection to the night editor, the chief sub-editor, and the other executives responsible for the production of the paper.

The news room and the foreign news room will have their own copy-tasters assessing the flow of information, picking up stories from news agencies or from outside correspondents which might be worth developing by a staff man, and keeping the news executives in constant touch with what is going on.

Since it is part of the copy-taster's job to put through out of the mass of material he receives just enough copy to fit the space available in the paper, he is more concerned with what to leave out than with what to pass on.

The chief sub-editor is in charge of the processing of copy and, with the night editor and the picture editor, determines the physical appearance of the paper. He directs a staff of sub-editors ('subs') who take copy that has originated either inside or outside the office, check it, correct it, rewrite it into the newspaper's own style or from a different angle, cut it to length, write headlines, and mark instructions to the printer. Other subs lay out pages and direct the compositors in putting them together. For the late news pages they work in the composing room—'on the stone'—alongside the printers.

The inter-relationship of activities and departments is a most complex matter, requiring both co-operation on the part of executives and skilled direction from the top. For example, if a financial scandal breaks concerning an internationally promoted golf tournament it would be more than likely to involve financial writers to interpret the ins and outs of the deal, the golf correspondent to explain the tournament itself, crime reporters to follow up police investigations, photographers to get pictures of leading participants, feature writers to prepare a background piece on the promoters or on the sponsored tournament business, gossip writers to dig out the life story of the chief sponsor, a leader writer to comment on the iniquities of the situation, and even a cartoonist to poke fun at the whole affair. With practically every department of the paper concerned except the foreign desk and the women's page, the editor would depute one of his senior executives to control the whole operation.

Lesser issues requiring co-ordination of action come up in any case at the editor's conferences, morning and late afternoon, when the news and feature, picture and sport situation is discussed among the heads of departments, the shape of the day's paper is considered and the policy line on major stories is laid down.

There are often other executives in a newspaper office with titles and duties that are not immediately apparent to outsiders and may vary widely from paper to paper. There are, for example, managing editors who are business managers and managing editors who are responsible for production.

A daily newspaper contains thousands of words, which have in turn been selected from thousands more. Where does all this material come from? A news story may emanate from a variety of sources. A passer-by may telephone the news desk to say that he has seen an attempted bank robbery before the paper's own crime reporter picks up the same information from his own official or unofficial sources. An industrial press officer may telephone to say that a major statement is on its way round by messenger or a government information officer may warn that a minister will be holding a press conference in two hours' time. The first flash from Reuters may reveal the assassination of an American politician. A free-lance in Cornwall, phoning from a coastguard hut, may be dictating to the telephone typists (copy-takers) a description of a tanker that has gone aground. A staff industrial correspondent on a press facility visit to a new factory may decide that there is a good story in the trip after all and call the news editor to advise him of its significance before dictating his story. The women's page editor may receive in her mail a contributed article from a distinguished lady she has been pressing for months to write for her. The news editor's calendar will have indicated several stock events that will need to be covered by staff reporters. The parliamentary sketch writer may come up with a colourful piece about a row in the Commons in the early hours of the morning. A big debate in the United Nations may be on the foreign editor's mind.

These are just a few of the ways in which material floods into newspaper offices in the form of agency tape, tips, releases, official statements, contributed articles, ordered and speculative stories from free-lances, pictures hawked round by the photo agencies, and material turned in by staff men who are in the office, out on assignments or based in other places. In the face of all this competition for attention, the PR man can feel himself fortunate when he has a story that is good enough in itself and well enough presented to be published in a national daily.

The provincial daily papers operate on broadly the same pattern, but with smaller staffs, fewer departments, and less specialization. The industrial correspondent may also be the air correspondent and help out with football on Saturday. The one girl reporter may be expected to produce a women's page once a week. The foreign coverage will come from the news agencies or from links with other papers. The London news will come from a small staff backed by Press Association copy. The top executives will be more closely involved in the nuts and bolts of getting the paper out.

Evening papers have the additional problem of having to work even faster to get their editions out during the day, and their internal organization is geared above all to speed of operation.

Weekly newspapers still follow the basic pattern of news-gathering and processing, but with many fewer journalists. The editor will almost always contribute directly both as leader writer and as a reporter of events to which he is invited socially as a civic figure. The chief reporter may be the news editor and some of the reporters (often most of them) will be juniors learning their business. There will be few subs and probably no specialists, other than for sport. There may be a women's page and an entertainment feature, but these may be made up of contributed copy or syndicated material, plus some local pieces written by an enthusiast on the staff. A single staff photographer is often supplemented by a local free-lance who may for most of the week be a commercial photographer. The wedding pictures will certainly come in from local commercial photographers. Minor out-of-town stories will come from village correspondents: the sub-postmistress or the local butcher earning a few shillings by scribbling a report on the flower show or the school sports day.

The weekly staff men will be supplementing their own incomes by relaying tips and stories on a free-lance basis to the agencies and to provincial and London papers; some of them may be 'stringers', regular correspondents for specific papers who may be asked by the news desk to cover a story but are not obliged to do so if their normal work intervenes, in contrast to the accredited free-lance correspondent receiving a retainer which gives a paper or agency first call on his services.

On the major women's magazines and those covering general interest subjects like homes and decoration there will also be an editorial structure of an editor, deputies or assistants, department heads, specialist writers, chief sub-editor, sub-editors, art editor, artist, and photographers, but the departments themselves will be different. There may be a fiction editor, a cookery editor, a beauty editor, a fashion editor, and so on, to fit the content of the paper. The elements of layout, illustration, and design will figure more prominently in editorial planning; colour photography for features will be planned months ahead; serials will be commissioned, studied, revised, and revised again to achieve the exact requirements of an editor who should be able to pick out a typical reader at a hundred paces on any High Street.

The smaller magazines and the more important trade and technical papers have a staff structure that usually consists of an editor and an assistant, both of whom contribute directly to the running of the paper, a sub-editor or two, several reporters, one of whom may function as news editor, and a number of regular and occasional contributors on relevant subjects. If the paper is part of a publishing group it may use a central production department for layout and design and a central art and photographic unit.

At the lower end of the scale, an independent trade monthly may run on an editor and a secretary, with the advertisement manager lending a hand and a good deal of the production left in the hands of the printers, but even for this type of paper and its weekly newspaper counterpart in remote rural areas the procedures are in principle the same.

Common to all publications is the basic process of getting into print. The copy and pictures prepared by the editorial staff are processed by the printing staff, checked in proof form by the printer's readers and by the subs, and finally passed for press. Once the presses are running, it is for all practical purposes impossible to alter anything. Up to the point at which a page is sent away, corrections are technically possible, but the chances of getting a correction made to, say, a wrong figure in a press release are infinitesimal on an evening paper, although a weekly trade paper staff is likely to have more time to catch it before it is too late.

Also common to every publication is the point at which it is too late for anything more to be accepted. An evening paper will run a number of editions, each having its own press time. One minute after edition time is too late. A monthly magazine has a printing schedule (perhaps three months ahead of publication date for colour pages) that can be varied only very slightly. One day after a section is due to go to press is too late.

It is up to the public relations man to familiarize himself with the edition times or production schedules of the publications with which he is concerned and to gear his release of material to what he learns. For example, most weekly newspapers are published on Thursday and Friday, and this means that they begin printing a day (two days if their equipment is old) ahead. Monday and Tuesdays are therefore good days to present them with a story; on press day itself the PR story will have to compete for attention with last-minute local news.

One day might seem as good as another for giving an undated story to a daily paper. Yet Friday is a poor choice because Saturday papers tend to be smaller and have less space for news and be more devoted to sport and leisure subjects. Monday on the other hand is a day when industrial and commercial news is often scarce and a story delivered for editorial men on the Sunday turn, for them to work on for the next day's paper, may have less competition than on other days of the week.

Some journalists with a common interest in particular subjects have banded together in loosely organized groups and the public relations man needs to know who they are and how they operate. These groups may consist almost entirely of newspaper and agency men, as in the case of the Labour and Industrial Correspondents' Group (and the Association of Scottish Industrial Correspondents), or of both newspaper and periodical writers as with the Guild of Motoring Writers, or of staff men and free-lances as in the Circle of Wine Writers.

There are about a dozen such groups covering a variety of specialized interests. Each has an honorary secretary able to provide a list of members' names and addresses. There are occasions when a group invitation may be appropriate, like a general-interest background event, but this approach should be used with care as in some groups there is more than one representative of a paper in membership and it may be difficult to determine which is the senior man.

These groups of journalists constitute a network worth understanding, for purely practical reasons. There have been attempts over the years to establish group diaries of events to avoid the clashing of rival press conferences, but these have largely failed for lack of support. However, the PR man contemplating an invitation for, say, building trade press editors would do well to telephone one or two to check if they have another event in their diary for the time and the day he has in mind.

Many newspapers and publishing groups have their own promotional staff, although rarely public relations staff in the accepted sense. The PR man in commerce or consultancy may find himself working with a publication's promotional manager if he becomes involved in a reader competition, joint sponsorship of an event such as a car rally or an exhibition, or even an editorial feature on some subject of wide interest such as road safety or the conservation of wild life.

This in turn may lead him into contact with the circulation staff of a paper, since no publication can be expected to participate in a promotion or espouse a cause unless the editor believes it will be of interest to his readers and will therefore boost sales or subscriptions.

The task of the circulation manager and his staff is more complicated than is often realized. The business of getting newspapers to wholesalers and retailers on time is a matter of split-second timing and manipulation of the resources of public and private air, road, and rail transport. Bad weather, public holidays, and labour disputes can easily disrupt the intricate pattern of distribution by which the same paper (although in a different edition) can be read at the breakfast table on the same day in Falkirk and Farnborough, in Norwich and Newport, Mon.

The public relations man is not likely to come into frequent contact with papers' advertising staff, unless he is directly responsible for advertising in his own job, and even then he will probably be working through an advertising agency. There is, however, one issue on which advertising managers and space salesmen will approach him and that is in connection with advertising features, special supplements, sponsored editorial sections, or whatever name they may be given by a particular publication.

These are sections of a newspaper or magazine in which both editorial and advertisements are devoted to one topic, and in which all too frequently the editorial content is selected not on the basis of the journalists' professional judgment but is directly related to the booking of space. It must be realized that, almost without exception, the motivation on the part of the publishers in producing such specials is to increase their advertising revenue. The topicality of the subject, such as holidays in the immediate post-Christmas period (when advertising is scarce anyway) or a current exhibition (on the Monday before it opens, Monday being a thin day for advertising), may give an impression of genuine editorial interest. However, a study of the quality of the text in the average supplement—on the foundry industry in the north-west, or the new towns of Scotland, or the independence of a tiny African state, or the religious press of Northern Ireland, or Polish agriculture (all genuine examples)—is sufficient to indicate their true value to the reader and, therefore, to the PR man with a message to put over.

4.34 *Writing for the press*

In theory the ideal 'situations vacant' advertisement is one that is written so skilfully that it only produces a single reply—from the one man who precisely fits the job. It probably never happens. Similarly, the ideal concept of writing public relations material for the press is that it should be exactly suited to the paper for which it is intended: written in the correct style and to an acceptable length, exhibiting a clear understanding of the paper's approach to its readers, and offering an angle or an exclusive element that is characteristic of the publication. This may never happen either, at least in the editor's opinion, but it is a worthy aim.

Written material for the press falls largely into four categories: (*a*) press releases; (*b*) captions to illustrations, and (*c*) feature articles—all submitted for consideration; and (*d*) items commissioned or requested by editors. With the exception of the fourth category, no assumption should ever be made that there will be any inherent editorial interest in what is received. Even material supplied in response to an editorial request may be rejected or delayed, altered or reduced beyond recognition for a variety of reasons not necessarily anything to do with the material itself.

To achieve success in getting one's material published it is essential to follow a number of rules based upon standard journalistic practice. The element of luck also figures largely, although it is not always easy to explain this to clients or employers. A good story may fail on a day when there are better stories clamouring for space, while an indifferent story may get greater coverage than it merits on a day when the news editor's schedule looks sparse.

The first rule is to write and present copy that is instantly recognizable by professionals as having come from a professional. In the rushed, competitive world of journalism, there is no time to linger over material which does not look immediately acceptable.

The second rule is to provide information that can quickly be seen to be relevant to the publication to which it is offered.

The third rule is to write copy that is logical, unambiguous, and immediately intelligible and attractive to editorial staff with a thousand other things on their minds and with no prior knowledge of the subject.

And the fourth rule is to be ready to provide further information, corroboration, and justification if required. This involves being flexible enough to recognize that every paper will have its own approach to the subject, affecting the emphasis and treatment given to the information provided and maybe leading to unexpected lines of enquiry. For example, a release sent to two apparently similar papers might only make a filler in one which is under pressure on space in that issue, while it might become a major story in the other which has the space, time or imagination to develop it through follow-up work. Or a run-of-the-mill story issued widely might appear briefly in a number of papers but in one office touch an editorial raw spot and provoke an attacking leading article.

The ability to work within these four basic rules can be learned, by study, by practice, and by experience. A close and continuing study of the press is an essential element in all press relations work: observation of what the papers use; how they treat news stories, features, and pictures; how coverage of items varies from paper to paper. This applies equally whether one is interested in every daily newspaper in the country or mainly concerned with the weekly and monthly journals serving a particular trade or industry.

The attitude of mind that press relations is a service to the press helps to guide the writing and presentation of material along lines that are likely to meet editorial criteria. In other words, if the public relations man can start by trying to put himself into the editor's chair and considering how his material will be seen by those who receive it, he is more likely to produce what is needed.

What, then, does the editor ask? He has limited time; limited space; a clear idea of his readers and their interest; a concept of the paper's approach to life, which is usually known as the policy although seldom closely defined; a variety of personal preferences and prejudices; and, probably, a jaundiced outlook on public relations. This last is understandable, if not altogether justifiable, because of the amount of irrelevant material that still wastes the time of hard-pressed journalists, even those who rely upon public relations sources for a growing part of their copy.

The editor wants to recognize the source of material; to be able to see at once what it is about; to be able to sub-edit, rewrite or précis it without undue difficulty into a form suited to the immediate requirements of his paper; and to be told the individual to whom he can direct questions. If the material is of no interest to him, he wants to be able to discern this without delay. If it appears to be of potential interest to him, he wants to be able rapidly to confirm this by no more than a cursory study before beginning the processes by which the material may appear in print.

These criteria apply equally whichever of the four categories of press material is being supplied, but the means of ensuring that the editor gets what he wants vary greatly from subject to subject and from one type of publication to another. Yet one aspect is constant: the concept of news. What constitutes news also varies according to readership and editorial policy, but unless the public relations man can learn enough to understand what any given editor will consider to be news, he is not likely to succeed in press relations with any consistency. News in this context means what the editor believes his readers want to read or ought to read.

The most common form of dissemination of public relation information is the press release. This can have various purposes and is sometimes given other titles, such as news release, press statement, information release, background note, and so on, but is essentially one form of written presentation. The two elements of writing and physical presentation need to be considered separately, since the approach to writing a release must differ according to the subject and the media at which it is aimed, while the rules for physical presentation are similar for all types of release.

The basic elements of writing for the papers can be applied to virtually every form of press release. The rules taught to junior reporters are equally important for public relations people. Every story should answer the questions who? what? when? and where?—and usually why? The first paragraph should contain the essence of the story: the points that make it news, the identification of what it is all about. The succeeding paragraphs should expand the story, giving the additional facts in descending order of importance so that the whole is capable of being cut to length as required without having to be wholly rewritten.

Individuals should always be given title and forename (or initials) the first time they are mentioned. Titles of organizations, however well known, should always be given in full the first time; abbreviations may be used later. Company names or brand names should not be given all in capitals, in quotes or underlined for emphasis, because the style of the paper will determine how they appear in print. Dates, addresses, spellings (s or z in organization, for example) should be consistent and preferably in a style than can be seen to be followed by the majority of papers.

Every paper has its own style and will follow it. If it is not a paper's style to use the title Mr, then those who are written about have to get used to this. If the PR man observes that a paper does not use Mr, then he only irritates the editor by putting it before the managing director's name in a release, whatever the managing director may think. If the company secretary thinks that the organization should be dignified as The Company, he will have to bow to the editor who thinks it is only a company like any other. In press relations, the editor's decision is final.

The language of the press release should be plain English. There is no place for clichés, unthinking use of vogue words, colourful prose, adjectives, and expressions of opinion in a document which must express a piece of information briefly, crisply, and logically. If the editor feels that a different treatment is necessary he will do this himself; it is the public relations man's job to give him the basic facts and try later to provide whatever information may be required.

Knowledge of the content and approach of the publications relevant to a story is the best guide to the way to write a given release. Study and practice based on the way stories appear in the press can teach the disciplines necessary to successful release writing. These disciplines can then be applied to releases dealing with subjects as varied as a new dispenser for the grocery trade or a complex stock market operation, the launching of a new bicycle or a contract for building a power station abroad, the appointment of a company chairman or the closure of a department store.

Assessment of the value of the story to the publications to which it is being sent determines the detail in which it is written and this in turn determines the length. As in all journalism, brevity is preferred: it is better to leave the editor interested in finding out more than breathless after wading through far more information than he could possibly need. Indeed, he probably will not wade very far.

The PR man's interpretation of what the editor is likely to want also decides the treatment of a story. Every organization tends to feel that it is the centre of the world and that the press should therefore care what it is doing. Every editor knows this and is ready to cut the organization and its story down to size. If the public relations man can do the job for him, the story will be that much more acceptable.

To take a simple example, if a new director is being appointed to the board of a none-too-large company, a release intended to get this event into the appointments column of the *Financial Times* should be limited to the two or three lines needed to state the facts. The reality has to be faced that very few appointments rate more than a brief paragraph in the *Financial Times*. On the other hand the relevant trade press may be prepared to run a little of the director's life story.

In another area of press relations, if an extension to a range of popular children's wear is being introduced, the interest of the trade papers and the interest of the women's magazines and the women's page writers of the newspapers will be totally different. The editors of the trade papers want to be able to tell readers as much as possible, because the aim is to help them to run their businesses profitably. The women's press are not likely to be much interested in running stories about something that in their terms is only a marginal change, but they like to see up-to-date information and perhaps file it for possible future use.

The basic *news release* should, obviously, contain only news. It should be written as a self-contained story as near as possible in manner to the style of the publications for which it is intended. If there is a need for additional background information, like a brief history of developments leading to the story itself, this should be provided as a separate document.

The *background release*, on the other hand, may be longer and more detailed. Its purpose is to provide accurate information that journalists can draw upon, and on receipt it may well be filed straight away in the paper's library. When a large document is being sent as background information for reference, an accompanying release can serve as a précis indicating the content.

A *press statement* is the term usually applied to a release giving the exact text of a formal public announcement and no more; or the verbatim text of a speech with no additional details other than who is speaking to whom, when and where; or agreed wording issued as a progress report during negotiations.

A *feature release* may contain material suitable either for incorporation into features, such as cookery notes, gardening columns, motoring columns, and so on, or for specialist publications which want to be certain they have comprehensive information on their own subjects.

An *information release* is usually for guidance. With a covering note to the editor explaining that it is not intended for publication, it can cover a wide range of topics with the purpose of keeping him in touch with current developments.

If the ideal form of press release writing is to try to achieve a common denominator of style applicable to the type of publications that are relevant, then the ideal form of press release presentation is to create copy that looks like copy to a journalist. One further element beyond normal copy is necessary: visual identification of the source.

Copy for the press is typewritten on one side of the paper, double-spaced with wide margins, and with ample room at the head of the first sheet. This to allow sub-editors to correct, cut, rewrite, reduce from many pages to one with scissors and paste, and mark instructions to the printer. Press releases should be produced in this way, on paper that will withstand folding and mailing, and then ink, pencil or ball-pen subbing.

Quarto or A4 size sheets are most acceptable. A single staple is safer than pins or paper clips. Continuation headings (catchlines) using a key word or phrase from the main heading plus the page (or folio) number should be given on each sheet. Paragraphs should not be broken at the foot of the folio because in rapid newspaper work stories are often split into 'takes' and handed out to different operators to set in type. For the same reason, and to avoid confusion if pages are dropped or mislaid, it is customary to mark the foot of each folio 'more' or 'more follows' (sometimes 'mf' for short) until the last sheet which should be marked 'end' or 'ends'. These practices are universally recognized in the newspaper business.

The heading to a press release should state what it is about. It should be a label rather than a headline, for each publication will write its own headline according to the value and interpretation it puts on the story, the style of the paper, and the layout of the page. There is no point in trying to write clever headings to attract editorial attention. If the heading announces a story which is editorially relevant and the introductory paragraph clearly summarizes the facts, the release will be considered—no more. No amount of gimmickry will succeed in winning publication for stories that do not stand up on their own.

Every release should indicate the date of issue. Upon occasions, particularly when there is a need for a complicated story to be studied in advance, or for weekly and monthly papers to come out with something (like a new model at the Motor Show) at the same time as daily papers, it is necessary to place an embargo upon the publication of a story. Otherwise, editors assume that releases are for immediate publication. The usual form for an embargo is a phrase like: 'Not for publication before morning newspapers on Friday 13 October'. Sometimes when issuing the advance text of speeches, it is necessary to state: 'Not for publication or broadcast before 1500 hours . . .' and the warning 'To be checked against delivery'.

Embargoes should be used only when absolutely necessary. They are not popular with the newspapers, which like to get on at once with the material before them. Using embargoes pointlessly is liable to lead to impatience, and editorial impatience generally leads in turn to the spike upon which unwanted copy is impaled.

Every release should indicate a point of contact for further enquiries, preferably naming an individual and giving a phone number. Newspapers exist on telephone communication and an address without a phone number creates an unnecessary delay. Newspaper stories should always carry a home telephone number too. The reporter trying to develop a story in the early evening or the late duty sub trying to recheck a figure should be able to get hold of the PR man who knows the answers rather than have to look up the company chairman and then try to get him to the phone at dinnertime.

The Institute of Public Relations recommended-practice paper on press releases lists all these physical requirements most succinctly.

Many press releases are accompanied by photographs, drawings, and diagrams. Just like the release, every picture needs to be identifiable by source, to have a date of issue and a point of contact indicated. It also must have its content briefly described. These elements can all be contained in the caption. A picture and caption can often form the whole of a release by themselves.

In a newspaper office, caption writing is a specialized task, requiring the ability to summarize both the content of the picture and its news interest attractively in very few words. In a press office, the requirement for a caption is that it should describe the picture accurately and provide the information the picture editor and the caption writer will require, including the link with any accompanying release.

Pictures of groups of people, of rows of vehicles, or of large areas of buildings, for example, should be identified clearly by naming what can be seen from left to right, by foreground, centre, and background, or whatever may be appropriate.

Captions should also be readily detachable from pictures, as the typesetting of the caption and the platemaking for the illustration will be done separately. Captions attached with rubber gum or adhesive tape are removable. Those glued down firmly will merely annoy the busy journalist who has to retype or to salvage tattered fragments and paste them together afresh. Best of all is the caption lightly attached to the back of the picture and projecting below the bottom so that it can be read in conjunction with the illustration without any need for neck twisting and turning the picture over. Pins and paper clips should never be used, as they damage the print.

It is also desirable to rubber-stamp the back of each print to indicate its source, the reference number, the photographer, and the ownership of, or freedom from, copyright.

If a printed release paper is used, the caption paper should match it so that the two parts of an illustrated story can easily be recognized as coming from one source. The design of press release and caption paper is largely a matter of taste, but there is much to be said for having printed headings that, while identifiable, are not too aggressive. After all, a press release is not a piece of direct mail advertising. The release which is headed 'News from Bloggs' in four-inch purple letters is not likely to endear itself to the journalist who prefers to make up his own mind about what is or is not news for his purposes. A modest heading that states 'from the press office of The Bloggs Organization' is sufficient identification.

An industrial company will probably bring to its press releases a different design approach from a cosmetic manufacturer or a chain of food stores. All may wish to use their trade marks, but discreetly to avoid any appearance of advertising.

Much information of potential press value is not suitable for presentation in news release form. It may lack immediacy, it may need detailed treatment, it may call for numerous examples to be given, it may be highly technical, it may be discursive rather than concise. In other words, it may be suited to a feature article rather than to wide dissemination as a brief item.

While most publications will consider using news in the form of press releases in the full knowledge that others have received exactly the same material, few are prepared to publish longer articles that they know have been widely circulated. There is little point, therefore, in settling down to writing a feature and then sending it off in the hope that one or more editors may like it.

Study of the papers that might conceivably be interested is the first step. Do they use features of this kind? Are all their features contributed by staff writers and named contributors or are some anonymous? What length seems to be acceptable?

If the answers to questions such as these indicate that a feature might be placed, a synopsis should be prepared, including a list of illustrations, if any, and the selected editor should be asked if he is interested in seeing a draft. If he is not, then the next selected editor should be approached. When tentative acceptance has been won, the article should be written and submitted, with a clear indication that amendment to suit the paper's particular needs can be arranged. The article should be written as closely to the editor's requirements as possible and the style of the paper should be followed meticulously.

All the rules of presentation that apply to press releases and accompanying pictures must still be observed, but the text and captions should be individually typed. Carbon copy or, worse, duplicated manuscripts show that they are not the first and only attempt to meet a paper's needs and are an insult to the editor.

When an editor requests a public relations man to provide material, a slightly different set of circumstances arises. The brief must be discussed between them, whether the item is no more than a short message for a trade paper special issue or as complex as a full-scale review of developments in some technique to be published at the time of an internaional conference on the same subject. The editor must say what he wants; the public relations man must say if he can provide it and may offer suggestions on content and approach. When broad agreement has been reached it is up to the PR man to deliver the goods on time, and in the form agreed. He should not go off and write, or commission someone else to write, a feature that varies from the specification. If an expert writer suggests variations, these should be agreed with the editor before the final manuscript is submitted.

With both submitted and requested features a great part of the attraction for the editor lies in the knowledge that they are exclusive to his paper. This does not mean that some of the information they contain cannot be used for other publications, but it does imply that the essence of the material and the particular way in which it is presented is for that paper alone. A breach of this journalistic understanding is a serious black mark against any PR man.

Another instance of the need to write precisely to the style of a given publication is when preparing a letter to the editor. Here again, it is vital to study the content of the correspondence columns of the paper concerned. Where a learned journal may publish every letter it receives that is not frivolous or libellous, and may not be too concerned about length, most newspapers are overloaded with correspondence and select for publication only those letters that make an interesting point in an interesting way and with reasonable brevity.

Even if a letter to the editor is a contribution to a running correspondence on a topic of wide interest, it has to compete for space just like a press release. It must, therefore, make its points quickly. Any reference back to previous letters or to other items published in the paper must be clear and sufficiently informative for new readers to gather the gist of what has previously appeared.

Generally, letters signed by public relations people are frowned upon editorially (unless they are writing on a communication topic) and it is wise to draft a letter for signature by the most appropriate senior executive available in the client's or employer's organization.

Writing a letter on a tendentious issue is a dangerous move: someone else always has the chance of the last word before the editor decides to close the correspondence.

Before any piece of public relations material is written for the press, before all the practical considerations have been thought over, one question has to be asked and honestly answered. Is the subject worth writing about at all?

The fact that it is of interest to the public relations man's client or employer does not mean that it is of interest to any reader of any paper. The fact that skilled editorial work by the PR man can make a polished feature or a lively release out of certain facts and figures, opinions and pictures, does not mean that it has the vital ingredient of news that can make it a candidate for publication in a business where every paper is overloaded with copy, pictures, and other people's bright ideas.

The PR man who succumbs to the temptation to put out a release on every topic that his client mentions to him will saturate his editorial market with unusable material and in time his usable material will be disregarded because he will be recognized as a source of non-stories. No one can afford this reputation. The apparent importance of the story is not the criterion, only the news value.

For instance, a one-paragraph release covering a new trade catalogue can find its way legitimately into the columns of dozens of specialist magazines and produce thousands of enquiries. It constitutes news for the readers of those papers because it is something they need to know and this is recognized by the journalists who put the papers together. Yet a long-winded statement on the national economy by a captain of industry may not merit a line in the national papers, perhaps because he or someone else has said it all before, or because an even more important character has said it better on the same day.

Journalists assess news in relation not only to the policy and readership of the paper, but in comparison with whatever other material comes to hand or can be obtained at the same time. If the editor of a trade weekly has received, by coincidence, three stories about largely similar new products in one week, he will not give any one of them prominence over the others, although he may write them all into one item and thus give them greater collective coverage than any one would have been worth alone. As another example, the stories written overnight for use in the first edition of a London evening newspaper are superseded edition by edition by fresher items that have a higher news value. The relative news values are changed by time and by circumstances.

There is also the mysterious assessment of the 'hard' news story as opposed to others. This generally means the story that arises from an occurrence that is in itself of wide and genuine interest: disasters, deaths of famous people, coronations, general elections, landings on the moon, major strikes, financial crises—these are the stuff of hard news.

The PR man finds himself involved in handling hard news when his employer or his client sells ten million pounds worth of goods to Russia, raises the price of a basic raw material, announces a revolutionary method of transport, opens a plant that will provide five thousand jobs in a depressed area, or fights a major legal case. Much of the time he will be handling lesser news: 'thin' stories that are based on happenings of restricted interest; on events that have been organized to try to create attention, like factory openings or centenary celebrations or cross-Channel balloon races; stories that are derived from the opinions of notable people, or those who believe in their own importance, expressed in speeches, books or contentious articles.

Such material does not constitute hard news. It will not find its place in the papers automatically because every editor knows that every other editor can use it. It has to fight for attention. The PR man has every right to try to get that attention by the skills of press relations, provided that he retains sufficient objectivity to tell the difference between good stories and poor ones.

His success will depend upon an ability to write; upon an understanding of the needs, the methods, and the attitudes of the press; upon a sound judgment of news values; and upon his skill in seeing the 'angle', the fresh approach to a story, that will appeal to journalists. In the end it will depend, too, upon a commonsense acceptance of the hard fact that there is usually no reason why anyone can be expected to be interested in the story he has to tell.

4.35 *Dealing with journalists*

Dealings between a public relations man and journalists are not, of course, confined to the written word. There are many occasions when the contact is face-to-face or over the telephone. Equally, such contact may be with individuals or with groups, and it may be short, like a telephone enquiry, or long, as during a press facility visit. The maxim: 'For the papers nothing is too much trouble—even when it is' should always be remembered.

The observation of some simple rules is vital to the public relations man in this situation. He must be factual. He must be brief, even if that is a relative term. It is his judgment that will guide him into giving a journalist as much detail as he needs to be properly informed.

He must, of course, not mislead a journalist. He must recognize that, while he is entirely within his rights in giving off-the-record information and asking that it should not be published, a journalist may ignore the request. The fact that almost all of them abide by such requests, and are indeed grateful for being properly informed rather than half-informed, is not the point.

Above all, the public relations man must be available when the press want him. That is his simple duty. If he has laid his groundwork correctly, journalists who may need to talk to him will have his office and home telephone numbers (and direct night line for use after the office switchboard has closed) listed in their contact books. Although it may be irritating to be telephoned in the middle of the night the public relations man needs to understand that this is an inescapable part of the service he is offering. Naturally it also means that he must keep at home any information and other people's telephone numbers he may need to meet such late-night requests.

The initiative for personal contact between a journalist and a public relations man—especially over the telephone—can come from either side. As a result of a press release a journalist may call asking for more details or clarification of a point. The public relations man must then decide on the spot whether he will merely answer the questions, or whether he will try to suggest a way in which the particular journalist might develop the story. The conversation will soon show whether this possibility exists.

Some questions cannot be answered immediately by the public relations man, especially if they involve technical points. Then he must offer to get the information and return the call. As an alternative he can offer to put a technical expert, or some other executive, in direct touch with the journalist. Either way he must find out the time by which the journalist needs the information and he must be scrupulous about calling back before that time, especially if there are only minutes to spare before the publication goes to press.

The further situation that can arise is that it proves genuinely impossible to answer the question in the time available. In that instance, the public relations man must still call back with whatever information he can collect and explain why there is some missing.

There is a growing contact between journalists and company executives, especially chairmen and managing directors, particularly in financial or industrial press relations. This is no bad thing, and the public relations man should not discourage it. However, if it is a feature of his organization, he should take steps to ensure that any executives who come into contact with the press understand the rules by which it works.

A press man caught in the web of edition times cannot sit and wait for answers to his questions. He will go to the source that is reliable and efficient, and that plays the game by the same rules as he does himself. The rules are not complicated and it is well within the competence of most company executives to understand and observe them.

The public relations man may decide to follow up a press release by calling one or more journalists himself to suggest developments of, or angles on, the story. It is perfectly permissible to do this, provided that he either makes it clear that he is calling more than one paper, or that each development or angle is exclusive to the particular paper. He must make sure that he never breaks faith by giving the same angle to competing papers; exclusivity is dear to the heart of all journalists.

There are dangers in indiscriminate telephone calls to journalists. If the original story is well enough written it should stand up without too much extra promotion. The follow-up phone call should be used sparingly. A habit to avoid is excessive first-name familiarity with journalists who are little more than acquaintances It is unwelcome, besides being bad manners.

On certain difficult stories, the public relations man finds he cannot materially add to his release. There may, for instance, be legal reasons for issuing nothing more than a three-line statement. In such cases it is good sense for him to put himself in the place of the journalist and list all the awkward or difficult questions he may be asked over the telephone. He must try to be helpful, but he must not reveal any more than is permissible.

While most journalists understand the public relations man's problem, they would be failing to do their job if they did not try to get more information. Today's world is a peep-hole society, and journalists have to reflect it. The classic 'no comment' answer, while not absolutely excluded from the public relations man's armoury, nevertheless smacks of unhelpfulness. It is not difficult to find variations on it that sound helpful and pleasant. The public relations man must also always be ready to fill in whatever background he can.

The telephone is a beguiling instrument of communication. It is possible to inject into the voice all sorts of meanings, not one of which may be the true one. The situation is completely different in a face-to-face confrontation. A public relations man is entitled — even if misguided — to feel that a journalist he meets is a nuisance. He may be able to conceal that feeling on the telephone; he cannot do so face-to-face. Inevitably there is a great deal of personal contact between public relations man and journalists, especially in certain kinds of work, such as product publicity. There is no mystery about the techniques. They are based on good manners and a genuine desire to be helpful. Journalists are trained to find information and to sort out the genuine from the false. Most of them can recognize instantly an insincere public relations man.

Much of the individual personal contact may take place at lunch or over drinks and it will normally be on the suggestion of the public relations man (who is the seller to the journalist's buyer). When this happens, the public relations man should not assume that an opulent lunch, or liberal quantities of alcohol, are a substitute for real information, ideas or news. It has to be recognized that there is often no good reason for wining or dining journalists beyond the fact that journalists are also human beings and are mildly more likely to look favourably on a story coming from someone they know than from a complete stranger. Hospitality does not affect the acceptability of news. In the end, too, it must be remembered that most stories are assessed for publication by someone other than the actual writer.

All dealings with journalists must be based on useful facts and good ideas. Differing circumstances may dictate the ways in which they are presented, but they do not alter the principle.

The holding of a press or news conference is standard practice when a story needs amplification or explanation to a group of journalists. Before calling a conference, a public relations man must be sure that it is worthwhile and necessary. Hastily called and ill-conceived press conferences do no good to anyone. Used as an excuse to try to fill journalists with food and drink in the hope that they will give valuable space to a 'thin' story, they become a positive menace. If all the facts can be explained in a press release, even if it needs some pages of background attached to it, there is no need to call a conference. If the organization concerned does not wish to give further explanation than is in the written statement, it is pointless to ask the press to spend valuable time travelling to and from what turns out to be a non-event.

The only justification for calling a press conference is when a story needs amplification and detailed explanation. It can then be a useful method of dealing with the press.

There is a difference between a news conference and a press conference. A news conference is called on the basis that there is hard news to give: discovery of gas in the North Sea; the signing of a new trade treaty; the opening of a new factory. A press conference (possibly better called a press reception) is called when the news is soft: new product launches; cookery column material; fashion shows. In their way they are news, but they are likely to be of restricted interest. Press conferences are mostly attended by staff reporters or specialist news writers; press receptions are attended by columnists or feature writers, too. Both kinds of functions have value, provided they are not abused.

There can be several virtues in a conference. In the first place it can save time by allowing a speaker (or speakers) to inform a number of journalists all at one time. In the second place it permits the use of charts, graphs, films or other visual aids in explaining the intricacies or significance of a story. In the third place—and sometimes the most useful—it allows personal contact between spokesmen and journalists who want to dig deeper into particular aspects of a story.

There can be a number of angles in a story which will interest journalists who are also interested in the total story. For instance, the opening of a factory could contain the following stories: the design and architecture, the method of construction, the internal layout, the facilities for warehousing, production, and dispatch, the canteen arrangements, the welfare facilities, the job opportunities, the landscaping, the extent of automation or computerization, and so on. A wide range of publications can be interested in the different aspects, but all will be interested in the central fact of the opening itself. This is a clear example of a situation best handled by the calling of a press conference.

When the decision has been taken to use the conference as a tool, the public relations man must take charge. He must carefully select the location and the timing (both the day of the week and the time of day). In doing so he will bear in mind the needs of daily, weekly, and monthly papers, and times at which they go to press. He will also bear in mind that a mid-morning conference may give him good coverage in the evening papers but kill the story for the following morning.

Many press conferences, and almost all press receptions, can be planned some time ahead. It is normal practice to give ten to fourteen days' notice, with either a printed invitation or letter. Whichever method is used, it should be sufficiently explanatory to allow journalists to use their judgment in deciding whether to accept or not. It should not, of course, give away the whole story. In some instances, a 'stunt' invitation is permissible, like one printed on leather, or a miniature bottle of perfume, or something both novel and relevant. Such invitations should be used with caution; they tend to imply that the story is thin.

It is sometimes necessary to call a press conference at short notice, holding it within hours of the decision to convene it. The invitations can then be issued by telephone, or by telegram, or by the news agencies. To justify asking the Press Association to use its heavily occupied tapes to call a press conference, it must be a genuinely important occasion. It is, of course, possible for it to be handled by Universal News Services, whose coverage takes in almost all daily papers and many trade publications.

The public relations man must see that the equipment in the room chosen is adequate: tables for the speakers (raised above the level of the audience if it is more than a handful of people), chairs, ashtrays, and mechanical items like a projector, screen, display boards, and so on. Special arrangements may be needed for television or radio. He must have a table—sometimes two—by the entrance where visitors can sign in, receive badges and press kits, and be given general information.

The labelling of journalists and company officials at a press conference is open to discussion. It is undoubtedly desirable for company representatives to be labelled. It is seldom desirable for journalists at a news conference, but may be at a press reception. It depends largely on the size and type of occasion. When it is thought necessary, the labels must be distinctive and legible. The way by which they are affixed may be important. An evening press reception attended by women journalists is not perhaps a suitable occasion for labels fastened by large pins. An alternative method is a reel of sticky labels, on which details can by typed. The labels detach without harming a dress or suit.

If hospitality is provided, whether just drinks or food and drink, the PR man must ensure that the service is good and prompt. He must also ensure that there are non-alcoholic refreshments available. He must brief the catering staff on the opening and closing times he wishes to observe, and see that they are given ample notice of his requirements.

He must then carefully prepare his press information, so that it is as complete as possible. If he is inviting several categories of the press it may be sensible to give them all a general kit of information, but include in selected ones specially written sections on their particular interests. Any available photographs must either be included in the kits, or prominently displayed near the entrance, with order forms handy. Any orders handed in must be dealt with promptly. For most occasions it is enough to have a small stock of each picture available for the journalists who need them immediately and to deal with less urgent requests later in the day.

Briefing of speakers is of paramount importance. They must be clear; they should be provided with microphones if there is the slightest doubt of their audibility. If they are speaking from prepared texts, rehearsal is essential so that they do not mumble. If they are using visual aids, they must study them in advance so that their use helps the telling of the story and does not confuse it. Speeches should not be any longer than is necessary; many company executives are not practised at public speaking and often become boring.

The handling of questions is equally important. There is a disadvantage in public questioning in that it means that all the journalists present share the questioner's perspicacity in picking out a special angle to the story. It is allowable for the speaker to promise to deal with a particular question privately after the conference, provided that he does not make it look as if he is evading the issue. The speaker should repeat the salient points of the question, to ensure that everybody knows what he is answering (apart from the fact that it allows him a moment or so to compose his thoughts).

In some circumstances, there will be questions which the speaker does not want to answer, for whatever reason. This is a potentially dangerous situation, because there are few audiences more ruthless than pressmen convinced they have uncovered a story they were not meant to uncover. The public relations man can play a useful part here by preparing a list of possible awkward questions and going over them with his speaker beforehand. If there are good reasons for not answering a question, the speaker should try to indicate what they are. In the process, though, he must not leave an implication of an answer. There is nothing immoral or unethical in this approach—the dictates of commercial security need to be observed. After all, in a democracy the press has the right to ask questions. It often has the duty to ask them. However, it does not necessarily have a right to an answer.

It may prove sensible to plant some questions in advance. Although journalists are accustomed to attending conferences, it is often surprising to see the reluctance of any one of them to ask the first question. No questions, of course, may be a tribute to the efficiency of the public relations man in foreseeing all contingencies and answering them, but if that is so it is likely that he should not have called a press conference in the first place. Assuming there are going to be questions, it is not usually difficult to find a friendly journalist or two who can be pushed into starting the ball rolling.

Once questioning is over, there should be no delay before refreshments are served. The speaker or speakers should leave the platform quickly, and if they have promised to deal privately with any questions they must keep the promise immediately, They should also be encouraged to move about among the audience.

It is often preferable that the chairman of the conference should be a real chairman who is not encumbered with the need to speak. He can introduce the speakers and channel questions. This will help the proceedings to flow smoothly.

Just as the organization must be immaculate, so must the follow-through. Whether this is for a simple matter like the dispatch of photographs or for something more complicated like a specially written technical article, it must be handled promptly and efficiently and must be delivered by the time promised. A journalist may ask for special facilities such as a personal visit to a production unit, or an interview with a senior company executive.

Many company executives, especially technical experts, are frightened of meeting journalists. The public relations man should therefore attend any personal interviews (unless a journalist or executive particularly requests him not to do so). In doing this he should not try to dominate the occasion. He should have facts and figures available in case they are needed, but he must remember that his opinions are unimportant. The journalist wants the views, opinions or statements of the executive, not those of the public relations man. The main role the PR man can play is to help everyone to be at their ease and take whatever steps are needed to ensure that both parties get what they want from the interview.

Press facility visits are a form of press conference, although they often involve only one journalist or a small group, whereas a major ministerial conference might be attended by 200 newspapermen.

A facility visit involves travel. Whether it comes about because a journalist has asked for the facility or because a public relations man has suggested making it available, the administration must be closely controlled and efficient.

The purpose of providing facilities for a journalist to make a visit to, say, a factory is basically to allow him time to see the operation fully, to make his own assessment of its importance or interest, to question any experts or specialists involved in it, and thus to write a better story. If this premise is accepted, then the role of the public relations man becomes clear. He is the provider of the facility, and that carries the inference that when the facility has been enjoyed there will be a profitable result for the journalist. This is really another way of repeating one of the truly fundamental maxims of all public relations activity: nothing replaces good planning and administration.

The travel arrangements must be carefully made, both for comfort and speed. The accommodation arrangements, if an overnight stay is involved, must be the best possible. The experts or specialists the journalists wishes to question or meet must be available and adequately briefed. The press kit provided must contain all the basic information the journalist needs. The public relations man should keep in the background but be there to help when needed.

Somewhat obviously, the problems are compounded when a facility visit is arranged for a large group of journalists, both men and women. The principles of good organization and forethought remain the same, but their application presses harder on the public relations man than when he is organizing a visit for a few people.

One of the tricky aspects of a facility visit is the tour of the location. It is essential that the guides should be well briefed and knowledgeable, and equally essential that parties should be kept to a manageable size. Half a dozen is usually the maximum; how much smaller each party should be depends on the noise level. If the guide has to shout to make himself heard he is almost bound to become incoherent.

Journalists are, of course, human and perfectly capable of making human errors. This can be an awkward problem for a public relations man to handle. The error may be one of fact or one of interpretation. The first decision is whether or not it is absolutely necessary to have it corrected. Minor errors may well be best left alone. For something which does need correction, the public relations man should discuss with the publication the best method of handling it. Dashing off a solicitor's letter is probably the worst thing to do. Equally, the public relations man should not be surprised if he finds that the correction is tucked away in a corner in small type. Unjust as he may feel it to be, in most circumstances it is best to swallow hard and get on with the next job. Corrections are defensive and achieve little. If the organization has the right reputation it will be able to ride the consequences of an occasional mis-statement or misinterpretation.

The ability with which a public relations man handles people is critical to his success. This is nowhere more true than in his dealings with journalists. If he follows straightforward rules of frankness, honesty, efficiency, and organization he cannot go far wrong, particularly if he learns to think like journalists and to understand how they have to go about their job.

4.36 *Press office organization*

A press office exists to serve and service the press. To do this properly it needs to be adequately staffed and adequately equipped. The staffing and equipping involved are obviously related to the needs and opportunities of the particular organization. A press service may be a full-time operation employing a dozen or more people or it may be the part-time occupation of one man. An organization like a nationalized industry may need to provide a twenty-four-hour service across an immense range of activity, because it is permanently newsworthy. A manufacturer of cold rolled steel bars may have one news story to issue a year. The facilities he needs are minimal while the nationalized industry must have a full complement.

Journalists are now in the instinctive state where they pick up a telephone, call an organization, and ask for the press office. When they do this, they expect to find at the other end of the line someone who knows what they are talking about and understands how to answer their questions. The press is the *raison d'être* of the press office, for nobody but a journalist is likely to call it. The function of a press office is twofold: to provide material for the press (either actively by initiation or passively by response to queries), and to interpret the press to its clients or employers. It is different from an information office, which may supply information to many other people than journalists.

It follows that the calibre and type of people who make up a press office are important. While time can teach a man how to serve journalists or write for publication without actually having worked on a newspaper, it is obviously more convenient and better sense if he has had that experience. The point is even more valid when it is remembered that a press officer acts as a journalist in actively seeking out stories about his organization.

Be that as it may, he must start with a facility for expressing himself clearly and simply in words. He needs certain other qualities too. He must be a man of integrity. He must be able to work quickly and accurately under pressure. He must not be a clock-watcher, since he must be available whenever journalists want him and not only at the times he chooses. He must be mentally agile, since he can easily be dealing with half-a-dozen things at once, and able to cope with them without putting a foot wrong. He should be an avid reader of newspapers and periodicals.

He will also need a clearly defined status in his organization. There is an extremely good reason for this. Most press enquiries have to be dealt with quickly, and many of them create the need for the press officer to find the answer from someone else. The someone else may be the chairman of the company or a backroom scientist in a laboratory 200 miles away. The press officer does not have the time (because the journalist pressing him does not have it either) to explain why he is calling the chairman or scientist, to justify the original call from the journalist, or instil confidence in his ability to do his job. He must not only be senior enough in the hierarchy for all these points to be immediately accepted, but be known to be senior enough.

When a press officer is appointed (whether he is a staff man or an executive in an outside consultancy) it is practical commonsense for a note describing him, his duties, and his likely needs to be circulated to anybody in the organization with whom he may come into contact.

Whether his experience is journalistic or not, he needs the

facility to be able to grasp facts quickly, and to acquire encyclo-
paedic knowledge about his organization, even if that is somewhat
of a counsel of perfection. It is even more important that he should
know where and from whom to obtain facts, figures or interpretations quickly. With all this allied to the knowledge of the
press he either has or acquires, he then stands a good chance of
being the kind of press officer journalists are willing to contact.

The number of people in a press office can only be decided in the
light of the circumstances of the organization. Is it in the news
every day? News does not happen only between Monday and
Friday, although many organizations seem to think it does. Is
the news in it of restricted interest, or does it range over a wide
field? Does it produce news only at certain times of the week,
month or year (like a football pools company)? Is it an organization that creates news, or one to which the press wants to come
or has to come regularly for information (like a government
department)? With what sort of press will it usually be dealing?
A manufacturer of fashion clothes will normally be in contact
with women's magazines and the women's departments of
newspapers; a manufacturer of motor cars will be talking to
motoring writers and industrial or labour correspondents; a
government department will often deal with non-specialist staff
reporters.

If the flow of news is small, whether it covers a wide area or not,
it can probably be handled by one press officer (who may also be
the public relations officer). It is an unfortunate fact that the one
person may be extended to the limits of endurance, but that is
another issue. If the news flow is large, the office may need
half-a-dozen press officers. The situation is further complicated
if the organization has a regional network, or branch offices, or
factories in other parts of the country. In certain circumstances,
each of these may need a full-time press officer, or a part-time
one. Some organizations approach this problem by using local
public relations consultants in the out-of-town areas where they
have interests.

The type of press handled decides the qualifications desirable
for each press officer. If the news flow (whether outgoing or
incoming) is general material, then the press officer needs general
experience of journalism. If there is a heavy weighting towards

women's interests, or quasi-medical interests, or technical subjects, then press officers with relevant experience are necessary. At the same time, the more specialized the interest, the more difficult it can be to decide who should fill a post. Occasionally it may be advisable to employ a technical expert with some small experience of writing, rather than a writer with some small technical experience. It may, in the end, be quicker to teach a man to write than to teach him technical expertise. It is also not too difficult to vet the material before it is issued.

Whether or not there is a need for explanatory job titles can only be settled after a detailed study of the needs. The work flow (by type and quantity) may indicate the need for a chief or senior press officer, a technical press officer, a woman's press officer, or it may not. Giving people titles may even create more problems than it settles. One of its minor advantages is the fact that in a busy office a journalist can be put in touch quickly with the press officer best qualified to handle his particular kind of enquiry instead of being switched from one person to another.

A side consequence of this thought, of course, is the need to brief telephone operators properly. Indeed, the contribution that telephone operators can make to the smooth operation of a press office can be enormous. At times of peak pressure they can save journalists from hanging on the other end of the line. They can help to see that incoming calls are dealt with quickly and in rotation, and see that outgoing calls are made quickly. A wise press officer will go out of his way to ensure that all the switchboard staff of his organization understand the demands of his job (just as he will try to understand the demands and problems of their job).

A one-man press officer may only be able to do a successful job by working incessantly day and night and weekends. Long before that point is reached, he should have a colleague. How many press officers there need to be is partly governed by the working hours of the press. For all practical purposes these are 7 a.m. for the earliest evening paper duty turns to around 3 a.m. for the last of the morning paper editions. Within these times there are peak periods as each edition goes to press, and slacker periods in between. If necessary, the hours worked in the press office will have to conform to the flow of enquiries or releases. This will mean establishing a rota in the same way as a newspaper does. Experience will soon show the hours of the day when it is necessary to have more than one person available. It will also show when it is helpful to have someone available even if they are not fully occupied throughout their turn of duty.

A twenty-four-hour office service is only feasible or necessary in an intensely busy organization. For most people it is sufficient to provide a sound daytime service (which should end at 6.30 p.m. and not 5.30 p.m. if only because morning papers do not really start operating before 10 a.m. but become exceedingly busy just before the editorial conference held around 6 p.m.); there should be ready accessibility at other times.

The degree of accessibility is difficult to gauge. It starts from the point that when a journalist wants to reach the press officer he must be able to do so without excessive difficulty. It is possible to instal an answering service at home, although this is only practical if a journalist does not have to wait long for a return call. A helpful wife is the best answering service.

The method by which journalists come to know alternative telephone numbers is again open to individual choice. It should be included on press releases. It may be included on a business card, or on an information sheet circulated to news rooms or specialist writers. Or it may prove most useful to insert it in the various press reference books, either editorially or as an advertisement.

In any event, the press office will remain open at times when it is known that a story is happening out of regular hours. Evening and weekend coverage can also be arranged by a rota system, though this is normally only needed in big organizations.

The press office is not only responsible for sending news outward; it is equally responsible for scanning the papers and feeding material inwards. This is a job which must be properly organized. It does not need to go as far as studying each edition of the national mornings, although it should take in the early and late editions of the evenings, which change greatly. It is a job which must largely be handled first thing, and can thus be the duty of the early morning press officer. The extent to which it is done varies. A large organization which is constantly in the news, or which, for one reason or another, needs to know what is appearing in the papers will require a daily circulation of press references, as a duplicated summary or as photocopies of clippings. For this to be of any value it should be with the people who need it before 10 a.m. To read, mark, and cut ten morning nationals properly cannot be done in a few minutes, although practice enables it to be done fairly quickly. For an organization with out-of-town locations, it may also be necessary to see the relevant provincial or Scottish dailies. The daily check will be supplemented by coverage of the weekly or monthly trade or specialized publications.

In undertaking this process, the press officer will be alert not only to direct mentions of his organization but also to stories which can affect it and opportunities for follow-up activity. A newspaper may start a new feature or series; the press officer should consider whether he has any material that might fit into it. Seeking and making openings like this are a measure of the ability of the press officer and whoever hires him should be looking for evidence of this kind of quality in his previous experience. It is one reason why so many press officers are ex-journalists and why it is desirable that they should be. Thinking of this type comes as second nature to most newspapermen.

It will also be the duty of the press officer to monitor radio and television programmes when there is a possibility of relevant material being included.

At the same time, a limit must be kept on the extent of newspaper scanning. It is time-consuming, and while valuable it should not be allowed to get out of hand. For many purposes, the services of press-cuttings agencies and radio and television monitoring agencies are sufficient for anything other than the main daily papers and the most relevant trade periodicals.

Press-cuttings agencies have an unhappy reputation for missing nearly as much as they find, but they are still essential. The press officer can materially help them by sending them copies of his press releases, or telephoning to warn them when he believes something of interest is going to appear. His brief to them on the names, subjects or interests he wants covered must also be clear. Early in his career, a press officer should tour a press-cuttings agency to see how it works. He should meet a principal of the agency (as well as that of a television and radio monitoring agency) to discuss his needs personally. Their reading lists and viewing coverage should be on his bookshelf.

People need equipment to be able to do their jobs. This is entirely true of a press office. Whether it is an active office, issuing material constantly, or a passive one answering many incoming calls, or whether it is a quiet office handling only a few stories a year, it cannot exist without mechanical aids.

Chief among these are two telephones. They may both go through the switchboard, or one of them may be a direct line, but there is no doubt that two are needed. (And that means two for each press officer on the staff.) Further, one of them should be usable on the internal system. If this cannot be done, he will need a separate internal telephone. There is nothing but commonsense behind this advocacy of a battery of telephones. A press enquiry may need to be answered in a matter of minutes. Often the journalist can hold on while the press officer gets the answer on the other telephone. In the end that is quicker than laboriously noting the number and telephoning back (only to find that the journalist is by then engaged on another call or has gone out).

Beside the telephone, the press officer should have a typewriter. If he has journalistic experience he will be accustomed to using a machine and will probably find it quicker than writing by hand. It will also avoid the dangers of illegible handwriting. If he has not used a typwriter before, he should learn to do so; he does not have to become a touch-typist.

Third in line of priority is a typist, preferably also able to do shorthand. A press office must never be asked to use central secretarial facilities because there is usually not the time to wait while the central unit processes other departments' work. Press officers are often not good at dictating copy or even letters, but when they have produced rough versions on their own typewriters they should be handed over to be properly typed.

In a busy press office no typist should be expected to work for more than two men, and it will be understood that they will be busy at different times. While a man is reading the morning papers, the girl will be filing; while he is drafting one story she will be typing another. At times he will have to sit and wait while she finishes typing some material; at others she will have to wait for him to finish. In a well-run press office, the typists become much more than typists; they become personal assistants. They should be given opportunities to visit a newspaper office so that they get the feel of the business they are in.

Of equal importance is a proper library of reference books. These must include current telephone directories; *Whitaker's Almanack; Willing's Press Guide;* the *Newspaper Press Directory; Who's Who in Journalism;* the *PR Planner* (published by Romeike and Curtice Ltd., the press-cuttings agency); the *Hollis Press and PR Contact Directory;* the National Union of Journalists' *Free-Lance Directory;* the list of members of the Foreign Press Association; the list of members of The Institute of Public Relations (who may be useful contacts from time to time); the *BBC Handbook;* a good dictionary (for most practical purposes, the *Concise Oxford*); Collins's *Authors' and Printers' Dictionary;* the AA or RAC handbook; the *Treasure Chest for Teachers* (an excellent source of information); Vacher's *Parliamentary Companion;* the Central Office of Information contact book; and any trade directories or other reference works particularly relevant.

These must be regarded as the press officer's working tools of his trade, constantly in use. He should not have fewer than he needs, but he also need not have more than he can use properly. The reference library must also contain facts, figures, and statements of policy on the press officer's company or client. This information must be kept up to date with copies circulated within the office.

Fifth comes the equipment needed to process stories for release to the press. This means a good duplicating machine, either the standard type using wax stencils or, if the quantity of work justifies it, a small offset-litho machine.

An office regularly issuing material to a long list of newspapers and periodicals may find it useful to have a collating or folding machine readily available. There is an immense range of office equipment which can be used with offset, but the press officer should guard against the danger of buying equipment just for the sake of having it. He should be sure that it is going to be used and worth using before incurring the expense. The only justification for the purchase of expensive equipment is that it enables him and his staff to do their job either better or more quickly.

Certainly in the category of essentials is a postal franking machine, which is infinitely quicker than licking stamps and sticking them on.

To be regarded as less essential, except for large outfits, is a tape machine (hired from a news agency) and a GPO Telex machine. The Telex—best described as a private cabling machine —is becoming more and more useful, but its value is closely linked to the amount it is used. If only one message a day is being transmitted the cost is not justified. Its great advantage is that messages can be transmitted and received at almost the same speed as over the telephone but there are no dangers of mis-hearing or misinterpretation, since the messages are written ones.

Finally, there must be a good copying machine for processing cuttings or reports for internal circulation.

Press-cuttings are a guide to what the press (as representing the trends of thought and action in society) is thinking. They are also a yardstick by which the press officer (and his employer) can judge his work. If he constantly issues releases which are not published there is obviously something wrong with them. It may just be bad luck if a good release fails to see the light of day anywhere, but it cannot be bad luck if they go on failing. A simple way of checking this is through press-cuttings. However, they are not collected just to make the press officer feel good. Other people in the organization may need to see them, or want to see them. What they see, too, is not only complimentary refer-ences. They must see criticisms, and they may need to see general background material or examples of what is being written about competitors. In a sense this is a passive use of cuttings. There are active uses, as when they are reproduced for distribution to sales-men to provide them with talking points with customers.

Sometimes, a company will wish to take reprints of an article in a newspaper or magazine for direct distribution to share-holders, or some other group. The duty of arranging this will fall to the press officer. Faced with it, he must check with the publica-tion concerned its rules about reproductions; most papers will provide reprints at a nominal cost. Whatever arrangements are made should be confirmed in writing. One point to remember is that type matter is broken up fairly quickly, so that a decision to ask for a reprint must be taken promptly. It is always possible to re-set the type but it is unnecessarily costly. An alternative method is to reproduce cuttings by litho from actual sheets taken out of a publication.

The press office should have its own messenger facility, or access to a general one, with priority understood when it is used. Despite the speed of modern communications, there are times when nothing is more valuable than a messenger boy who understands the urgency of press relations work.

The most efficient press officer, aided by an able staff, and equipped with all the latest mechanical and electronic aids, will not succeed unless he pays proper and constant attention to his distribution lists. These are created by a mixture of personal experience and recourse to reference books. They must be regularly updated. The basic list will come from reference books. To this will be added new names as the job progresses. Equally important, names will be deleted as necessary. It does not always matter if a new publication is not added to a list for a week or two; it is crass inefficiency if material is sent to a publication the day after it has folded. The press officer should make it his business to read the trade press—*AdWeekly, Campaign,* and the *UK Press Gazette*—each week and mark any news about changes in publications or discontinued or new papers. His secretary should see that this information is translated into the press lists the same day. Depending on the frequency with which he is issuing material, the press officer should go over his lists monthly or quarterly. He should not do it less frequently.

Stocks of pre-printed envelopes or labels should be kept so that a release can be distributed speedily. They may be prepared on one of the recognized address-plate systems or they can be individually typed. There should be an index system of some sort, either in a loose-leaf book or on cards. The system used for preparing envelopes and keeping a master list is unimportant. What is important is that it should be done and done efficiently.

There is constant discussion on the point of whether press releases should be addressed to an individual by name or in his capacity as a specialist or departmental head. It is unwise to send them to an individual, unless his job is also specified, as A. Bloggs, Agricultural Correspondent. The safest procedure is to address news material to the news editor; feature ideas or synopses to the features editor; financial material to the City (sometimes called financial) editor; and so on.

To achieve simplicity in procedure it is permissible to address all newspaper material (other than financial, since City offices are often in separate locations) to the news editor, who will pass it on. In the instance of trade papers and magazines, the variation on this is to address material to the editor (who probably acts also as news editor, especially when he is working with few staff). An alternative which is also permissible is to send material to a specialist correspondent, with a copy to the news editor for information. When this is done the release should be clearly marked to that effect. Material should not be addressed to individual members of the general reporting staff. Equally, for a national daily or evening paper it should never be sent to the editor by name. The best guide is normal courtesy and commonsense. Although more and more reference books appear which give the names of senior management and editorial staff, their names should be used by the press officer with care. A contact is somebody known personally, not someone whose name appears in a reference book.

Each press officer will also build up his own particular list for provincial stories. It will include free-lance journalists and the correspondents for papers published outside the area, whether regional or national. Maintaining these names demands just as much care as any other list.

There are exceptions to all these rules. A journalist may specifically ask to be included on a press list, even if he has no apparent professional interest in it. When this happens the press officer should comply with the request. A journalist may ask to have releases sent to his home address; again there is no reason not to comply. A news editor may specifically demand that all releases are sent to him and him alone; the press officer can do nothing but agree.

An unclassified general press list is mostly useless. It should be broken into categories, according to need. At the same time, the press officer should always look critically at each story he puts out to see whether it contains an element of interest to publications which do not normally appear on his lists. These will seldom amount to more than a handful and envelopes for them can be individually typed. If there is a likelihood that they will appear again they can be transferred into the index and address-plate system.

The press officer who is capable and lively is an asset to both his client or employer and to the press. To become capable means a great deal of hard work, not only in doing the job but in learning about it. The press is a constantly changing, ever-challenging business and few emotions are more satisfying than that experienced by a press officer who succeeds in handling and placing a difficult story. He can then justifiably feel that he has done a good day's work. Proper preparation will make it more likely that he will succeed.

4.4 PRINT

Printing is the oldest mechanical technique of communication. In the western world it has been possible for more than 500 years to reproduce words on paper as a service for anyone who can pay. For most of that time, up to the last twenty years, the basic principles of assembling characters and impressing them on surfaces were little changed, although enormously refined. Today, printing is undergoing a technological revolution which is altering both the structure and economy of the industry and the possibilities open to the customer. Yet much printing is still undertaken by highly mechanized versions of methods that Caxton and Gutenberg would recognise.

As with any complex technique, it is easy for a communicator to become too deeply involved in methods and to lose sight of the essential requirements of finding the best medium and the right way to reach his audience. Print is a specialized subject, in which a little knowledge is often a costly as well as a dangerous thing.

The public relations man needs to know enough to make a judgment on what process to use, on which printer to choose, and how much to pay. While his knowledge should be sufficient to prevent the wool being pulled over his eyes, he must always recognize that the skills of the printer are not acquired by reading books or even by a few years of print buying. In other words, he must know when to seek advice and when to take it.

Just as there are several different printing processes, so there are varieties of printers, large and small, specialized and general. The first task of a print buyer is to decide which process to use for his message and which printer to choose to carry it out. This is a decision he may be able to make for himself if the subject is simple or if his experience is extensive; alternatively he may employ a print consultant to advise him or obtain advice from a graphic designer; or he may ask printers what they would suggest. In the last case, it is as well to remember that only the most enlightened printer's sales representative is likely to refuse work for which his company may not be wholly suited. It is as well therefore to discover what a printer's strengths and weaknesses may be before asking his advice on a particular job.

To make even the beginnings of a choice practicable, it is necessary to understand what the main printing processes are and how they are used. The industry itself divides fairly neatly into printers capable of handling work by these processes on a large or small scale, and with gradations of quality and expense.

Printing is broadly divided into three main processes: letterpress, offset-lithography, and gravure, representing three ways of reproducing words, figures, and illustrations on paper or other surfaces. Broadly common to each of these are the various processes by which paper and ink are made, words and figures are assembled, and printed sheets are collated and bound. Each process has its advantages for particular types of work.

Letterpress is relief printing from a raised surface. A rubber stamp is the crudest example, a daily newspaper one of the most complex. In letterpress work, the beginning is with the text (copy) which has to be set (composed) in type or on film. Continuous passages (body or text matter) are almost always set mechanically, using machines which set either complete lines of type of the required length (measure) or cast lines of individual characters. The Linotype and Intertype machines cast lines (slugs) and the Monotype machine produces separate characters.

The slug casters, as used on newspapers, offer speed and therefore economy, both of setting and correction; the Monotype offers better reproduction possibilities, easier setting of mathematical or other complex copy, and a wider choice of alphabet designs (typefaces).

Heading and display lines can be set by hand by the compositor (comp for short) using founder's type (reusable individual characters bought individually, as sorts, or in complete sets—founts—from type founders); they can also be produced as slugs on keyboard typesetting machines adapted for larger sizes, or on the Ludlow, a machine which casts slugs in display sizes.

Both text sizes and display sizes of types are available in great profusion. The makers of typesetting machines and the type-founders provide display sheets (type specimens) of what they can offer. Most printers make up their own type books to indicate what they have available; other faces can be bought in as founts or, alternatively, special settings can be obtained from trade typesetting houses.

Printers work in measurements of their own. In Britain the size of the characters is measured in points, approximately seventy-two to the inch, and the widths in ems, the square of the point size. Measures (widths) are always based on the pica, or 12-point em, approximately six to the inch.

Incidentally, the basic point system seems likely to be unchanged by decimalization and metrication. It is by no means universal even now, with differences between the British, American, and continental systems in spite of years of discussion about standardization within the printing industry.

The type set by hand or by machine is assembled by the compositor, tied up to hold it together temporarily, and placed in trays (galleys). First proofs (galley proofs, or pulls) are pulled on a simple proofing press so that the setting can be read for correction. Errors made in the setting are rectified (house corrections) at the printer's expense and clean (corrected) proofs are offered to the customer. His amendments and afterthoughts (author's corrections) are charged as an extra and may be expensive as this is time-consuming work. If there are extensive corrections, fresh proofs (revises) are supplied.

When the corrections have been completed, the text and display type, with the illustration plates (blocks), are combined (made up) into pages according to the design (layout) for the job. The whole, when locked into a frame (chase) ready to put on the printing press is a printable unit called a forme. Before printing, further proofs (page proofs) may be pulled for the customer to make a final check on accuracy, spacing, alignment, and so on. When the forme is ready to print, after adjustments have been made (make-ready) to ensure the best image (impression), final proofs (machine proofs) may be offered for a last-minute scrutiny. However much the printer's readers may check, the ultimate responsibility for accuracy lies with the customer.

Only at this point, with the actual ink and paper for the job on the machine, can colour work be finally assessed. Earlier proofs may be deceptive.

Letterpress printing presses vary from small hand-operated presses that might be used to produce a few dozen posters, through small motorized machines printing quantities of stationery, to vast and complex high-speed rotary presses that can print and fold a whole newspaper.

Some presses print both sides of the sheet at once (perfectors); others can print more than one colour on the same side of the sheet in one operation. As many as sixty-four pages of a book are often printed on a single sheet at one time, the pages being arranged (imposed) in a mathematically calculated pattern that allows the sheet to be folded and cut (trimmed) to make a book section (signature) of consecutive pages.

Illustrations for letterpress reproduction, both black and white and colour, are printed from etched metal or plastic blocks, mounted on wood, metal or patented mounting systems to bring them to precisely the same height as the type. Blocks are measured in inches; after metrication they will be measured in centimetres.

There are two types of plate made by the process engraver (blockmaker): line and half-tone.

Line blocks (zincos) are made from outline illustrations without too complex a degree of pattern: sketch maps, lettering, pen and ink drawings, and so on. The illustration (original) is reduced or enlarged photographically to the size required to fit the layout, is transferred (printed down) to a sensitized plate, and the non-printing parts etched away by the engraver.

Many uniform patterns (mechanical tints) can be applied to shade, enliven or emphasize parts of line blocks. Blockmakers supply specimens to show what their studios can do. Alternatively, the original can be treated with transfer shading material, of the Letraset variety, which is also suitable for line reproduction.

Half-tones are made from photographs, wash drawings, paintings, and other complex originals. Here the subject is photographed through a cross-lined glass screen on which the rulings are measured in so many lines to the inch. This converts the image into varying sized dots corresponding to the gradation of tones in the original. The dot pattern is transferred to a sensitized plate and again the unwanted parts are etched away to leave the tonal areas as a relief surface.

The screens used are coarse or fine according to the quality of the paper on which the illustration is to be printed. Fine art reproductions on glossy (art, or coated) paper might be 135 screen (also written as 135 #), while photographs in a local newspaper, in which the screen dots can be seen with the naked eye, might be as coarse as 65 screen.

To reproduce colour originals it is necessary to make sets of blocks and print one over the other. A simple black and red line illustration needs only two plates and two printings; to reproduce a painting in full colour would require at least four plates and four printings: yellow, blue, red, and black.

To make these the original is photographed through coloured filters to separate out the basic colour values and blocks are made for each. These blocks are then printed one precisely on top of the other (in register) so that the dots of various colours combine to give a rendering of the original. Some loss of colour accuracy is inevitable and the assessment of the quality of colour plates is a skilled matter. If the final colour proofs from the engraver do not offer a satisfactory rendering, certain further correction can be made on the plates themselves.

Colour plates are expensive to make and should be carefully preserved for further use, whereas line or half-tone blocks are less often worth keeping unless the subject is one likely to be reproduced again, in exactly the same shape and size.

Beyond the straightforward line and half-tone blocks there are endless treatments available through the skill of the engraver. Solids and half-tone can be reproduced on the same plate (line and tone combinations). Lettering or line illustrations can be shown overprinted on photographic subjects. White lettering can appear in solid or shaded backgrounds (reversed line blocks). Half-tones can be squared-up, or framed, or with the edges softening away to nothing (vignetted), or with only the subject visible without any background (cut-out), or with highlights appearing pure white (deep-etched). Blocks and mounts can be pierced for type to be inserted for printing within the picture.

Because of the expense involved in process engraving and the time taken to send originals out to a blockmaker, many printers, particularly local newspapers, instal electronic engraving machines, such as the Klischograph. These offer sound reproductive quality, but less variety of treatment, and many models are not capable of enlarging or reducing the size of original artwork.

As a general rule it pays to give the engraver an original that is larger than the size required for the finished block. Enlargement invariably means loss of sharpness (definition), while reduction can sometimes appear to sharpen an indifferent original. When in doubt, ask the printer's advice.

If a block is to be used repeatedly, as with a trade mark or a titlepiece, or if duplicates are required for distribution, facsimiles may be made relatively cheaply. Simple duplicates are castings (stereotypes, or stereos) made by pouring molten metal in papier-mâché moulds (flongs or matrices, mats for short) taken from the original type or line block or even from coarse screen half-tone. For finer screen half-tones duplicates are made by an electrolytic deposition process (electrotypes, or electros).

Display advertisements, other than those set by the printer (house-set) are supplied to publications by advertising agencies in stereo or electro form. To ensure uniform quality and accuracy, such advertisements are generally produced by taking reproduction proofs (repro pulls) from type matter set by a specialist house (trade setter) for blockmaking along with illustrations.

Letterpress is still the most widely understood printing process (although offset now rivals it in output and versatility), partly because it is readily available and partly because it is flexible and economic for a great variety of jobs. For example, any work which requires frequent or last-minute correction is more conveniently handled by letterpress; any job which is mainly typesetting without much illustration is likely to be capable of higher quality reproduction; and for small quantities (runs) required to be produced swiftly and cheaply letterpress remains preferable.

The next most common form of printing is offset-lithography, known as offset. Originally lithography was a system of creating an original on a smooth stone and then using the mutually repellent qualities of grease and water to determine which parts of the image should retain the ink and thus give an impression when paper was pressed on to it. This laborious process was the method used by Toulouse-Lautrec for his famous posters. Litho is planographic printing, using a flat surface, as opposed to the relief process of letterpress.

Nowadays the original—text and illustrations—is printed photographically on to a grained aluminium plate, the plate is clipped round the cylinder on the press, damped and inked, and brought into contact with another cylinder rotating at the same speed which has a rubber or composition blanket upon it. The image is transferred to the blanket which in turn transfers it to the sheet of paper by the pressure of a third cylinder, the impression roller.

Thus the litho plate, being transferred twice, or offset, differs from letterpress type and illustrations in being a readable, left-to-right image instead of a mirror image.

Since the offset plates are prepared photographically, everything required to be printed has to be reproduced on film. Type matter can be produced either by conventional letterpress setting, high-quality proofing, and photographic reversal for printing down, or by setting direct on film by photocomposition machines.

Proofs of type matter, whether on paper or as contact photos, need to be corrected as for letterpress, but it is essential that all changes and alterations of mind are settled before the complete original is photographed for platemaking. Whereas in letterpress the type can be altered up to the moment the press starts to run (or even during the run in case of disasters), once a litho plate is printed down no change can be made without making an entirely new plate.

Just as for letterpress, illustrations may be line or half-tone, and colour work follows the same general pattern. There is, however, greater flexibility in producing combinations. All illustrations are photographed to the required size and made up with the text in film form on one master sheet according to the layout. Once the plate is made, printing can begin without the costly make-ready procedure necessary for a quality letterpress impression. The standard of reproduction can be quite as good as letterpress.

Litho has the advantage of economy compared to letterpress, particularly for heavily illustrated jobs and when using colour, for quantities of more than about 20,000. Much shorter runs are economical, too, using the small offset machines, like the Multilith and the Rotaprint. These are widely employed as a high-class method of duplication, offering better quality than stencil duplicators, with metal or paper plates that can be made on an ordinary typewriter using a special ribbon. However, despite the limits on the size of sheet they can take, these machines have considerable flexibility and versatility and can produce a great variety of work provided that not too many colours are required.

A useful advantage of litho is that not only can old jobs be stored economically in plate form, but that existing letterpress jobs can be reproduced cheaply and easily by photographing finished copies, thus avoiding the expense of re-setting.

The term web-offset is widely used as if it were some magical formula for solving the economic ills of the printing and publishing industry. It refers simply to continous printing by offset litho with the paper fed from a reel, as with rotary letterpress, instead of in individual sheets. This system is growing steadily for the production of weekly newspapers and newspaper-format specialized publications; a few evening newspapers are also produced by this system, which can offer economies in both capital costs and machine time over rotary letterpress. It is particularly suited to long runs and multicolour jobs with many illustrations.

Associated with web-offset in many people's minds is photo-composition. This is a means of typesetting without metal, the characters being stored as photographic negatives and assembled on film. Photocomposition is, however, also used for book printing and, as its relationship with computer control mechanisms matures, will undoubtedly increase, although the era of conventional metal type is far from over.

The third major printing process is gravure, the short term for photogravure, the process by which almost all the mass circulation colour magazines and most postage stamps are produced. In this process the whole image is reproduced through a fine screen and there is a consequent loss of quality in the reproduction of type for the sake of the pictures.

Since gravure is only economically justified with extremely large runs, measured in hundreds of thousands at least, it does not often figure in the processes likely to be used by the public relations man and the different editorial production procedures involved are more the realm of the magazine journalist. Suffice it to explain that the whole image is photographed on to a cylinder and the areas to print are etched into hollows. This is called an intaglio process, as opposed to the relief and planographic process.

The etched hollows contain the ink according to the weight of colour required and a blade removes excess ink from the non-printing surface of the cylinder. An impression cylinder presses the sheet of paper against the etched cylinder and the ink is transferred to print the image.

Gravure can offer exceedingly fine results in reproducing photographs and paintings, and smaller machines are available for shorter runs, although initial costs are still high.

Another, totally different, form of printing which is particularly useful for short-tun colour work such as posters and display cards, is screen printing. Originally, like litho, this was exclusively a hand process involving a stencilled image and a fine mesh silk screen through which ink was squeegeed on to paper or card. Today it is more sophisticated and photographic processing is employed for the production of illustrations and type, as well as the opaque solids for which the method is particularly suited.

The technology of the printing industry is changing fast and as a consequence the economic structure is altering too. The tendency is for more and more firms to specialize and the day of the all-purpose jobbing printer who would attempt almost any kind of work is probably numbered. More and more it is necessary for the print buyer, expert or inexperienced, to try to match his work to the printer best able to carry it out.

The printer who has made vast capital investment in gravure presses capable of printing full-colour periodicals by the million is not likely to be at his best tackling the last-minute corrections to setting of financial tables that are usually required when annual reports are prepared. The progressive group of provincial weekly newspapers that has retooled its production to take advantage of the economies of web-offset is not the place to look for a low price for 500 business cards. These examples are elementary, but the specializations of printers are endless.

Some houses are experienced in mathematical setting or are equipped to cope with foreign languages and have correctors (readers) with advanced skills. Some are geared to the production of the long-run complicated stationery required for mechanized accounting; others have arranged their composing rooms, their labour force, and their presses to cope with the rapid production of a clutch of trade papers.

It is the print buyer's responsibility to find out for himself whether or not a printer may be the right one to handle a particular job. There is no substitute for visiting a plant to see what is offered; specimens of finished work are little guide in themselves other than to the ultimate quality that can be achieved; they tell nothing of cost, time or trouble. It is also always worth obtaining competitive estimates for a job and insisting that quoted prices are broken down into their elements. The British Federation of Master Printers has a widely used standard costing system, details of which are available to all.

It is frequently forgotten that about one-third of the cost of any printed material is represented by the paper. The purchasing and selection of paper is a specialized task. Printers have their own tastes and know their own presses, but the choice of paper should be based first of all on the effect it is desired to achieve, together with the printing process being used and the purpose for which the piece of print is intended. A reference leaflet has to withstand much handling; a sales brochure may have as a first requirement maximum quality of reproduction of illustrations; a long-run pamphlet may have to be produced as cheaply as possible; and so on.

The paper merchant is the source of technical and economic advice on what paper to use for which job. He can not only talk about quality and suitability, but can also indicate sizes from which an unusually shaped job can most economically be cut or suggest bulk purchases for similar jobs or for potential reprints to obtain a better price.

The sizes of printing paper are still based to a large extent on traditions going back hundreds of years and printers use terms like quarto and demy in relation both to the size of the printed sheet and the capacity of the printing press. International paper sizes, popularly known as A sizes, have been gaining ground for some years. By the early 1970s it is probable that metrication will have produced a situation in which all printing paper will be produced in these sizes, although not all printers will have machines suitable for their most economic use.

The other essential physical ingredient, ink, is a matter for the printer, perhaps in consultation with the engraver if particular illustrative problems are involved. The public relations man seldom needs to involve himself, other than in a simple matter such as ensuring accurate colour matching.

The final, vital ingredient is design. Anyone can design a piece of print, even with no technical knowledge of the processes involved, by the age-old system of scribbling on the back of an envelope and asking the printer for 'something like this'. The result is what is often called a comp's layout, a putting together of the elements of the job in a balanced, mechanical way according to the compositor's craft training and his view of what the customer ought to have.

Design for print is a delicate matter, involving a subtle assessment of the aim of the job, the money available to carry it out, the nature of the audience, the visual style that is relevant, the resources of the printer, and the imaginative possibilities of the subject matter. It is an art and a craft, and, as such, is grossly under-rated by all those who declare that they know nothing about design but know what they like.

A graphic designer costs money, but he does more for his fee than prepare a layout for the printer. He may check and prepare copy for setting; obtain and advise on illustrations, including retouching and commissioning original artwork; find printers and compare estimates; organize a production schedule, pursue the printer and blockmaker, pass proofs, and in every way make certain that the job is completed to the client's satisfaction. He can save the client a great deal of time and money.

A graphic designer is also a typographer, who knows the character and suitabilities of the vast range of typefaces that have been designed over the years (and the lesser number available on film), who understands what is fashionable and what will shortly be dated, who never loses sight of the fundamental point that typography and graphic design are not only a matter of making attractive patterns but of creating a legible message for easy absorption.

The public relations man who can recognize half-a-dozen typefaces and tell newsprint from art paper is as far from being capable of graphic design as a child who can say its ABC is from reading an adult book.

Advertising agents are almost always capable of designing print, although there is a need to be wary of the artist in the studio who may understand design but has no practical experience of putting ideas into print. There is no substitute for this practical experience. A designer who specifies a rare type for a job being undertaken hastily by a provincial printer does not recognize the delay he will cause while it is found and trade-set elsewhere. The graphic artist who produces a rough based on a non-standard (or bastard) size of paper may have forgotten that cutting to waste to follow his design may considerably increase the cost of the job. And so on.

Many large printers have design studios either of their own or which they employ on a regular basis; these have the advantage of knowing the printer's capabilities. Some large concerns have their own design departments, which can work readily within a given style but are liable, for obvious reasons, to get into a rut. When good design is the most important element in the job, the independent graphic designer, with many different clients and a limitless range of printers to choose from can bring a fresh approach to bear that will justify his generally higher cost.

Whatever the skills of the designer and the printer, the co-operation of the client is still necessary to the efficient, and therefore economic, completion of a job. In the first place, having defined his audience and his message, he must make up his mind how much he is prepared to spend, what effect he wishes to achieve, what time schedule is involved for production, and what quantities are required immediately and for the future. He must be prepared to amend his ideas if the designer and printer demonstrate that they are not practicable or economic.

It is the client's task to provide the text and the headings, the illustrations and the captions, and to undertake sub-editing, indexing, and other editorial work, unless he deputes this to the graphic designer or an editorial agency. It is up to the client to ensure that material is not covered by someone else's copyright or, if it is, to obtain permission to reproduce it. It it his responsibility to keep libellous matter out of the copy, although the printer legally shares culpability for what may be published.

The client must also accept that upon him must rest the ultimate decision for what is to appear in print. Material should be checked and cleared, technically, legally or however may be appropriate, to the nth degree at the copy stage and a clean manuscript given to the printer for setting. Thereafter, every change of mind, even down to a single comma, costs time and money.

Likewise, layouts should be discussed and approved before the image is committed to the page. This requires an ability to visualize, which the PR man can acquire with practice. Most employers and clients lack this ability and want to see finished proofs before they are prepared to give an opinion. To avoid the costly risk of major changes when the job is almost complete, it is often worth asking the designer to produce finished artwork for a cover design or getting the printer to set up one specimen page to demonstrate the style. In this way approval can be obtained before too great a financial commitment has been incurred.

For the average public relations man, it is probably best to find a range of designers and printers who can be trusted and then to use them fully and wisely. For those who need to buy print regularly, there is ample scope for education, in books, in the part-time courses run by art colleges and print schools in all major centres, and by reading the technical press.

5

Visual Communication

PHOTOGRAPHY IS AN ASPECT of public relations work that many people find difficult to understand, let alone to use well. It is bedevilled by the number of amateurs—some admittedly skilful—who surround the public relations man at every turn. Yet if it achieves its purpose, which is to tell a story in a picture or to help words to tell it better, it is one of the most powerful techniques a public relations man can command.

Mastery of the technique comes from logical thinking, clear planning, and the understanding of a number of rules. To know the rules and apply them will assist the process of thinking and planning.

Somewhat obviously, the first and fundamental rule is to determine whether a picture is needed at all. A photograph, however good, may detract from a story, or may confuse the audience. A drawing may put over a point more successfully.

If it is decided that a picture is necessary (which is not at all the same as deciding that it would be useful or pleasant to have one), it is then absolutely vital to know the use to which it is to be put. Photography is not just a matter of pointing a camera at an object and taking a picture. It is a highly skilled trade and one in which it is easy to waste money. Before any photography is undertaken, the photographer—and the public relations man—must know the reason for the photograph and the public relations purpose behind it. For instance, if a photograph is needed to illustrate the power of a fork-lift truck, it will be different from what is needed to show the ease of operation of the foot controls. For the former, the picture might show the truck with an obviously heavy load fully extended on the forks. For the latter, the picture could be a close-up of the controls.

In any event, there is always a great need for genuine imagination on the part of both photographer and public relations man, particularly when dealing with standard subjects, like the presentation of long-service awards to employees.

The public relations man has the task of briefing the photographer, but not the task of taking the picture. Properly briefed— that is, told all the reasons for taking the picture—a competent photographer should know what to do. Nothing infuriates him more than a public relations man who interferes too closely. His fury is justified.

It is always essential to pick the photographer for the job. Clearly it is pointless to hire a fashion photographer to take pictures of industrial manufacturing equipment, and vice versa. Yet this simple rule is often forgotten. The most sensible practice is to build up a list of photographers who can meet particular requirements. Keep it up to date and always be on the look-out for new ones. Photography, especially in public relations, is a partnership. There is often little to choose between different photographers. Each public relations man's list should include those with whom he can work most successfully. This is no reflection on the personality of the others; it is merely a matter of convenience.

In picking a photographer for the first time care is needed, especially when the job is outside London or away from one's normal base of operations. It is risky to choose a photographer without seeing examples of his work, and checking his methods. There are subtleties to this which must be considered. A news photographer may be accustomed to working for newspapers or news magazines; there are slight differences in their methods. A local photographer who specializes in wedding groups is unlikely to be much good at handling close-ups of intricate machinery. Equally, the public relations man must find out whether the cameraman works quickly or slowly, with flash or set lights (which have to be plugged into the mains), and so on. It is always well to remember that photography can cause considerable upheaval, especially in a factory. The public relations man must be sure to minimize this.

Relatively large sums of money are involved in taking pictures, and it is thus wise to take a great deal of care before settling on the photographer to commission for a job.

It is a truism that every picture tells a story. Certainly newspapers, magazines, and other periodicals would be dull without pictures. Even the most learned technical and professional journals find it necessary to illustrate some articles with photographs.

The value of a photograph can be twofold. It can either illustrate a point which it would be difficult to explain easily in words, or it can act as an eye-catcher.

There are many examples that explain this thought, but one or two will suffice. A public relations practitioner working for an internationally known china company wanted to demonstrate dramatically the strength of the company's bone china. So he stood a sheet of armour-plated glass on four bone china cups and then had an elephant stand on the glass. The cups did not break; pictures were taken; and the public relations man had striking visual evidence of his story. Another man was faced with the task of showing the strength of steel-capped safety footwear. To do so, he hired a double-deck bus and had it drive over the feet of a man wearing what looked like ordinary shoes. He made his point.

Both photographs fulfilled both values: illustrating a point more graphically than in words and catching the eye. Their success was partly based on the old claim that the camera cannot lie. Although this is not true (and never has been) it is generally believed instinctively by most people.

Of course, the camera itself does not lie. It records what is before it, even though it may be distorted by the lens. It is later that retouching in the photographer's studio may change the original. However, it is necessary to be clear on the subject of retouching. Think back to the elephant standing on the glass on the china cups. It would be possible to take a picture of the elephant standing on the glass and later paint in four china cups. This would be wrong, because it would be a lie. But there would be nothing wrong in using retouching techniques to emphasize the cups and make them stand out more. An even more simple example is the retouching which is commonly undertaken for photographs used in catalogues. Here the emphasis is required on the actual product and the objective is more nearly achieved by painting out all the background. Providing that retouching, painting in, highlighting, air-brushing, and similar techniques are used only to emphasize something which is true, there can be no objection.

The same principles apply to some of the tricks of the trade used in studio photography. A particular example of this is the photography of cooked food. If a recipe appearing in a magazine is of a way of cooking a joint of gammon, decorated with cloves, it is made more lively with a photograph of the finished result. When it is actually cooked for consumption, this joint is glazed with brown sugar. However, under the intense lighting used for this kind of photography, the glazing soon dries up and the end product looks dull and uninteresting. To overcome this problem, the joint is cooked, decorated, and then glazed with a clear spirit varnish (such as painters use). The varnish holds its gloss even under the lights. The result—whether the picture is in colour or in black and white—is that the picture shows what the joint really looks like. The fact that the varnish has made the joint uneatable is irrelevant.

At the same time, it would be a mistake to think that retouching can make a bad picture into a good one. On the other hand, it is not correct that retouching is essential before a photograph is suitable for reproduction. A good photographer will take a picture that is suitable for blockmaking without excessive retouching.

If a photographic assignment has to include pictures needed for different purposes, it is wise to make sure the photographer knows beforehand and to consider the advantages of separate sessions to get different angles.

The cardinal rule—worth constant repetition—is: the right brief coupled with imagination. The wise public relations man asks himself a few questions before he starts his brief. Why do I want these pictures? Where am I hoping to use them? Do they need a long caption or just a line? Will they need later enlargement for display purposes at an exhibition? Summed up, he will ask himself: What am I trying to say with this picture and to whom am I trying to say it?

Broadly speaking, there are two ways in which the public relations man will come into contact with photographers. One is when the photographer wants to take pictures for a publication, or for use in a book, or in an exhibition, or in some other way, and requires or receives facilities, services or products from the public relations man. The other is when the public relations man commissions a photographer to take pictures for him, for whatever purpose.

In the first instance, the public relations man is only partially involved, and he must concentrate on being efficient. If he has set up a press event in which there are picture possibilities he will have invited the newspapers and picture agencies to send photographers. In his invitation he will have tried to indicate what pictures he believes could be taken, or what parts of the event lend themselves to photography

A factory opening gives the opportunity to show off a dramatic piece of machinery; a fashion show features the latest creations of a dress designer; a lunch includes a speech by a minister or an internationally known figure whose face the papers may want to print. Two points must be remembered in such situations. The public relations man must have his facts readily at hand in brief, concise form. Photographers often have to work quickly, especially for daily papers, and do not want to have to take down notes if they can avoid it. It is easier for them (and safer for the PR man) and, incidentally, easier for those handling the pictures back at the office, if they can take a brief captions with them.

The second point is that photographers need different facilities and services from those required by journalists. A journalist can take notes of a speech when he is sitting at the back of the room: the photographer must be in the right position, close-up or far-away as needs be. If the chairman of the company, or the chief guest, is cutting a tape to inaugurate a new production line, space must be left for photographers to ensure that they can get their pictures with an uninterrupted view. If the surroundings are normally dark or shadowy, they will appreciate the thoughtfulness of the public relations man who has arranged for extra lighting.

A final thought: some photographers may wish to send first pictures back to their offices as quickly as possible, but remain themselves to take later shots of another feature. Sometimes they arrange for their own motor-cyclist or messenger to call; it is then the duty of the public relations man to see that photographer and messenger can make quick contact.

Timing is important and must be borne in mind. A reporter can collect a story, write it in the office, send it down to the sub-editors in a matter of minutes. The minimum time for a photograph, after developing and printing, to be marked up for size and turned into a half-tone block is between thirty and forty minutes.

There are also fewer photographers than reporters, so that a cameraman may get through more assignments in a day than a reporter. Never forget that a reporter can collect his story by telephone; a photographer has to be on the scene.

For these and other reasons it has become fairly standard practice at many press events to have a photo call: a session specially set up for photographers before the main event, sometimes even the day before. When this is possible it is desirable on all sides. It allows the photographers to work in peace and it allows the public relations man to concentrate on providing them with the facilities they need. Clearly this applies to certain kinds of press event only. These include fashion shows, factory visits—indeed any situation where the pictures that can be taken are not dependent on something happening at a particular moment. The guest of honour cuts the cake only once; the winners of the company's sports day prizes receive their trophies at only one moment. It can make very good sense to arrange a photo call separately from a main event.

If the public relations man is in doubt he will usually find that a picture editor or the news editor of a photographic agency will seldom mind giving some advice or indicating what sort of material might interest them. This approach should be used with some discretion, since picture editors are busy and do not want to waste their time. It might only be used if it is accompanied by an offer of exclusivity.

On the occasions when the PR man is commissioning a photographer the method of working is slightly different, and the demands on the public relation's man skills are different, too. For one thing he is dealing with only one photographer; for another he is able to pick his time for dealing with him. He does not normally have to provide a caption on the spot. What he has to do is to ensure that he has picked the right photographer and that he has briefed him properly. Also, he must brief his client or employer properly. Client and employer organizations are full of amateur photographers who are full of amateur advice. They should be kept away from the professional photographer.

Reference has already been made to the partnership between the photographer and the public relations man. It is at the planning stage that this is most in evidence. Indeed, a reconnaissance may have to take place some time ahead, particularly if there is any likelihood of repainting or refurbishing the surroundings or the actual subject to be photographed. The photographer must be allowed time to walk round and see the factory, or other location. There must be someone in authority available to smooth the path, but not someone who becomes officious. Normal activities should not be disrupted more than absolutely necessary (for one thing, doing so avoids excessive self-consciousness in the people being photographed). Discussing the pictures with any technical people involved saves argument afterwards. Finally, the points to be emphasized must be detailed, but the photographer's advice should be accepted if he says something is not possible or will not make a good picture. The photographer should be left to decide how he will make the essential points visually.

Of course, not all photography is of machines or things. There is also the photography of people, once again calling for particular skills on the part of the photographer, particularly when the subjects are posed in their offices or against exterior backgrounds. It is part of the job of the public relations man to help the subject to be natural, as well as to advise the photographer of any of the subject's idiosyncracies as far as they affect pictures. It is often sensible to allow the photographer to roam around shooting pictures continuously while the subject continues to work or talk. The alternative, a plate camera on a stand, frequently proves unnerving for the average businessman, resulting in stiffness. Studio portrait sessions can produce even more artificial results.

So far, the situations dealt with have been location photography, that is, pictures taken outside the studio. Within a studio conditions are naturally much different. There is time to arrange lights and backgrounds. There is usually less urgency. The subjects are mostly smaller and inanimate. Here the photographer is the lord in his kingdom and the public relations man may well find it best to be as unobtrusive as possible. It is also an intensive world of specialists who must therefore be chosen with great care. To hark back to the earlier example of food photography: the specialists in this field have cooking facilities in their studios.

The point is important since studio time is at a premium and the right facilities on hand can shorten the time needed to take a picture. Working in the studio also means that the public relations man should plan his requirements carefully. He should see if he can get a series of pictures for different uses at one session, again to save time and money.

It is normal practice to provide whole plate ($8\frac{1}{2} \times 6\frac{1}{2}$ in.) glossy prints to the press, although a few papers prefer 10×8 in. prints. Print ordering seems to cause constant headaches, yet again planning solves most of the problems. The public relations man should carefully work out the immediate use of the picture (thus deciding how many he needs) and add to it extra prints for stock purposes. Bulk ordering reduces print costs but, at the same time, he should not order wastefully.

Maintaining a library of photographs is not difficult, but is essential. There should be a master book or file, with each picture clearly dated and captioned, showing its reference number, and the name of the photographer or photographic agency. Prints kept in stock should be in cardboard-backed envelopes, with all the essential details, including the caption, on the envelope itself. Each print inside should be captioned, so that if a request for it is received it can be handled promptly.

When photographs are issued to the press, the caption should be lightly attached with rubber solution so that it can be stripped off easily. There should not be too much solution, since it tends to soak through to the front, particularly on single-weight paper. The caption should carry all essential information, including any details of restrictions on reproduction, time or date of publication, the source, and an address and telephone number for further information.

Publications pay agencies a fee for reproducing pictures, but public relations pictures are usually free of charge for reproduction. If this is so, it should be clearly stated: 'No fee for reproduction'. On the other hand, if any copyright is involved this, too, should be clearly stated, with, if possible, the name of someone who can authorize the waiving of the copyright.

The copyright law is extremely complicated, but in normal circumstances a photograph commissioned by a public relations man becomes his copyright. Some photographers insist on retaining the copyright in the negative, while undertaking not to make prints for anyone other than the company which ordered the pictures to be taken. Almost all photographers retain the negatives of their work and will not part with them. This is understandable, since print orders represent good continuing business for them. At the same time, they will produce and sell duplicate negatives (which may be necessary for use abroad, for instance). It is sensible to clarify the points early in any discussions with a photographer.

A common problem is faced when a portrait of, say, a company chairman is needed. In many instances, he will have had his picture taken by a specialist portrait photographer, who will have retained the copyright. It needs only a telephone call to release the copyright for a fee each time the picture is needed, or reproduction rights may be purchased at the outset.

A photographic library is a living thing. It should be kept constantly up-to-date. Photographs of factory exteriors, or senior personnel, or machinery, for instance, should be studied regularly and retaken as needed.

There are useful possibilities in issuing stock pictures to libraries, particularly those of publishing houses and those of official organizations like the Central Office of Information. The public relations man should include these in his distribution and ordering plans, and make certain that he keeps note of where pictures have gone so that they can be changed if necessary.

Finally there is the question of colour photography. This is even more highly specialized than black and white, and certainly more costly. Its use for editorial purposes is normally limited to exclusive arrangements made with one publication. It is usually better to offer facilities rather than colour pictures. However, there is one exception to this. Certain types of books carry colour photographs. The publishers often appreciate being given actual pictures rather than facilities, and they will normally agree to the pictures being released for other publications once the book itself has appeared.

Colour has enormous potential for exhibition work, for leaflets, and for annual reports. Most of the same rules apply as for black-and-white work, but extra care is called for before going into colour. Many subjects which lend themselves perfectly to black-and-white treatment cannot be shown in colour, for a variety of reasons. External shots need good natural light, as a rule. For interiors, lighting needs are different and more preparation is necessary. Used properly, colour can sufficiently dramatize an exhibition stand or booklet to justify the time, trouble, and cost of obtaining it.

One of the most worn clichés is: 'Every picture tells a story'. The good public relations man makes sure that his pictures are good and that they tell the story in the best way. To achieve this result he will have to work hard and carefully. He will find it repays itself time and time again.

5.2 FILMS AND FILMSTRIPS

Film is the most potent and emotionally penetrating medium of visual and aural communication. The theatricality of the darkened room; the hypnotic effect of the brilliant oblong of moving light and pattern; the impact of colour, voices, music, and effects; the sense of shared experience in the close-packed audience—all these, plus the many subtle skills of the film-maker, contribute to the power of film to convey feelings, impressions, and information.

Relatively few public relations people become physically involved in the making of films, but to be able to commission and guide the making of a film, and even to decide whether or not film is the most effective way to put over a message, it is necessary to have an understanding of the production process.

It is not difficult to make a film. It is very difficult to make a good film—technically polished, suited to its audience, and telling its story clearly through the precise balance of picture and sound. Film-making is a job for professionals; the amateur approach is almost always a disaster, even if the ciné enthusiast has talent.

The only reasonable exception is the local newsreel made on a shoe-string and intended to serve the same purpose as a parish magazine or works news-sheet. Here the content can overcome the limitations of the maker and his resources, but the temptation to try to use such a production more widely and for different audiences should be firmly resisted.

This tendency to think vaguely that any film can be used for any audience is symptomatic of many people's approach to the medium. Too often a film begins because someone suggests brightly, 'Why don't we make a film about this?' The idea of film is generally attractive, provided that not too much money is required. A film is then made, frequently without adequate planning or budget and usually with only the sketchiest concept of how it might be used.

This is not the way to do it. It is right that film should nearly always be considered as a possible way of putting a story over but, like any other form of PR communication, the objective must be clear and the nature of the audience understood first. Then the suitability of film (both economically and technically) for achieving the aim must be assessed and the means of reaching the audience by film ensured. Only then is it advisable to go ahead and find the money before embarking on the complex process of getting the film made.

Few organizations maintain film production units of their own, because of the expensive overheads when a film programme may not involve all members of the unit in full activity all the time. Some large concerns employ a films officer, a man with professional experience of production and distribution who guides outside production units. There are also nowadays one or two experts who have set up as film advisers, acting as brokers between the sponsor and the production company. Usually, however, the public relations man is on his own and has to find a producer to work for him.

There are scores of production companies, ranging from large groups with many full-time technicians, their own studios, and full technical facilities, to small outfits with only a handful of permanent production staff, who retain the services of other specialists as required, and hire their studio space and post-production facilities. Either can do good work, although the larger groups tend to be more expensive and the smaller units need to be scrutinized more carefully.

The first move is to see a selection of the films made by several different producers and to ask in each case about the audience and objective of the film, the cost, the way in which it was distributed, and the time taken to make it. Naturally, producers show their best wares but, just as a portfolio of beautiful photographs does not tell you how much time and trouble was taken to achieve good results, so an attractive film does not reveal what agonies, confusions, and expense were involved in getting it finished.

The sponsor may have to decide whether he would rather have calm competence and efficiency or suffer temperament and extra expense in the hope of producing an award-winner. Many fine films are made on time, within budget, and according to plan, and the public relations man should be wary of the producer who is more interested in making a film to flatter his reputation than in getting the message across in the best way.

A producer should be asked who he has worked for, how many regular staff he employs, how many films he has completed in the past year, what his technical resources are, and whether he has any understanding of the subject being considered.

Naturally, it is also essential to choose a producer who is personally amenable to acceptance of the client's wishes and reasonably likely to work amiably with other people in the sponsoring organization.

The routine by which a film is created can vary in many ways, but there is a basic system common to most production companies which can be made simpler or more complicated to suit given circumstances.

The starting point is the brief. This is a straightforward statement by the sponsor to the producer naming the object of the film, the audiences it is desired to reach, the general content, the approximate length, the main facilities the sponsor will provide, the completion date required, the sum of money available, the name of the sponsor's representative who will act as liaison and approve himself or with others the various stages of the production, and any special notes about such things as colour, overseas travel, underwater filming, and so on.

The next stage is the investigation, usually by the writer and the producer, for the writer has to create the script upon which the film is based and will often write any commentary too, and the producer has to see the production as a whole and guide it to completion to the client's satisfaction. It is essential that the sponsor should provide all the information and facilities necessary to ensure that the investigation is thorough and that the film-makers are not left in the dark on any important point.

The result of the investigation is a treatment. This is the term used for the document which outlines the suggested nature of the film in a narrative form, written in such a way that it is possible for the non-expert sponsor to visualize the shape, style, and content. The treatment is also both the point of decision and the first of five possible stages at which the sponsor approves the producer's work. Until a treatment is offered, it can not be decided if a suggested way of making the film is workable, or indeed if it is possible to make the film effectively at all, or if it can be made adequately within the money available. If there is any doubt, a hard look must be taken again at the objective, the message, and the money. Usually it is better not to proceed than to go ahead knowing that all is not well.

There is nothing wrong in deciding not to make a film after all. Sometimes investigation shows that the visual possibilities are limited, that action would necessarily be repetitive, that certain results cannot be achieved without extra cost, that necessary ingredients will not be available in time or any number of other unforeseen disappointments. At this point it may be right to give up the idea, or to defer the film for a while, or to ask the producer to approach the subject in another way.

With the treatment the producer should give an outline of production costs. At this stage it is not possible to provide a detailed budget. The treatment itself involves time and expense and it is wise to agree in advance on a fee, which is the sponsor's sole financial commitment at this point. If the decision is taken not to proceed, the fee is paid and the treatment becomes the sponsor's copyright. If the decision is to go ahead, no fee is paid because this item will be included in the total price later agreed for the film.

It is vital for full agreement to be reached at the treatment stage. It costs little to alter ideas on paper, but it can be very expensive to alter the course of a film once production has started.

Incidentally, it is well to be wary of offers to produce speculative treatments for nothing. No serious study can be undertaken without the expenditure of time and skill, and a facile sketch of how a film might be made is no substitute for a treatment based on a full investigation.

Occasionally, a detailed treatment can be used as a basis for filming, generally when the subject is one which cannot be fully scripted in advance. For example, an industrial film may consist of coverage of the laying of a pipeline by methods which have never before been used and which may have to be adapted by the engineers as they go along. In such a case it is not possible to write a shot-by-shot shooting script, only a clear indication of what the camera should record. This action will then have to be shot newsreel fashion and edited to fit the commentary the pictures require.

While this can be done successfully when the producer and director have a sound idea of what is wanted, the temptation to do without a shooting script and to film 'off the cuff' should otherwise be firmly avoided. The shooting script is the blueprint of the film and as such is as necessary as the engineer's drawing or the architect's plan. It is usually prepared by the writer in collaboration with the director who has the responsibility for controlling the filming, for turning the written word into pictures and sound, guiding the action, and combining life and movement into a logical presentation.

In a shooting script the action of the film is broken down into shots, indicating what will be seen on the screen and heard on the sound track. The content appears in the order in which it will be seen in the final film, and the director and cameraman use it as the basis for their creative work as the shooting proceeds.

Films are rarely shot in sequence, that is to say in the chronological order in which the shooting script is written. To save time and money, scenes which can easily and economically be shot in groups are brought together. For instance, if a film has three sequences in a factory, one at the beginning, one in the middle, and one at the end of the script, all three sequences would probably be filmed one after the other. This is planned in a breakdown, or shooting schedule. The editor who assembles, adjusts, and times the final film later places them in their proper position as set out in the shooting script.

When the shooting script has been broken down and the estimated times have been assessed for studio or location shooting, for travelling, and for the post-production phases of editing, recording, processing, and so on, it is possible for the producer to quote a firm price for the film. This may include artistes' fees, commentator, hire of special equipment, copyright, and an agreed number of prints.

It is highly desirable to have a contract with the producer based on a quotation which in itself has been based on a detailed shooting script.

It is also essential to make sure that the producer has arranged to obtain whatever copyrights may be necessary. There is an overriding copyright in a film, but it is the producer's task to deal with music and other rights, for overseas as well as home performances if necessary, so that he can pass the full copyright in the production to the sponsor.

All this preparatory work has to take place before filming can begin. Time-consuming as it may seem, every minute spent on pre-production planning and discussion can save an hour during shooting and post-production work and, in films more than most other media of communication, time is very expensive.

From this point on, almost all films follow a basic pattern of production, variable according to the complexity of the subject and the presentation and differing somewhat between large and small film units. The stages in production are shown in the chart opposite, with the five usual points at which the sponsor can exercise his powers of approval marked with an asterisk.

Before shooting begins, the producer usually calls a production conference. This settles all the administrative planning and a timetable for the film, and most of the senior creative personnel take part.

Photography then starts, according to the shooting schedule, and any animation work (cartoon and diagrams) which may be required is put in hand. All the exposed film footage is sent to the laboratories for rapid processing, and returned to the director for viewing. These rushes, as they are known, provide an immediate check on the photographic quality and on the content.

Footage selected from the rushes is assembled by the editor in the order laid down in the shooting script to form the rough-cut. At the same time, the commentary is drafted.

It is worth noting that commentary writing is a specialized skill. True, any competent professional writer can learn to pro-

The stages of production in a sponsored film

Briefing the producer
Investigation by the writer
Submission of treatment and indication of price*
Submission of shooting script and firm price quotation*
Contract, including copyright arrangements
Production conference
Shooting
Assembly
Screening of rough-cut, with commentary*
Sound recording
Track-laying
Double-head screening*
Dubbing
Negative cutting, optical effects, titles, complete print
Picture and sound processing on to one print
Married print*
Grading
Show print

* Points at which sponsor's approval is normally exercised

---

duce effective commentary, but that does not mean that commentary can be written well by any writer or by any expert capable of expressing himself. It is as well to be wary of amateur commentary writers who have no knowledge of the nuances of timing required nor of the difference between just writing and writing words to be spoken aloud at the same time as moving pictures are seen. The professional commentary writer can master a subject well enough to draft on any subject; technical specialists can then check his work for accuracy and emphasis.

It is unwise to allow a commentary to be read for approval as a manuscript. It should always be read and checked against the film itself: words to go with pictures follow rules of their own and convey different meanings when read separately.

Film commentary is probably the most ephemeral form of writing. It has been scientifically established that two-thirds of the viewer's mental attention is taken up with the visuals moving before his eyes, leaving only one-third for words, music, and sound effects. It is not advisable, therefore, except in instructional films which can have a repetitive form, to attempt to pack too many facts and figures into a commentary. The sponsored film, like any entertainment production, works best when the pictures tell most of the story on their own. Commentary is an enhancement, a strengthening factor, not the main means of getting the message across.

When the rough-cut has been completed to the director's satisfaction, it is shown to the sponsor, with the commentary read live, plus any sounds or dialogue that may have been shot in synchronization (sync for short) with the pictures. At this stage none of the optical effects, such as dissolves, fades, and mixes, have been made and the work print which is usually shown will be marked with lines and crosses to guide the editor and the laboratory.

The editor produces a fine-cut version, which includes all timing adjustments necessary to give the finished film the correct pace and emphasis. Shots included in the rough-cut may be discarded and others inserted at this stage. Until a picture is seen in something approaching its finished form it is difficult to be sure that the writer's original concept has worked properly.

Next the sound is recorded: voices on one track and music and effects on another. Foreign language versions can then be prepared if required without altering the music and effects (or M and E) track.

The sound engineers then lay the tracks to the fine-cut print, meticulously timing the process to fractions of a second. Now the film can be shown double-headed, with the picture on one print and the sound on another. At this stage it is still possible to make major adjustments without too much trouble and expense.

Given approval, the two sound tracks are re-recorded into a final balanced form on one complete track. This is the process known as dubbing.

The negative of the film is then cut to match the fine-cut edited version, the optical effects (opticals) are done in the laboratory, the titles are added, and the completed picture printed.

It is still possible to show the whole film double-headed for a final check, but in the interests of avoiding tinkering and last-minute brainwaves many producers and sponsors prudently skip this stage rather than risk incurring further expense.

The picture and sound are then processed on to one print, known as the married print, which is shown to the sponsor for final, formal approval. Only after this is the finishing touch put to the film when the print is graded by the laboratory for the balance of the photographic quality; this applies equally to black and white and to colour. The producer having accepted the graded print, the show print is delivered, the print order put in hand, and the film is ready for use.

Film production is a highly technical business involving a great many artistic and craft skills, and physical and chemical processes which are constantly progressing. It is easy for the public relations man to become fascinated by techniques and to lose sight of the essential point: whether or not the message is being conveyed in the best way for the audience. It helps to know enough about the production process to be able to understand what the film-makers are talking about, but it is more important to be able to influence their work as it goes along to ensure that their own understandable enthusiasm for making the film does not lead them to diverge from the original brief.

While it is unwise to become too involved in the technicalities of someone else's business, it is necessary to know that, unless a film is being made for commercial (or theatrical) distribution, it will almost certainly be made on 16-mm gauge, as opposed to the more expensive 35-mm gauge. It is also important to remember that while sound and picture are married on one print, because of the way a film is projected the sound on 16-mm film is twenty-six frames ahead of the picture to which it relates. It is not, therefore, possible to chop pieces out of a finished print and join it up with a few feet missing, as some afterthought experts in management try to suggest.

Audiences today are so conditioned to colour in the cinema, and to a growing extent in television too, that a hard look should be taken at any suggestion that a film should be made in black and white as an economy. The impact and persuasive power of colour is such that it is almost essential for anything other than a simple record film or an instructional production. The extra cost lies largely in the stock, the laboratory processing, the additional time required for shooting, and for extra lighting of interiors.

No film has any value as a means of conveying information if it lies in a can on the shelf. It has to be distributed to the chosen audience and this may be a brief and simple matter or a complex, long-term operation.

To take the simplest example, if a film is made to describe a new machine to the factories of a major industrial company, all over the world, there is no problem in making sure that the right people see it. All that has to be decided is the number of prints required and the best itinerary to send them on their way.

On the other hand, if a film has content of wide popular appeal, or contains material capable of being interesting to audiences at more than one level, then its distribution may be undertaken in more than one way.

Basically, distribution falls into two classes: theatrical and non-theatrical, although the second category can be broken down further.

Theatrical distribution of sponsored productions is relatively unusual. The subject and the approach to the audience have to be very broad—such as a travelogue made by a major oil company or an exciting display of aerobatics recorded by an aero-engine manufacturer—for acceptability either to the commercial cinema or to television.

If the general public is being aimed at and an adequate budget is available—for production values have to be high for a film to be commercially considered—then the producer can approach a registered film distributor (also called a renter) who may take the production for hiring to cinema exhibitors.

Neither in this case nor if television screenings are being sought is it feasible to seek a guarantee of distribution until the finished film can be shown. Whatever any producer may say, the men who book films will not buy a pig in a poke. And in both cases the content must exclude any direct or blatant advertising. This does not mean that the sponsor can get no direct value from the commercial audience seeing the film. At its crudest, a shot showing in passing the name of the company on a building would be acceptable whereas dwelling lovingly on close-ups of packs showing the brand name would not.

If there is any thought of theatrical distribution being achieved, the producer should be consulted from the start, as not only will many points in the writing and shooting need a different approach, but even the exact length of the finished film will be affected. Both cinema and television bookers work to accepted disciplines covering the running times which can be fitted in to their programmes.

For the great preponderance of sponsors, non-theatrical distribution is the main outlet, and this may be to general or to specialized audiences.

There are established film library organizations capable of providing a service for both home and overseas distribution and any film producer can advise on their use. The Central Film Library operated by the Central Office of Information and the commercial non-entertainment library of Sound Services Ltd. are the most effective means of distributing sponsored films in Britain. The COI can also help with overseas distribution through the British Information Services; the films acquisition department is always prepared to offer advice. Foreign government officials in London can usually give information about non-theatrical distribution facilities in their own countries.

Specialized audiences can also be reached through the film libraries by making arrangements to limit acceptance of bookings to a defined group of viewers.

The remaining large range of specialized audiences, from architects to women's institutes, may be reached by the sponsor's own efforts. Wherever an existing audience forms part of a group it can be approached direct or through whatever national or regional organization may exist. If the sponsor wishes to do no more than send the film, he can either rely on local projection facilities being available or—and this is safer—arrange for projector, screen, operator, and sound equipment to be provided by one of the many concerns which offer this service. If the audience is one which meets regularly and is accustomed to accepting films on this basis, then there is no particular difficulty beyond the administration involved.

When distributing films direct, it is essential to have more than enough prints to meet demand and to allow ample time for dispatch and return. It is also vital to re-run prints when they come back to check that they have not suffered damage. (The film libraries do this as a matter of routine.)

If, on the other hand, the desired audience, although available through an existing organization, is not one which has a programme of events suitable for film screenings, then the sponsor must build his own programme of events to attract the audience to see the film. This may involve tea and biscuits in a village hall, or a full-scale cocktail reception in a big hotel—whatever may be applicable to the nature of the audience.

Indeed, it is the nature of the audience that governs almost every aspect of film sponsorship. There is no substitute for the sponsor knowing his audience and understanding its ability to accept and remember the message he wishes to have conveyed by film. The practical means necessary to achieve this can then be purchased, provided he has the budget to meet the situation.

Sometimes, if the money available is wholly inadequate, it is possible to produce a reasonable substitute for a film in the form of a filmstrip. Sometimes, too, the subject matter for a proposed film may on examination seem not to offer the necessary potential for interesting moving pictures; here again filmstrip may be the answer.

Not that filmstrip should be regarded as a mere substitute: for many subjects, particularly for training use, it may be preferable to film. The lengthy holding of a single frame to show an intricate piece of machinery or a complicated flow diagram while the commentary explains it in detail is often more acceptable within the context of a series of still pictures than in the series of moving shots that constitute a film. Likewise, repetition of a picture for emphasis jars less than on film.

The transition from a general shot to a closer view and then to a very detailed close shot to concentrate the viewer's attention on some vital aspect of the image is sometimes more effective in successive stills than in moving pictures. This is particularly so if there is inherent movement in the film image which may distract the eye's attention from the point the commentary is making.

Filmstrip has moved a long way from the time when it was merely a convenient way of projecting a series of still photographs one at a time on 35-mm film instead of struggling with a box of slides. Production techniques have advanced greatly. Methods of photography, artwork, synchronized commentary, dialogue, colour, music and effects, have been polished to such an extent that much of the hypnotic power of the cinema can be reproduced.

Like film, anyone with a camera can make a filmstrip, but the production of first-class work, including the writing of effective commentary, is a specialized task. There are a number of filmstrip producers with the necessary skills and a knowledge of refinements that surprise those sponsors who still have the 'lantern lecture' approach in their minds.

5.3 TELEVISION

Television could be one of man's greatest inventions, or one of his most disastrous. Its power to hypnotize, its power to educate, its incredible power to be completely unmemorable all add up to its being a medium of communication that a public relations man should study deeply.

It is not the purpose of this chapter to consider the social implications of television, but to advise on the part it can play in a public relations campaign. Nevertheless, some thoughts on the medium are necessary.

The world's first regular television service started in Britain in the mid-thirties. It was then the eighth wonder of the world: a little flickering picture on a tiny screen. Today it is a worldwide part of daily life, with pictures sent in colour from one continent to another, with audiences for single programmes reaching into the hundreds of millions. It is used to educate backward peasants, or to sell American presidential candidates. It gobbles up and pours out the limited creative talents of hundreds of average playrights, scriptwriters, and performers with the same enthusiasm with which it puts out the work of the world's greatest authors, composers or actors.

It has refashioned society, and especially home and family life, replacing the fireplace with the screen. People have a unique love-hate relationship with their television set. It brings the world's most dramatic happenings into homes in exactly the same way as it continually screens the world's worst movies. It creates, and then destroys, a steady series of 'non-personalities', or 'plastic people'. Its discussion programmes are often 'instant think', in which both genuine and false authorities on any subject disappear behind meaningless words which no one can remember the day after.

One British Prime Minister of recent years appeared as little as possible on television, whether in party political broadcasts, studio interviews or in airport interviews. His reasoning was that he could never win; with luck he would draw, but he was most likely to lose. Whatever he said, in whatever context, he knew people would say things like 'he looks cocky', or 'he looks tired'. They were unlikely to listen to his words. Again, the effect of his appearance or his words would mean different things to different people (and governments) in different countries, and in the relatively short time usually available to him his chances of achieving an allround satisfactory result were too remote for his liking.

On the other side of the coin, a student of television as a method of education once claimed that its virtue was its ability to enthuse viewers, especially children. An example he gave was map reading. He said that the most fruitful steps were the appearance on television of a 'character' who bubbled over with excitement about maps, stood knee-deep in them, and talked entertainingly about them. This had to be followed by a talk in school, within a day or two, by a teacher with a relatively small group who could accept him as a genuine authority. The lesson would finally take effect when the children went out with a map and read it for themselves.

Above all, the effect of television on the future of the world is not understood. At the moment, it is undoubtedly a mass of trivialities, with a tiny proportion of important, valuable or even vital material.

At the same time, however true these generalizations may be, for most purposes the public relations man just has to accept that television is there, that it has a particular place in the communications world, and that he should thus consider how it can help his work.

While doing this, he must avoid one of the dangers of all creative people: that of doing something in order to be able to show off to his contemporaries that he has done it. Few public relations people can resist boasting to their friends that they have had their client or employer on television. This must be resisted.

There is no point in dropping all other work to achieve even a full-scale 'Panorama'-type debate if the audience is wrong, or the time is wrong, or if other media could produce a better result. Television has great strengths, but it also has great weaknesses.

The secret of getting on to television lies in two points: understanding its mechanics, and remembering that its greatest demand is for visual quality. This makes television no different from any other medium, as far as the public relations man is concerned.

To understand the mechanics means watching television and studying the programme publications. This has to be done, and it has to be done regularly, although with discrimination.

The need for visual quality is almost too obvious, yet seems often to be forgotten. Whatever appears on television ought to look interesting, exciting, dramatic or unusual. A study of television commercials will demonstrate this quite easily. In them, the producers have to cram into half a minute, or even seven seconds, a visual image that will stay in the mind. Often they achieve that objective.

However, it is the 'editorial' content of television with which the public relations man will more often be concerned. For example, a company may invent a new kind of chain-link fence which prevents cows from straying. This can be a first-class story, which can even lend itself to description in a radio farming programme. But it has limited visual quality, and is thus unlikely to appeal to television producers.

A range of furniture may be the best buy in the country, but if it looks (as indeed is probable) like most other ranges of furniture, no television producer is going to rush to film it.

A regularly recurring exhibition like the Motor Show makes the point in another way, but in one that has great meaning for many public relations people. Basically, the Motor Show is the same every year. Only occasionally does it now throw up an example of car design so radically different that television features it. More usually, what happens is that a commentator talks about the interesting variations from the previous year against a background of a general view of a throng of people. The occasion is too important to be missed out altogether, but it gets less and less television time each year.

A popular public relations ploy in such circumstances is to use a scantily clad pretty girl, or an expensively clad pretty girl. Although this may achieve ten seconds of television time it is debatable how much it achieves for the manufacturer concerned. The viewers concentrate on the girl.

The rules for offering ideas to television producers are no different from any other medium of mass communication: offer them at the right time, and make sure before offering them that the ideas have at least some possibilities.

Advance notice, with explanations of any visual aspects, is usually sufficient. If a television programme wants to cover an event as an outside broadcast, the technicians will soon enough explain to the public relations man what special facilities they may need for things like lighting, position of cameras, and so on. Clearly, there are differences between events televised live, and those filmed for later use. When an event is televised live, there have to be special arrangements for the siting of the outside broadcast van, the laying of cables, and the placing of the cameras.

If the item is to be incorporated into a studio programme, it may need rearrangement of the schedule planned by the public relations man to ensure that the item is actually happening at the time it fits into the programme. Sometimes, this situation arises at a moment's notice. When it does, the quality the public relations man needs above all else is to be able to emulate the boy on the burning deck and remain calm. Everybody else will be getting excited, not least the television technicians themselves, and a panicky public relations man is useless.

Filmed events are much easier to handle. The cameraman may be there alone. In certain circumstances he may take material from the public relations man so that someone at his office can write a commentary. Alternatively, he may be accompanied by a reporter. Experience will have taught them how to work together and the public relations man should not make himself too obtrusive. He is there to help, not to control.

Filming only becomes complicated when there is a need for simultaneous sound recording. This means a team of perhaps four to six men: reporter, cameraman, sound recordist, lighting man, and so on. They often create a fair deal of chaos and they sometimes seem to work in a state of utter confusion. However, they know what they want and how to get it, and they will not thank the public relations man who tries to do their job for them.

Studio programmes present different problems. Someone who has to appear on a programme may have to be at the studio hours ahead to rehearse his part. This creates its own complications. For, say, a research specialist, appearing on television for the first time can be a daunting experience. The expressionless eye of the camera, the lights, the obvious superiority of the practised people around him, perhaps also the strange feeling of make-up— all these can easily combine to throw him out of his stride. Television producers are well aware of this and go to considerable lengths to help newcomers to calm down. There is little the public relations man can do, although he may be able to warn the television people in advance of any idiosyncracies or foibles of his client or employer.

It is always best to be led by the television producer and his staff in matters of appearance, mannerism, and the like. However, there are one or two rules which the public relations man should remember to pass on in advance. Anyone speaking on television should try to keep fairly still. Too much movement, either of the head or body, is distracting to the viewer and makes it difficult for the camera to maintain a steady picture. For men, a striped or coloured shirt is better than a white one; for women, ornate and sparkling jewellery create a flashback which is equally distracting. Advances in camera technique mean that these points are less important than they used to be, but they are examples worth bearing in mind.

In particular, time spent mastering facts and figures is vital. One of the effects of television interviewing is that it diminishes a speaker's authority if he has to refer constantly to notes. Because it is mostly shot in close-up, it picks up any nervousness easily. It equally puts into sharp relief any hesitation and magnifies it. Speakers should be briefed in the art of over-simplification and compression, since they may have only sixty seconds at a time in which to put over a point. At normal speaking speed this is probably 120–150 words: enough to do the job but appearing too few and tending to induce panic in an unpractised speaker. It is not difficult to avoid these obstacles, provided advance time is used sensibly.

The output of both BBC and independent television is controlled strictly. It must contain a proportion of regional material, and it is in this area that many public relations people can find opportunities to put over their story. Each BBC region and each commercial television programme contractor runs local news magazines, whose producers are always ready to consider ideas. The only thing to remember is that they still must have visual quality.

Over and above this, both networks carry educational and specialist programmes, such as on farming. The public relations man with a specialized interest should keep an eye on the programmes. He should remember to include their producers or regular speakers in invitations to facility visits, and in the circulation of background material or press releases.

Outside the main centres of production—London, Birmingham, Manchester, Glasgow and so on—conditions and people are different. Free-lance journalists are used extensively and there is more doubling-up of jobs (for instance the news-reader also being the reporter). At the smaller independent companies, producers and directors have a wider range of duties and responsibilities. The public relations man who operates regularly in these areas should get to know his people, in exactly the same way as when he is dealing with provincial newspapers.

It is possible to interest the producers of magazine programmes and those devoted to specialized interests, such as motoring or the arts, in relevant films or extracts from films. If a film is new, then the producer or editor can be invited to send one of his research staff to the press view. If it is not new, but is seen to have topical possibilities, then a letter describing the content briefly and offering to lend a print or arrange a screening will sometimes produce results.

Particularly away from London, the number of camera crews available to attend news events is limited and here again film may be the answer to obtaining visual coverage. For example, if a major factory is being opened, it would be normal practice to offer the television newsmen the opportunity of a shooting session on the buildings and the production process the day before. A department store fire, a murder, a royal visit—any form of hard news story might offer better material on the day in question and the television camera crew might be diverted. Alternatively, film commissioned and shot in advance, and edited into a very brief sequence with commentary notes, could be delivered to the television newsroom to provide visual to back up the news-reader's words about the event.

In some circumstances, such as the presentation of a prize for architecture, the weather might not be good enough on the day of the ceremony for favourable film to be shot. Footage obtained in advance, taking time to show the building at its best, might then be welcomed by the news editor.

Apart from participation in programmes (outside or studio) by people, or by the provision of written material or film, there is one other area which can repay study. The props departments can be supplied with either charts or handbooks of equipment, apparatus or appliances which a public relations man can lend them. An obvious example here is domestic electricity or gas appliances, regularly featured in plays and domestic settings. However, if this is done, the public relations man must remember to keep the equipment up to date, or issue revised versions of either charts or handbooks.

There is another use of television of which the PR man needs to be aware: closed-circuit facilities. That merely means hiring a specialized company—of which there are a handful—who will shoot an event and relay it live over special lines to an audience somewhere else. The method is undoubtedly expensive, and the major job of the public relations man is to ensure that the cost is justified. Typical uses could include the inauguration of a large new production line at a factory televised to a meeting of shareholders held 200 miles away; basic statements of major company policy televised to staff meetings in half-a-dozen locations; or a royal visit to one factory televised to workers at another.

In these circumstances, the only real knowledge needed by the public relations man is the names and addresses of the companies able to provide this service. They will tell him exactly what is needed and what it will cost. He will need to brief them on his objectives, and work in collaboration with them in the same way as with a journalist or photographer.

Finally, some organizations can be commissioned to film an event for distribution to television networks either in Britain or abroad. This is a straight commissioning operation. Its value can lie in the firms' knowledge of how to film material and edit it to make it interesting for television, and also in the speed at which they can distribute it worldwide. As a variation, the Visnews organization has a network of cameramen around the world who can send material back to this country to be offered to British television. The costs are relatively low, and the use of the service is suggested for such news as the award of a major export order, or a visit overseas by the nationally known chairman or chief executive of a company.

Television, by necessity, compresses much of its material into few words and few pictures, especially in news coverage. By watching it, the public relations man can learn a good deal of the art of picking out the essential from the verbiage.

5.4 EXHIBITIONS

There are two ways in which a public relations man can become involved in an exhibition. Either he mounts an entire exhibition, or he participates in somebody else's show by taking a stand or handling publicity for an exhibitor.

The word 'exhibition' usually conjures up in people's minds a large-scale operation, such as the International Boat Show. It would be wrong to assume that an exhibition has to be enormous to qualify for the description. Exhibitions can be limited to small local shows, even down to a display of products in a staff canteen.

The purpose of an exhibition is to show visually a range of products, services or ideas, backed with descriptive literature and personal explanation by salesmen or experts. An external exhibition, whether staged by a commercial promoter, a trade association or a professional body, usually has as its objective the sale of more goods or the wider use of services. An internal exhibition, such as might be put on in a canteen, usually has the objective of explaining graphically a new development by a company, or presenting in a relatively small space its normal work in an interesting and easily comprehensive manner. Between these two extremes lie a whole series of different types of exhibition, display or touring show.

Large or small, external or internal, exhibitions must always come about only after a set of questions has been asked and satisfactorily answered.

An exhibition must be seen to be the most effective way of putting over the story before the public relations man decides to become involved, whether he is staging a whole show or just taking part in somebody else's project. This means clearly stating the target, and also clearly understanding what an exhibition will do and what it will not do. This includes remembering that exhibitions and exhibition stands are costly.

A total exhibition has a theme. This is the first point to settle. It may be to promote the idea that containerization offers the best way of shipping goods around the country or exporting them to other countries. It may be that the better conduct of companies depends on business efficiency. Once the theme has been decided the consequential decisions on location, timing, and exhibitors fall into place. However, the decision to stage an exhibition of this type normally does not enter the life of a public relations man, unless he is working for a professional or trade association. Even then, his first duty is only to conceive the idea. After that, he will hand over the job to the companies which specialize in mounting exhibitions. They will take over all the detailed administration involved in selecting the site and the date, and selling space to individual companies.

Basically, an exhibition exists because it can bring under one roof, or into a reasonably small area, all the concerns that can benefit from showing their wares to likely customers. An exhibition does no more than allow actual and potential customers to get through their business quickly by being able to see developments, products, new ideas, and new services in one place instead of travelling all round the country.

This fact creates other facts, which the public relations man must remember. It has become a tradition that companies launch new products at their annual trade exhibition, but this has only happened because the launch allows exhibitors more easily to publicize their participation, and provides customers with good reasons for visiting particular stands. It has also become a tradition that customers—especially at trade shows—should be entertained, probably lavishly. Thirdly, it has become traditional that special stunts are mounted by some exhibitors to gain publicity and thus attract more visitors to their stands.

It may be the duty of the public relations man to recommend participation in an exhibition. He will do so in consultation with other executives in his client's or employer's organization: marketing, sales, advertising, technical, and so on. To reach the decision, and help others reach it, he will need to be armed with certain facts. Is the exhibition new or long-established? If the latter, what is its record of attendances, general publicity, and trade or public acceptance. Does it appeal to a wide section of the community or to a narrow section? Does its audience include enough who are relevant to the potential exhibitor? Is it unique in its appeal, or does it have competitors? What return is expected from it by the different departments (for example, marketing, sales, production) concerned?

Some exhibitions are little more than an excuse for social meetings between salesmen and customers, although they may justify their cost on these grounds alone. Others are serious technical displays. Others again are linked to national or international conferences or seminars. Some can only be justified because the sales made from the stand could not be made in any other way.

If a new product is to be launched, can it be ready in time or will there be impossible development or production department problems? If the product can be ready in time, will stocks be sufficient to meet any anticipated demand? It can be disastrous to launch a product and then fail to deliver orders speedily.

Participation in an exhibition can easily cost £10,000, including the time of staff involved at all levels. Preparation, participation, and follow-through also distract staff attention from other necessary, if mundane, duties. The effect of the distraction should be assessed. The public relations man must ask himself whether there is a better way of spending the money. It is a question he must ask himself constantly, if he is to be sure that he is making the most useful contribution he can to the success of his employer or client.

Assuming that the decision is made to take part, the job of the public relations man becomes easy to define. He will have to hand over the physical design and production to outside contractors (or, in certain circumstances, to departments within his organization) and merely brief them initially on the public relations objective he seeks. He will be more closely involved in some of the administrative procedures. These are immense. They cover entry in the exhibition catalogue, issue of tickets or special passes, special events on the stand, advance publicity (including advertising), the design and printing of special leaflets or descriptive literature, photography, and press exploitation. Some of these may be handled by other experts, but it will be the duty of the public relations man to keep an eye on them.

For a major national exhibition, it may be necessary to have a planning committee, of which the public relations man will be a member. At the end of the exhibition, it will be his task to prepare (either single-handed or in collaboration with others) an assessment of the exhibition. This will not only provide facts and figures for the future but will also include his opinion of the success of the stand and of the exhibition as a whole. Such a report should be produced within a few days of the end of the show, while everything is still fresh in people's minds, and also because the space booking for successful annual exhibitions has to be made twelve months in advance.

An exhibition mounted by an individual company, whether for external or internal purposes, follows the same broad rules. It also presents some different problems for the public relations man. It can take various forms, such as a special display in a showroom, or in a part of a department store, or in a town hall, or a hotel, or in a specially erected marquee, or as a travelling show in a caravan or even in a train. It will sometimes be for a controlled audience—named invitations—and sometimes for a general audience attracted by advertising or posters or distribution of handbills. It will naturally be smaller in scope, and less widely appealing, than a national show since it will be displaying only the products, services or ideas of one organization.

This being so, it is even more important that the administration should be immaculate. Instead of a catalogue entry, the form of which is dictated by somebody else, there will be a whole catalogue (even if it is only a four-page fold-over). Exhibitions of this kind are usually easier to justify since it is likely that the results will be easier to see. There is not the problem of competing against other organizations. However, the public relations man must carefully survey the ground before he goes too far. Do other companies in his field run exhibitions? If so, what kind are they, when are they held, and are they reckoned to be successful? It is not difficult to collect opinions on these questions, although it is obviously difficult to collect facts. Above all, what is the objective, and is it either impossible or too costly to achieve it any other way?

It is for the public relations man to decide the use of the budget and therefore whether the administration should be handled internally or put out to a contractor. The chances are that for anything more ambitious than simple display of products in a town hall (which may be perfectly acceptable) he will be wise to call in a contractor. If not, he must be prepared to take responsibility for a host of detail—as diverse as insurance, lighting facilities, permitted floor load factor, cleaning and maintenance, cost estimating, furniture, transport, and so on.

If he does decide to use a firm of contractors, he will commission them by following procedures similar to those used for film-making or photography. He will ask to see examples of their work and he will invite them to submit written proposals. He will brief them correctly by telling them what he wants to achieve and how much money he has to spend.

There is a distinct place in may public relations campaigns for the purely internal exhibition, put on to inform employees. It may be to show them plans for expansion of the company, or the development of a new product range. It can be particularly effective for factory workpeople who make parts of a product the whole of which they never see at close quarters (like roller bearings for helicopters, for example). It can also be relevant for factory open days, when the relatives of staff, or other members of the community, come in to see what the company does. And it can throw up the chance to co-operate with other public relations people handling end products to which the factory contributes.

One of the outstanding values of an exhibition is that it enables people to see and touch. If they can see a working model so much the better. If they can actually operate it they will be delighted. This is seldom easier to see than with an internal show. It can have the merit of enthusing personnel, or allowing them to identify themselves more closely with what they labour at each day. The manufacturer of woollen cloth can arrange a fashion show for his staff, so that they can see the clothes they are helping to create, and which may quite possibly be beyond their own financial capabilities. The maker of machine tools used in the manufacture of toy cars can put on an exhibition of the toys—remembering that many of his workers will have children of their own who buy the models.

In the area of community relations, and certainly for local authorities, exhibitions of town development or plans for extended amenities are necessary. Here there comes the chance to use large-scale maps, architects' models, and enlarged photographs. Blown-up maps and photographs are telling parts of any exhibition. If nothing else, their size commands attention.

The construction of exhibitions is neither difficult nor easy. If the design has been properly thought out, and the brief has been good, the work will flow as smoothly as the people involved can work together happily. Constant changes in the plan upset everybody and will result in a bad exhibition or a bad stand. It is the initial planning that is vital. A clever designer and competent stand-builder can keep costs down, and parts of the necessary equipment can be hired or even borrowed, but all their cleverness will come to nothing if they start from the wrong point and are not clear about their aims.

Exploiting participation in an exhibition is another question. Like most public relations jobs, it needs good organization and advance planning.

National exhibitions have their own press officers, either on the staff or as outside consultants. It is their job to attract visitors to the exhibition through editorial publicity. It is, of course, up to the individual exhibitors to make the most of their participation for themselves. The fact of an exhibition, especially if it is new, is enough to make some publicity, particularly if it is one of the growing number of specialized shows or trade events. Some exhibition organizers try to focus interest on their show by setting up a central exhibit, often with an apparently non-commercial angle. Thus an exhibition of printing equipment might feature an exhibition of some of the world's most beautiful stamps or colour reproductions of great masters. An exhibition of musical instruments could feature concerts of classical or pop music. It is becoming more common to link exhibitions with seminars or conferences. All this will act to bring visitors to the show, whether just on the opening day or throughout the run.

Normally, there is a press call or press conference at the time of the opening, or just before it or just after it. The public relations man should attend this, but he should remember that he will not be welcome if he tries to take it over by forcing his attention on the journalists there. Discretion is the better part of enthusiasm. Often enough the press simply come in during the first day. There is much to be said, on both sides, for allowing journalists the freedom to move around without clashing with customers or members of the public. It can be particularly valuable for photographers, although less valuable for film or television cameramen, who often prefer to add atmosphere by showing real visitors at the exhibition.

The exhibition press officer will look to individual exhibitors to provide him with advance information (often at the same time as the organizers are asking for catalogue entries) to help him promote the show. When it is international in scope and visitors are coming in from overseas, press information is needed well ahead. This is a situation which presents regular difficulties. A company may not wish to reveal to competition that it will have a new product to show. It may not have made up its mind what to show in sufficient time. The public relations man (and the exhibition press officer) usually and sensibly have to bow to commercial prudence.

The individual exhibitor is free to invite his own list of visitors and if any of them are interesting in press terms the public relations man will lose nothing by giving advance warning to the exhibition press office. At the same time, he will again have to watch that he is not giving the competition enough time to get in a counter-invitation.

There will certainly be an exhibition press office, which is a magnet for all visiting journalists. The public relations man for an exhibitor will provide copies of all press releases and photographs to this office, where he will usually find special racks or boards erected for their display. He should find out whether copies are required to be translated, and may decide to supply these himself. He will make a point of visiting the press room regularly to see that there are proper stocks of his material and that it has not been hidden under piles of other exhibitors' releases.

He will co-operate with the exhibition press officer, who can make life easy or difficult for him. If any stories arise during the show or if he wants to invite journalists to visit his stand at a particular time, he will usually find that the press office will be willing to lend a hand.

Apart from posting up material in the press room, it is vital to issue it direct to newspapers or periodicals before the show opens.

When a show is opened by a member of the royal family, or by a minister or other public personality, their tour of the show is settled by the exhibition organizers. If it happens to include the stand of the public relations man's company, he should have a photographer standing by, although it is fair to recognize that the pictures he takes will usually achieve little more than a page or two in the commemorative album the company keeps, or be framed on the wall of the chairman's office. The pictures used by the press are almost invariably those taken and circulated by agencies.

It is standard practice at a commercial exhibition for one photographic company to have the sole rights for the taking of pictures of the stands. The public relations man has to decide whether these are of any publicity value (as opposed to record value) and if so he has to have them taken by that photographic agency. This does not preclude him from using his own photographer or another agency to take news pictures to circulate to the press if he wishes.

A trade exhibition will be widely reported in its own trade papers, usually by a catalogue-type listing of all the exhibitors. This may appear the week or month before the show opens, or on the opening day. Within the trade this information is part of the method for attracting attendance. It is therefore important to the public relations man that he should get the best possible showing in pre-exhibition or exhibition issues of the relevant trade press. He can either do this direct with the publications, or via the exhibition press office.

The opening speech will be reported in subsequent issues of the trade papers, with a review of the show. The review section is also important to the public relations man, since it is the channel he uses for communicating with those people in the trade who did not come to the exhibition.

The daily press may or may not report the opening speech. Equally, they may or may not report some of the contents of the show. When it is a trade show, the daily paper reports are bound to be of something exciting or novel or dramatic. They will seldom have much effect in attracting genuinely useful visitors who have a direct interest and really want to do business or keep themselves informed. It is trade publicity, direct mail, and overseas publicity (when it is relevant) on which the public relations man should concentrate his attention.

Nevertheless, many companies, when they have spent a great deal of money on taking part in a trade exhibition, appreciate the warm feeling that goes with national newspaper publicity. The public relations man must judge for himself whether it is a justifiable means to a justifiable end (it may have some small side-effect on shareholders, to take just one example).

If he decides that national publicity will help in his public relations campaign he must then study how to achieve it. He must also remember that if he is taking part in an exhibition with, say, 200 other companies, trying to get daily papers or television to single him out is a bit like entering a lottery. And only in exceptional circumstances is he justified in spending a disproportionate sum of money in making the attempt. This applies with equal force in a popular show attended by members of the general public.

How he does it must be dictated by his knowledge of the press and by the type of show. Nine times in ten the chances are that he will use a pretty girl or a 'personality'. However, it is not a bad rule to consider the value of contrasts, particularly for pictures. A piece of machinery weighing ten tons may make a good picture if it can be demonstrated that it is used for producing pins. The attempt to get publicity on this occasion is an unashamed stunt and all stunts are governed by the same two rules. They must either be so demonstrably logical or relevant that the stunt is accepted as the only way of graphically presenting the situation, or they must be so outrageously illogical or irrelevant that everybody is prepared to join in the fun.

For example, making a car with a transparent plastic body,

cutting it in halves to show the works, and then putting it on a turntable is logical and will thus stand a chance of being photographed. Putting a pretty girl into a bikini made of real gold wire is illogical, but it is harmless fun and stands an equal chance of being photographed.

The important point to bear in mind is to keep stunt attempts in perspective.

Many public relations men make the mistake of thinking that their work is done once the exhibition has opened. It is often in the follow-through operations that public relations men lose some obvious opportunities to capitalize on an exhibition stand. Pictures taken on the opening day can be sent direct to local papers apart from trade press. If possible or desirable, pictures should also be sent overseas. A daily visit to the stand, or a daily call to the senior company representative on the stand, may produce stories of interesting but unexpected visitors or exciting orders.

Good pictures should be set aside for use in the annual report. There is no reason why a set of pictures and press cuttings should not be mounted on portable stands and toured round company factories or branch offices when the show has finished. Overseas radio services may be interested in stories or exclusive interviews during the show. At the end, there may be round-up stories of business done to be issued.

The exploitation of a company exhibition is naturally much easier, even though the public relations man has to do it all himself without the extra opportunities created for him by an exhibition press officer. Allowing for this small disadvantage— against which he can weigh the considerable advantage of no competition—he will merely follow the same pattern as for a commercial show. The one difference is that he is unlikely to need any stunt.

This will be especially true of an exhibition mounted for solely internal purposes. For that type of show, the other media of communication which ought to receive special attention are company publications. An external house magazine should carry a story and pictures of the exhibition. The story should be rewritten with slightly different angles for a staff magazine. If there is normally only an external publication it may be worth printing extra copies to distribute to staff.

5.5 HOUSE STYLE

Starting with the premise that reputation matters, it follows that easy visual recognition of the existence of an organization is necessary to the establishment and maintenance of a reputation. It also follows that recognition implies an assessment of the nature of an organization by what is seen of it: products, packaging, print, advertisements, vehicles, and so on. If that assessment is to be favourable, in other words if the ready recognition is to be of value in the public relations sense, then the creation of an appropriate house style is essential.

This may be a major exercise involving much time and money, or it may be a relatively simple matter, depending on the nature of the organization; but in either case, a clear and controlled design policy is vital.

The responsibility for design policy may lie wholly with the public relations executive, although it is more likely that he will share it with others; certainly others within any organization are bound to be concerned in any design policy and its implementation.

What is house style? Basically it is the sum of all those elements which give a definable character, recognizable at sight, to everything connected with an organization. The 'house' may be a business, a trade association, a charity, a nationalized industry, a professional institution or any other corporate entity.

Often, house style is thought of as being mainly a matter of stationery and other printed material; this is understandable, since the phrase 'house style' originated in publishing and printing and, indeed, is still used in a particular sense there. Publishers and printers standardize the varying usages of the English language and use consistently one set of rules in all their productions. It is the reason, for example, why 'organization' is spelled thus in this book and does not appear as 'organisation'. The 'z' spelling is Heinemann house style.

However, if a style is to achieve its maximum benefit for the organization, it should permeate every aspect of its activities. There is no point, to take an extreme but not unreal example, in spending money on a well-designed letterheading if correspondence goes out in envelopes exhibiting a conflicting typographical approach. Similarly, if a new trade mark is being exploited expensively through advertising, it is futile to leave the previous trade mark visible on company vehicles on grounds of economy.

While it is perhaps not difficult to gain support for the concept that everyone who recognizes the organization in one form or another should get a favourable impression of it, achieving approval for design recommendations is quite another matter. Design is a subjective issue, and everyone believes he knows what is right. The chief accountant is firmly convinced that his views on design are as up-to-date as those of the advertising manager; the managing director knows what he likes and will rarely be prepared to agree that his judgments on design are highly subjective.

The public relations man has to deal with every point of view inside the organization if he is, firstly, to win consent to embark on a house style exercise and, secondly, to pilot it through to a successful conclusion. For a good deal of the time he will find himself dealing with intangibles. It is therefore helpful to involve others as much as possible in the practical aspects of the operation.

This falls into two parts: ensuring that the value of creating a house style is appreciated, and consulting all concerned on the practicability of design proposals (but *not* on their aesthetic merits).

Clearly, presenting a good face to the world can have a beneficial effect on various segments of the organization's public. Through good design, the sales representative, for example, can rely upon the company and its products being recognized by customers and potential customers.

A consistent visual expression of the character of the organization, recognizable throughout all its activities, can contribute to a sense of unity, to the morale of employees, and the loyalty of shareholders.

A consistent design policy applied to packaging can make each product a link with and a recommendation for other related products. In large and diverse companies the family resemblance needs to be flexible to allow for products with their own brand identities being sold separately, or even in competition with one another. The decision between central identification or individual brand image is a straightforward commercial issue.

The mundane elements of trade and industry, such as invoices, packing cases, and tarpaulin covers on trucks, can be given a public relations value, when in fact they are not promotional media in the normal sense.

Advertising within a recognizable style, or using consistent elements of design, can be made more effective by the creation of reminder value, each advertisement linking with the others through visual elements.

In overseas selling, an identity for a company or a range of products can help familiarization among audiences unaccustomed to the English language. A house style has no language barriers.

In the case of a large group of companies, or a parent company with subsidiaries, a firm design policy can have alternative values. In a closely unified group, the relationship of the parts to the whole can be shown clearly; or the different identities of units within a looser group can be indicated while still being under the umbrella of the group's house style.

For instance, a group may have a consistent style, but component companies may be allowed to retain their individual names, trade marks, and logotypes (symbols) within it. Alternatively, a group might apply its visual style rigidly to all its constituent units, but differentiate them simply by colour.

If design proposals are to work, it is vital for them not only to be attractive, but to be seen to be practicable. There is no sense in alienating a manager by presenting him with a *fait accompli* which he will resent, when he could well be consulted about practical aspects of a designer's proposals. Failure to consult, failure to accept people's human desire not to be overridden, is asking for proposals to be condemned out of hand as the worthless nonsense of starry-eyed designers. Even given top level approval, a design policy is difficult to carry through consistently and comprehensively without the consent of many people down the line.

It is right that the office manager should be consulted to see if proposed changes in stationery sizes will present filing difficulties or offer savings in purchasing. It is fair that the managing director's secretary should be invited to type a letter on the new heading to see how well it can look. It is vital that the safety officer be asked to check that proposed colours, if used in the factory, will not conflict with established safety codings. It is necessary to check with the finance director that functional aspects of stationery design fit in with any mechanized accounting system. It is only commonsense to talk with the transport officer about the repainting cycle of vehicles and the nature of loads carried before considering ideas for a revised livery. Examples could be multiplied for any kind of organization.

The possibilities for savings in costs and increases in efficiency as a result of rationalization of excessive varieties of stationery, greater opportunities for bulk buying, quicker identification of products in the warehouse, and so on, should be carefully explored with the relevant departments.

So far, all of this could be the responsibility of the public relations man, but it should not be assumed that house style can be a do-it-yourself job. It is up to him to make out a case and later to ensure that agreed recommendations are carried out, but design is a professional task. The outside designer can also offer the voice of experience and authority, which is invaluable in presenting recommendations and arguing against the inevitable conservatives and philistines; after all, the public relations man's opinions will be held to be no better than those of any other executive. Incidentally, conservative values can be right for some types of organization: the average insurance company might make a mistake if it advanced too far into modern design idioms.

Selecting and briefing a designer is often a delicate business, but it is worth spending time over it. There are design consultancies, large and small; many advertising agencies can offer design services; and there are individual free-lance designers in profusion. The Council of Industrial Design maintains a register of designers; the Society of Industrial Artists and the Design and Industries Association can offer advice. Often the recommendation of another satisfied organization is the best beginning.

First, it is desirable to see a wide range of the designer's work for other organizations, preferably including some that are directly comparable. It is necessary for instance, to be sure that a designer asked to make recommendations for a voluntary body is capable of thinking within much more modest limits than he would for a giant industrial complex. Some indication of an appreciation of the nature of similar organizations' affairs is helpful. For example, a trade association may need to create a unified identity exemplifying a variety of member companies, whereas the sole objective of a consumer goods firm may be to achieve better recognition than its competitors.

Curious as it may seem, it is also desirable to ensure that the designer has no doubt that the object of the exercise is not to express his personality or enhance his reputation, but to achieve a distinctive, coherent, and wholly practicable means of recognition appropriate to the client's organization.

A designer is no better than his brief and it is the public relations man's task to brief him on the structure, character, and operations of the organization, its market situation, the areas to be covered by recommendations, the timetable suggested for changes, the amount of money available, the history of any previous design exercises, and any existing elements (such as an established trade mark) which should be considered for inclusion within proposed changes. There may also be legal problems over registered marks and names. An opportunity to see parts of the organization and meet some of the executives usually helps the designer gauge its character for himself.

When, after a period of study, a designer has submitted his initial proposals, the public relations man must satisfy himself of their suitability and relevance before attempting to start the process of gaining approval for action. Obviously he will assess proposals on the basis of the criteria he has laid down during the briefing, but it is inadvisable to be too rigid in this. One of the side benefits of designers is their ability to dispose of sacred cows. If a hallowed company colour has outrun its usefulness because it has become hackneyed, then the designer must be free to say so and recommend an alternative, even if the chairman has specifically told his public relations man that he wants the colour to stay. Until alternatives are proposed as part of a logical plan, even company chairmen should not be regarded as competent to declare categorically that one element of design is immutable.

It is also the PR man's responsibility, perhaps with advertising, marketing or product design colleagues, to consider the designer's proposals from the point of view of their workability. For instance, there is an obvious danger in too strong a recommendation on colours in a business like clothing or cosmetics, where colour itself is an ever-changing factor. Then again, a designer may make an otherwise sound recommendation that unwittingly creates a chance of confusion with another organization of which he may not be aware; this is a particular problem when using sets of initials. For all the trouble taken over briefing, a designer may make suggestions that are too rigid to fit an organization's multifarious activities, and revisions must be considered to prevent a total proposal being turned down on this one point.

It is normal for designers to put forward their proposals in the form of key designs plus recommendations for further work and implementation. For example, the proposals themselves might consist of a written document covering the main elements of the job, a handful of design specimens in finished form or as finished artwork, perhaps some roughs to indicate the treatment of additional items within the same style, and a timetable outlining the succeeding phases of implementation and control.

A portfolio containing these recommendations, plus a persuasive introduction by the designer and the public relations man may suffice to carry through the proposals and the way the budget is to be spent in a small concern or an organization where one man's word is law. If, on the other hand, a board of directors or a trade association committee have to be satisfied, then it may be worth having the designer go to the extra expense of preparing a presentation, with slides, flip-over charts, large-scale reproductions, and even a 'rogue's gallery' of the mess (and it usually is a mess when seen as a whole) the organization's public face is in already.

When proposals are under discussion one recurrent problem is with trade marks, name-plates, symbols, and logotypes. The commercial value of an established visual form cannot be denied, although many of the longer-term successes have been modified over the years without most people noticing. This single element may be the centre-piece of a style. It may be basically words, letters or figures, such as British Rail, ICI or 57. It may be abstract shape, like the red triangle of Bass or the cross-barred circle of London Transport. It may be purely pictorial to illustrate a product or service, or symbolically pictorial, like the shell of Shell or the International Wool Secretariat's Woolmark. Or it may have started in one form and become another with the passage of time, as Esso started as a word expressing the initials of Standard Oil and has become both a trade mark and an established visual form.

A great deal of confused thinking goes on in this area of design. It is up to the client to define his market circumstances, his audience, his brand policy and the competitive situation so that the designer can recommend retention or adaptation of existing names, marks or symbols, their replacement by new ones, or the refining of various elements into fewer and more unified items.

Unless policy is thought out, logotypes of company names which may originally have been devised quite legitimately for narrow advertising purposes may be built up as if they were over-riding trade marks; similarly, symbols slavishly derived from initials may be forced into a design proposal in spite of the excess of marks of this kind already before an indifferent public.

The purpose of the name, mark or whatever it may be is the governing factor in deciding the form it should take and the use that should be made of it. And no two organizations have quite the same requirements.

Ultimately—apart from the subjective opinion of everyone concerned—the criteria for assessing design proposals are three: Do they accord with the character of the organization? Are they wholly practicable? And do they offer a consistent policy that can be applied throughout every aspect of the client's activities?

There are, of course, many other points to watch, most of which should not arise with a competent designer. Here are a few simple examples. If a design policy is to have an extended life (which it should if its full value is to be derived), recommendations for modishly fashionable typefaces should be critically examined; fashions change too quickly. Also, it should be established without doubt that the text and display typefaces proposed are readily available without delay and expense.

Suggestions for logotypes that appear to be unacceptably close to some current vogue should be viewed sceptically; a study of competitive advertising will soon reveal if this is a danger. Any mark or logotype suggested should be capable of easy reproduction in all forms and sizes ever likely to be required, from woven cap badges and minute engravings on company pens, to flags and illuminated signs. Many more potential problems can be seen after a thoughtful inward look at an organization's particular needs.

At the heart of most design policies is typography. This is reasonable, since there are few man-made objects that do not involve or include words. The range is vast: from the company name on the letterheading to the style of standard direction signs like 'exit'. Typography is the most permeating form of design and also one of the most powerful means of evoking the nature of an organization. The typeface on the letterheading can suggest the femininity of a fashion house, the solidity of a merchant bank or the vigour of an engineering contractor. It can be good, bad or—most often—indifferent. It can catch the eye and the imagination, and be recognizable on a desk littered with papers; it can look like thousands of others; or, even today, it can give every appearance of having come out of the nineteenth century.

It is on the area of print that most internal critics of design proposals concentrate, for here they feel they are on their home ground—even if they are not. The PR man and his design advisers may often do well to start with print proposals and then build outwards from the initial acceptability of these to all the other areas of the organization's design that form the complete plan.

Advertising and basic stationery happen also to be the areas in which it is easiest to bring agreed changes into use, for they are more ephemeral visual forms than truck liveries, reference books, branded consumer durables and other such items that may be stocked in large quantities, revised only over a period of years or require capital expenditure before alterations can be made.

A timetable for changes is therefore necessary. Some can be put into effect immediately; others can, in the interests of economy, only be brought in when existing stocks are used; still others will have to be fitted in with a schedule of repainting, or the programmed replacement of dies, and so on. A target date for completion of the whole plan is desirable, after which any surviving relics of the earlier designs should be discarded ruthlessly. A date from which new designs become mandatory is also desirable, if only to defeat those obstinate traditionalists who will persist in using the old style as long as they can.

A top management directive on the organization's design policy and its implementation is always worthwhile, but this alone is not sufficient to ensure that what has been agreed is in fact consistently carried out. A method of control is essential and the centre of this is the design manual, which is another important part of the designer's work.

A design manual may be no more than a couple of sheets of specifications and examples dealing with stationery sizes, typefaces, colour, and trade marks; on the other hand, it may run into several volumes dealing with every conceivable aspect of design for an organization with all the ramifications of a nationalized industry. In either case it is vital.

Only if colour samples are printed in a manual is it possible to ensure accuracy of matching for a variety of uses, as specified inks and paints look different according to the surface to which they are applied. Only if typefaces, the relationship of one typographic element to another, and paper specifications are laid down in a manual is it possible to maintain a visual consistency in the teeth of local managers' insistence (for which they may be able to make a sound economic case) on getting their print done by a little man round the corner. Only if the various physical forms of the logotype are shown in a manual is it possible to resist the curious variations of signwriters who like to add their own personal touch.

Moreover, the design manual is a constant point of reference for all within the organization and can save the public relations man and the designer endless hours of advice-giving on minor issues.

Policing a design policy, if that is not too strong a term, is not often a task that the PR executive can undertake alone. The office manager, the printing manager, the purchasing department, the organization and methods department, and maybe the company secretary are frequent and useful allies, for a clear approach to design is often of direct assistance to them in their own jobs.

6

Audio Communication

UNTIL THE ADVENT of television, radio was unique and supreme in its ability to convey news and information immediately, while it was happening, to any part of the world. Despite the dominance of the television screen today, radio remains a powerful communications method. It can play a vital part in a public relations programme, although it presents the public relations man with certain special problems. If newspapers, magazines or periodicals fail to print the material issued by a public relations man there is nothing—in theory—to prevent him starting his own publication. He cannot set up his own radio station, at least in Britain. He can, of course, set up as a 'ham' (an amateur broadcaster) but he is then severely restricted in the range and nature of his transmissions.

For all practical purposes, radio transmission in Britain is entirely controlled by the BBC, backed by statutory authority. Thus the public relations man who wants his stories used in radio programmes must play absolutely by the rules of the BBC. It follows that he must learn those rules.

Learning the mechanics of obtaining air time is in the end only a matter of application. But all the application will achieve nothing unless the public relations man remembers one simple fact; anything offered to a radio producer must be capable of description in words, or make a sound that identifies it clearly to the listener.

To take an extreme example, it would obviously be pointless to send a photograph or a piece of film to the producer of a sound radio programme, unless it were of historic importance or interest and could be described in words as part of a total story. There is little appeal for the listener in hearing someone say 'I am looking at a photograph' when the listener cannot see the photograph. Equally, there is little appeal for the broadcaster, if only because

175

of the difficulty of describing something as static as a still picture. The point needs no further labouring.

The BBC has a fairly well-known rule of not using trade names or manufacturers' names unless it is impossible to tell the story without them. That it does this does not make it all that different from many national newspapers, at least in principle. The rule is applied fairly strictly, sometimes to the point of absurdity ('a well-known north-east seaside resort had six inches of rain' was once included in a weather report), but is not applied universally. On certain programmes, particularly in overseas services, the names of companies are freely used.

Just as when he deals with a newspaper, the public relations man should not conceal the name of his client and should place it where it belongs in stories. He should not be surprised if it is deleted, and should be grateful if it is left in. In today's circumstances, of course, it is becoming almost impossible for the BBC to be completely inflexible on this point, although there are troubled times when perhaps the public relations man would indeed by grateful for the omission of his client's or employer's name. It would be ridiculous for a radio report of a labour dispute affecting British exports of, say, cars to refer to it as a strike 'at the Midlands factory of a car manufacturer'. The name of the manufacturer is important to the telling of the story.

As a general rule, not to be taken too literally, it can be said that in major stories of national interest the names of companies involved are mentioned. The sensible public relations man will accept the BBC's approach and will not try to circumvent it by 'pulling a fast one' to get his client's name used. In the long run he would suffer more than he would gain.

Many public relations men, of course, have a perfectly legitimate reason to feed material to radio programmes and to feature the names of their organizations. Road traffic information is a classic example. The local consequences of Parliamentary Acts— such as those allowing certain people to claim rent or rates rebates—would be another.

The output of the BBC is phenomenal. In an average twelve months it will broadcast for about 20,000 hours. Of this total, about three-quarters is music or light entertainment; the remainder covers features, news, talks, schools and other educational broadcasts, and programmes for minority groups. It will be this section which will generally provide possibilities for most public relations people.

The BBC service is divided into four categories: Radios 1 and 2, which concentrate mainly on music and entertainment; Radio 3, covering serious music, poetry, drama, talks, sports commentaries, current events, and the like; and Radio 4 (formerly the Home Service) which is regarded as the main programme for comprehensive coverage of news, coupled with background and comments, both for general and specialized interests, although it also broadcasts music and drama.

Apart from the national services, there are the regions— Midlands, North, Northern Ireland, Scotland, South and West, and Wales—and the experiment of local stations broadcasting on VHF in Leicester, Sheffield, Merseyside, Nottingham, Stoke-on-Trent, Brighton, Durham, and Leeds.

The news comes into the BBC from news agencies, its own monitoring service, and the news-gathering resources of each region, plus free-lance journalists, the study of publications, and public relations sources. There are two news rooms in London, and eleven in the regions, handling almost half a million words a day. Further still, the Corporation has its own staff of correspondents and reporters, including specialists and overseas men, just like a newspaper.

More than fifty separate news broadcasts are issued every day, from full-scale programmes to two-minute summaries.

Required reading for any public relations man is the annual *BBC Handbook,* a mass of vital information, statistics, and details.

The public relations man who wants to get his client or employer on the air starts with a simply stated task: he must listen to as many programmes as possible. Only in this way can he learn what kind of material is likely to interest their producers or editors. Only in this way can he master the medium. He must learn the times at which to put up news material, remembering to relate it to newspaper edition times and copy deadlines. He will hear how a radio news item is compressed into a few words without losing any essential information. He will discover how complicated stories which need long explanations are usually not acceptable, except for specialized programmes.

He will also learn how to present a basic item differently for different programmes or different regions. The original piece of news may be suitable for a national bulletin, and may comprise only one sentence. Extra localized information may be added for regional bulletins, making the item up to two or three sentences. 'Colour' material, often lighter or less serious, may also be offered for news magazines. All this calls for skill and judgment on the part of the public relations man and these qualities cannot be developed without spending a good deal of time just listening to programmes.

When he has studied the needs of radio and thinks he has something to offer, he should contact the producer or editor and state his idea clearly. This is sometimes fairly easy and sometimes fairly difficult.

If the item is a piece of straightforward news which is also being released to other media, it is normally sufficient to send a copy to the news editor (either national or regional) in the form of a press release. It should also be remembered that the BBC takes the tape services of the Press Association, Exchange Telegraph, and Universal News Services. Thus material issued by these bodies will automatically be considered for radio news bulletins.

If the item is more than a short piece of news, then the public relations man needs to remember that the BBC works in much the same way as a newspaper. As with newspapers, it is often better for the material to be sent to the news editor rather than to a specialist correspondent direct, although there can be no harm in sending an extra copy to the correspondent as a matter of courtesy.

There is one variation worth remembering. The public relations man who finds that he deals regularly with one particular correspondent (say, the motoring man) will clearly be better advised to reverse the previous procedure. He will send his material to the correspondent, with a copy to the news editor, or perhaps the editor or producer of a particular specialized programme.

The BBC has one facility which can reduce the distribution problem for the public relations man. Its Future Events Unit at Broadcasting House will take any press release, whatever the subject, and circulate it to all editors or producers who might be interested, including those in the regions. Three or four copies should be sent, although the Unit will make its own copies as needed. The service covers overseas as well as domestic programmes. It is up to the public relations man to decide whether he operates direct to individuals or not, though the BBC claims to prefer material circulated through the Unit.

Radio should be treated the same as newspapers in the offering of facility visits and general background material. Put another way, it is just as important and just as sensible to maintain regular contact with radio men as with newspaper journalists. The difference lies only in what is offered to them, and also in remembering that the basic need is for something which can be described easily or which has a distinctive sound.

However, apart from these considerations, there are areas in which the medium presents both the radio man and the public relations man with technical problems.

If the BBC sends a reporter to an event, or to cover a story, he will most probably only bring equipment with him if the material has to be recorded on the spot. Almost without exception the equipment will be battery-operated, obviating the need for plugging into a mains installation. When this happens, the public relations man does not need to make any special preparation. He should just be ready to co-operate as with any other journalists.

When an interview is needed, he should be ready to provide a quiet place where it can be conducted. A newspaper journalist can interview someone in any circumstances. A radio reporter will often find it helpful to get away from background noises, unless they are essential to the story. Microphones are extremely sensitive and can pick up sounds which make an interview into a jumble. The public relations man should plan for this. For instance, it can help if he indicates in a letter of invitation or covering note to an invitation card what steps he has taken. Equally, he should be prepared to make arrangements for a representative of his company or client to go to a studio, if this is requested by the BBC.

Advance planning is the wise course. If the extraneous noise is too great to allow a sensible interview to take place, but the sound is essential to the telling of the story, it may be possible to record it separately and match it into the tape before actual transmission.

The public relations man who is in doubt can always suggest

to the BBC that they might like to reconnoitre the ground in advance. They can advise him whether they need any special arrangements.

All this is possible when there has been time to plan. But at, say, a railway disaster such counsels of perfection become meaningless. Here the public relations man who has done his best to learn the technical problems of radio can help a reporter to get over them.

Again, it is worth remembering that there is today much interchange of news and background items between radio and television. The reporter may cover for both. When he does and has cameras with him, the conditions are different. (This is dealt with in the chapter on television.)

Several years ago, recording equipment was cumbersome and bulky. Today, the radio reporter usually takes with him only a small tape recorder. Nevertheless, many company executives, unused to speaking on radio, are still made nervous by the sight of a microphone. The public relations man can take some easy precautions to guard against an interview being a flop by briefing his company spokesman or client. He should tell him not to look at the microphone but to be certain to speak towards it. There is no need to shout. The reporter will hold it or place it at the right distance to allow for a normal conversational tone.

Most people, when they speak, tend to drop their voices at the end of a sentence. For broadcasting this can be calamitous, and anyone being interviewed should remember to keep his voice up as he reaches the end of a sentence or phrase. A little practice ensures that the right effect is achieved without sounding unnatural. The person speaking should remember, too, that he is not addressing a public gathering. He is having an ordinary conversation, usually in simple questions and answer form. A declamatory style of oratory sounds unreal and false in a radio interview.

Finally, the speaker should be natural, especially in his speaking. At one time everybody on radio tried to achieve an 'accentless accent', but this has gone. Often a broad accent adds something special to a radio interview. In a curious way it adds to the authority and standing of the speaker.

The public relations man who believes that his chief executive or client is likely to have to broadcast regularly can arrange for him to attend a brief training course. It may not be worthwhile for the chairman of a normal commercial company, but it would be sensible for the chairman of, for instance, a nationalized undertaking or a development board. It could be sensible, too, for the manager of a football club. If it is felt that this is too time-consuming or expensive, it is possible to achieve a certain amount by experimenting with a tape recorder. At least this will let a company spokesman hear some of his more obvious faults.

If the chairman or managing director proves to be a bad speaker, the public relations man must say so. He must stick out for the right to depute another company spokesman. Otherwise he will find that his organization is not asked to provide speakers.

The overseas services of the BBC present different opportunities, and have some slightly different rules of operation. One of the most important is that there is not the same strictness about the use of company or brand names. There is a good reason for this: the BBC can play a part in helping British exporters by publicizing their products. Good stories of British achievements can help the growth of overseas business, but they become less useful if they do not mention an actual company. After all, a potential customer in Mexico is hardly likely to write to the BBC to discover the name and address of a 'north country button manufacturer'. He is much more likely to go to a local manufacturer or the agent for a competitor and see whether something near to the British product can be turned out.

There are two aspects of this situation that the public relations man needs to remember. One of them—the same as for domestic radio services—is to become familiar with the network of overseas services so that he offers them material they are really likely to want. The second is to inform people in his organization who can capitalize on a broadcast. If he has succeeded in gaining the interest of a producer in an item and thinks it likely that it will be used in one or more overseas programmes, he should advise the export manager. Then, either through the export department or direct, he should advise representatives or agents in the countries concerned. The advice should include suggestions for making the most of any broadcast.

The BBC External Services are based on Bush House, in London, where ninety-five hours of news and programmes in forty languages are broadcast every day. Direct transmission is handled from thirty-nine studios in Bush House, while recorded material is sent on to other radio stations abroad. The ninety-five hours includes more than fifty news bulletins a day. Export achievements, and scientific and industrial news, claim some emphasis with regular special programmes.

Comprehensive details of the scope and extent of overseas services are also listed in the *BBC Handbook*.

There is no substitute for the hard work it needs to understand the medium. A public relations man who offers a radio producer ideas or stories which are clearly no good for broadcasting will fail. Unless he listens assiduously to the radio he will never learn what is good and what is bad. Once he has learned what is good, he will find that radio can help him put over his story in an unrivalled fashion. At the same time, if he is working on something which has no radio value, he should not waste either his time or that of producers in trying to force his way in.

7

Specialized Communication

NEWS IS SOMETHING WHICH HAPPENS. *Why* it happened may be immaterial. *Who* made it happen may also be immaterial. At the same time, *why* and *who* may be the reasons that make the fact news. Strictly speaking, news is something unusual, something noteworthy. In terms of the general news pages in a newspaper, the unusual part of a fact is most often what makes it news in the journalistic sense.

However, there are many departments in a newspaper—features, the women's page, sport, gardening, cookery, food, and so on—for which the unusual or the unexpected are not necessarily the whole criteria. Put simply, at the time of a glut in the stocks of butter, a further fall in the price to the housewife does not really merit front-page treatment, unless the fall itself is exceptional. It may well merit top-of-the-story treatment in the weekly food coloumn on an inside page. In the circumstances in which the food journalist is writing, the standard of what is news and what is not is different from that of the news editor looking for a front-page lead story.

It is an understanding of these conditions and approaches that should be in the mind of the public relations man who sets out to 'create' news, especially when the vehicle for so doing is a promotion campaign or a sponsored event.

Having made that point, it is equally important to make two more of comparable validity. Sales promotion is not normally the province of a public relations man. It belongs in the sales or advertising departments of an organization. The public relations man can become involved, and some aspects of his duties will be considered later. A sponsored event—a golf tournament is an easy illustration—is very much the province of the public relations man.

Both promotion campaigns and sponsored events have as their eventual objectives the sale of more products or greater use of services. They reach their objectives in different ways.

Often the involvement of a public relations man in a sales promotion drive is to attempt to obtain editorial coverage on the campaign. Too often, a sponsored event is undertaken solely for the same reason: to get space in newspapers. Sales promotion and sponsored events are both entirely legitimate enterprises, but the public relations man should be wary of being drawn into playing a part in a sales promotion effort or organizing a sponsored event solely for publicity, with no clear intention to give benefit or impart genuine information. The exploitation of a sales promotion campaign or a sponsored event presents special challenges to the public relations man. To be successful, it calls for rigid adherence to high standards of presentation and meticulous attention to detail.

Sales promotion has been defined as the art of pushing the product towards the consumer. Thus the national tour of fifty theatrically costumed salesmen in specially labelled cars shouting the wares of a new synthetic detergent is sales promotion. So is the employing of half a dozen girls wearing some national costume to visit grocers' shops and decorate them with point-of-sale material advertising an imported food product. Sales promotion campaigns, of course, do not necessarily mean people. They include leaflet distribution, the merchandising of retail outlets with display material, and many other exercises.

News of sales promotion drives is usually acceptable to trade papers, since they can see it as part of their job of informing the trade they serve. For lay newspapers, they seldom make news without an excessive degree of stunting. Sales promotion is often based on a proposal put up by an advertising agency, whose news values are different from those of journalists. It is an understandable enthusiasm on the part of an advertising executive that leads him to call in the public relations man and ask him to try for editorial coverage.

If the public relations man sees that there is some genuine news value in a promotion, he will act in the same way as in the handling of any other story. If he wants to invite the press to see the departure of a team of bikini-clad girls on a national sales tour, he will work by exactly the same rules as if he were inviting the pressmen to a factory opening. He will have to resist the pressure to make his invitation and press information too excitable, or to use too florid a style of writing. In this way he will have a better chance that his story will be seen as a piece of possible news. He will still be fortunate if the brand name is mentioned anywhere, even in photographs.

It is, of course, perfectly within the rights and duties of a public relations man to suggest that a sales promotion campaign should be used to solve a particular public relations problem. However, if he does so, he will then exceed his rights if he does much more than make the proposal and afterwards hand it over to the experts, either in the sales department of an organization or its advertising agents.

A sponsored event is an entirely different proposition. Everybody has become familiar with major functions of this kind, and in modern society many sports, in particular, would be in a sorry state without sponsorship from commercial organizations. Golf, cricket, tennis, darts, horse racing, motor racing—these are only a handful of the sports which have drawn considerable benefit, not to say achieved survival, from the financial backing injected into them by industrial organizations.

In order to be acceptable (and this is not meant in any cynical sense), a sponsored event should aim either to bring obvious benefit, or improve standards, or encourage youth, or further participation in a worthwhile human activity. For a public relations man these ends should be sufficient. If the event merits editorial, television or radio coverage, so much the better. But no sponsored event can be forced to success against an unwilling audience. It may succeed once, but if its aims and objects are basically spurious, it will not succeed more than once.

If the reasons for undertaking a major sponsored event are genuine, it is almost inevitable that it should be seen as something which takes place several times. This may mean an annual exhibition or contest, or a bi-annual one, or even one which only comes up every five years.

A sponsored event will have short- and long-term objectives. It will be costly. It should thus not be recommended lightly. For example, an international architectural contest with a first prize of £5,000 will probably cost a total of £20,000 to administer. If it is to be kept up over a number of years it begins to add up to a great deal of money. Thus it is simple sense to work out carefully the value of such an event, its true cost, and its place in a public relations programme before making a firm recommendation.

To reach that point means taking a series of simple steps. A good example is a golf tournament, since this has become one of the most popular types of sponsored event. There are, of course, two reasons for holding a golf tournament. One of them is because golf is a popular game. A public relations man may decide that a golf day for his firm's or client's customers or suppliers may be a useful piece of promotion. Golf may have nothing to do with either his professional interests or those of the people he is inviting; it is simply a social occasion. A decision to hold such an event will then be based on whether there are enough executives in his company who are interested, and whether there are enough guests who want to play.

The decision once having been taken, the public relations man is only involved in making sure that the organization is right. He will need a working committee, a budget (he will often find that the day costs more than anyone thought it would) and enough planning time to ensure that everything is done properly. It is worth recording that one of the greatest problems is in matching players so that all enjoy the day. Incidentally, the public relations man can make a useful contribution to a memorable day by providing prizes which are slightly unusual. Certainly such a day can have a tremendous value in bringing together company executives and customers.

However, this is an entirely different operation from a tournament sponsored by a manufacturer of golf equipment or clothing. The company golf day may cost £1,000; the tournament can cost £100,000. The first is only intended to clothe business talking in a pleasant atmosphere; the second is intended to focus sharp attention on the manufacturer's products. The first is a relaxed day off; the second is a tense competitive occasion. The first can survive even if there are some small flaws in the administration; for the second any mistake is sudden death.

The first step is to survey the scene, to find out how many golf tournaments are already in existence, when and where they take place, what results they bring, and what sort of prizes they offer. This study will show whether there is a gap that could be filled with a new contest.

The public relations man will then consult experts—especially golf associations—to discover whether the gap has been noticed, and whether the initiative of yet another manufacturer in running an event designed to fill it would be welcomed. If there is immediate resistance it is usually not worth trying to pursue the idea. If, on the other hand, there is some interest, then the public relations man must go exhaustively into detailed planning. He must find out the form of tournament that would be welcomed, likely dates, and the prize structure that would make the event attractive. He must find out whether overseas entry would be acceptable or desirable. He will then have some basis for costing.

The first thing to remember, of course, is that planning for an event of this magnitude takes at least twelve months, and can quite easily take two years. It is unwise to try to cram the planning into less than a year and such an attempt can be disastrous.

To arrive at a final costing needs the creation of a timetable and a checklist. The timetable will work back from the date of the event, and forward to the eventual settlement of all outstanding details. It is important to be meticulous in the preparation of the checklist, and to make absolutely certain that everything is covered in it. What has to be covered includes: advertising; print (entry forms, handbills, posters, notices, rules, score cards, souvenir programme, menu cards, invitations); accommodation, travelling, and subsistence for competitors and staff, especially if overseas entries are being accepted; special amenities and facilities at the club where the tournament is staged; photography; press facilities; postage; prizes; souvenir wallets and the like; flags for each hole; caddies and stewards; transport; road signposting; extra policing; insurance; and so on. No item can be left out and the list is endless.

During all the work involved, the public relations man must also guard against the danger of becoming so immersed in the excitement of the event (and they *are* exciting to run) that he forgets the objective. The objective is to support the game and to draw attention to his organization and its products. He must ensure that it is attained. One obvious thought is to incorporate his organization's name in the title of the event.

For a sporting event such as a golf tournament it is the hope of most public relations men that it will earn television coverage. While this should not be a governing factor in a decision to stage an event, it is sensible to open discussions with special departments of the BBC or commercial television programme companies who consider the coverage of these functions. For one thing, their needs may dictate part of the timing of the event and it is as well to know this from as early in the planning as possible.

Other arrangements, such as advance press information and the provision of proper press facilities during the event, are important, but they need no special knowledge. They are the same as the arrangements made for anything which the press is to report.

The real key to staging an event is good organization. Of course, that implies that everybody who is involved anywhere along the line must know what is happening, why it is happening, when it is happening, and what part they have to play. Proper written briefs for everybody, as well as regular meetings of an organization committee, are essential. A simple but wise course is the appointment of an organizing secretary, who may become involved full-time in the work.

In events such as golf, where there are already a number of sponsors, it is fairly standard practice that the sponsoring organization should share the limelight with the professional body organizing the sport as a whole (for instance, the Professional Golfers' Association). This has some obvious advantages, not the least of which is the seal of authority that the name of the professional body puts on the event.

At the same time, professional bodies are helpful in making available to the sponsors case history material on other, similar events. The public relations man will find that studying this material will save him a good deal of time. He must also take heed of the advice and guidance the professional body gives him. After all, they know the framework, history, and traditions of the sport. He does not.

The work on the event does not finish at the end of the day on which it happens. Often the follow-up activity is what makes it a profitable and worthwhile investment for the sponsor. If it is an international tournament, there are advertising possibilities to consider. There are also endorsement possibilities: so-and-so used the maker's equipment when he won the tournament. This may lead into pack redesign jobs, window displays, and, indeed, sales promotion campaigns. For a sufficiently important event, the future value of a film should be considered. Golf clubs, for instance, are often willing to arrange special showings for their members of a film of an international tournament. It is at this stage that the real value of good advance planning will be realized.

The example of a golf tournament has been given at some length, since it contains most of the elements needed for the conduct of a successful event. In essence, the real need is attention to detail, whether the event is golf, table-tennis, pigeon racing or any other sport.

The growth of sponsorship of sporting events has come about for fairly obvious reasons. People's leisure pursuits engross them. As more people increase their leisure time they become even more interested. Thus the press devotes more space to sport. Television, too, has focused greater attention on it. Lastly, many sports attract great audiences of spectators. It is the devout hope of all salesmen that they can have a captive audience, that is, an audience whose almost total attention is riveted on what is happening in front of them.

However, sponsorship is not restricted to sport. Art, architecture, education, printing, journalism itself, all have attracted sponsors of awards, competitions, foundations, and the like. The backers have not only been commercial companies. They have included individuals, nationalized undertakings, charities, trade and professional associations, and many others.

In an increasingly competitive world, the standards of practice in any craft, trade or profession become more and more important. Only those with the highest standards will succeed. It is in the interests of manufacturers to help customers to attain high standards, and equally to identify themselves and their products with these standards. In any group of people with common interests there is the opportunity for a sponsor to advance standards by providing an award, trophy, or other prize. If it is truly relevant or sufficiently large it will attract the best people to compete. It should also set a target for entrants to the business.

Repetitive sponsored events—such as an annual competition—depend on good organization. This is no less true of a one-off event. A good example is an architectural competition to provide a design for the forecourt or entrance of the new head office of a company, or one to provide the landscape surroundings of a factory in a new estate. Once again, the advice of the professional body—in this instance, the Royal Institute of British Architects—should be sought. They can guide the public relations man into acceptable methods and prize structure. Even more, they may provide or recommend the judges.

The reasons for deciding to enter into something of this kind do not belong here—they have to do with community relations, or employee relations, or half-a-dozen other subjects. The only issue which arises in this context is one of method. A one-off event cannot be skimped any more than a repetitive event. Proper budgeting is essential. A single event may well draw more press attention than a regular one, since it satisfies the condition that it is unusual: it has not happened before and may not happen again. Unlike a regular event, there is no reason why press comment on a single event should not be seen as a major part of the reason for running it.

It is worth restating a principle: the reasons for entering into a sponsored event must be genuine if it is to succeed. It does not really matter if the event is international or purely local in scope. The public relations man must study carefully his objectives and decide whether he can attain them by creating something which excites the interest of any group he wishes to influence.

It is not possible to generalize beyond this point. The PR man needs to look at his own particular circumstances and forge his own particular method. A sponsored event may draw the attention of the general public, if that is what the public relations man wants. It may interest only a handful of highly erudite specialists. It may be used for great dramatic effect, or it may be used to add vital knowledge to research programmes.

Whichever of all these it does, it is based on the competitiveness inherent in all people. People either like taking part in a competition, or they like watching others take part. The desire for competition is a human attribute which the public relations man can use well, but he must use it for good reasons.

7.2 COMMUNITY RELATIONS

No man is an island. Today Donne's dictum is more than ever true for every type of organization. Every group has a relationship with the community around it, whether it thinks about it or not. A beneficial relationship can be sought and fostered, given the right attitude of mind and the application of much time, although not necessarily a great deal of money.

There are three basic motivations for operating a community relations policy: a sense of corporate social responsibility; an acknowledgment of the attitude that nowadays all organizations are expected to participate in life beyond their own doors; and, quite bluntly, because the understanding and appreciation of everyone around is of genuine practical value.

Community relations may involve many of the techniques of communication that are used in other areas of a company's public relations. It needs the same disciplines of selectivity and control, but it differs in that it is almost impossible to lay down general rules. The reason for this is simply that no two communities are the same and that no two relationships between an organization and the various communities in which it may find itself are the same either.

Even more than in other sensitive areas of public relations, careful study is vital before taking the first diffident steps to implement a programme. There is no substitute for local advice to ensure that an apparently good idea does not in fact turn out to be a local laughing-stock, or to identify a problem that is not obvious to the outsider.

The idea of community relations is not new; it might be said to be as old as organized society itself. The ancient city states like Athens existed on the strength of good relations with the citizens. In the middle ages, the powerful guilds set the pattern of charity and education in the towns, while sometimes benevolent landowners did the same in the countryside.

Even in the dark days of the industrial revolution there were an enlightened few, usually prompted by religious motives, who accepted that industry and society had mutual responsibilities. Unhappily, the majority of employers neglected the community as much as they neglected the welfare of their employees, and some sour social relationships which exist today can be traced back to their disregard of others.

On the one hand there are innumerable hospitals, schools, almshouses, and charitable trusts which are a welcome legacy of the past and have been integrated into the modern welfare state, and on the other hand there are rows of dwellings barely fit for animals, mountains of slag, and polluted rivers still besmirching the countryside.

Today there is power under the law to prevent irresponsible behaviour, such as the poisoning of the air with fumes or the uncontrolled dumping of waste. Yet the fear of transgression is not enough. It is quite possible to be a bad neighbour, or at least an indifferent one, without ever breaking the law. An attitude of mind has to be encouraged, a clear understanding of responsibilities has to be developed.

Few companies lack appreciation of their obligations to their customers and in the past twenty years or so progress in employee relations has been considerable. Yet the concept of a deliberate endeavour to build a good relationship with the community has lagged behind.

As with other facets of public relations, before action can be proposed, management must be satisfied that it is both necessary and viable. This means thinking out and putting across a clear case to show the value of a community relations programme. All too often, good intentions are believed to be enough.

Perhaps the simplest way to start is to formulate one or two questions relevant to the company's operations. Is it a good thing, for instance, for a wife to ask 'Who are they?' when her husband tells her that he is going after a job at a certain factory? Does the management think it would be helpful for the borough surveyor to recall the firm's unco-operativeness with disapproval when the factory needs permission to enlarge an effluent outflow? Will it assist recruitment of school-leavers for the headmaster of the local technical college to remember that the company never accepts visits by students to see the process? Is it desirable to let the plant next door gain all the kudos for helping youth organizations when the factory's own sports ground is hardly used?

Within the context of a particular organization and its surroundings, endless appropriate questions could be put. Even if the
general tenor of response to them is understanding and helpful,
both at top management level and on the part of the senior
executive at a given location, the difficulties of building and
applying a consistent community relations policy are only
starting.

The possibilities for action are probably many; the money and
time—particularly at local level—to carry them out are probably
limited. The individual situation has to be assessed meticulously
and the character of the community gauged to determine what
can most effectively be done. This means taking time to investigate the social structure and to listen to local people.

Attitudes vary enormously from one part of the country to
another. The approach which works in the Welsh valleys will not
necessarily go down well in the Lowlands of Scotland, and what
goes in the Lowlands will very likely not work in the Highlands.
One common factor in all regions is suspicion of interference from
the centre, whether that means London or Edinburgh, a head
office in Britain or a parent company in the United States.

Local affairs need to be handled locally, preferably by someone
who knows his community and is perhaps known in it. The public
relations man may establish the need, persuade the management
to act, create a programme, and provide the means to carry it out,
but its effectiveness is bound to be hindered if it all appears in the
community to be something artificially applied from outside.

A large organization building a huge project in a remote place
may be able to afford a full-time community relations man. A
company with a PR department or using a consultancy may be
able to put an executive on to a community project for a good part
of his working time. Mostly the handling of community affairs,
however, falls upon the management on the spot.

Usually, the public relations man must go beyond his programme to advise and assist those who will directly carry it out.
He will have the techniques and the resources; they will have the
awareness of local attitudes. The public relations man must learn
to understand those attitudes, to put himself in other people's
shoes.

Basic principles are easy to state: reputation depends not only on what is done but on how much is known about what is done and why. This means that communication is at the heart of community relations. But what needs to be communicated? Is it a precise message or a general impression of the nature of the organization?

The answer depends entirely upon the circumstances. The problems facing a mail order house moving from London to a market town are not the same as those of a contractor building a power station in a rural area. The needs of an established company which has long dominated a small town and is now liable to be swamped by a bigger newcomer are vastly different from those of an average engineering firm competing for labour in a flourishing new town.

All have in common the need to be understood. The local press, and this includes the provincial dailies and evenings and the regional radio and television services, are generally sympathetic to local stories. The independent endorsement of the editorial judgment of local media means that their stories are likely to be more acceptable among inhabitants than if the company blows its own trumpet.

This is not to say that direct published communication is not valuable. It may range from a selective outside distribution of the internal magazine to the issuing of an occasional open letter about progress on a large development; from making a background leaflet available through libraries, council offices, and so on, to buying advertisement space in the weekly papers to make an important announcement.

The possibilities for graphic communication are considerable, too. It may be expensive to set up a touring exhibition, but it costs little to organize a photographic display in a shop window. Permanent exhibits in local museums and libraries can keep the company's name, process, and product in the public eye (as long as 'permanent' is not taken to mean that they are allowed to become dusty and outdated).

Films can have a long and valuable life and are often in themselves an attraction for local groups, so that illustrated talks can be offered and human reactions and questions met face-to-face. It is not essential to have films of one's own; many film libraries have productions of sufficient relevance to be suitable for a company talk and most trade associations and technical institutions have film lists for the PR man to draw upon.

The provision of educational materials and guidance for schools is a subject in itself and may be of major importance in a community relations programme. This may mean lending a technician to lecture or demonstrate, or allowing craft classes to examine and use machinery. It may be a matter of giving information leaflets (sales literature is not usually acceptable to the teaching profession) or donating scrap material on which pupils may try their skill.

In the raw materials industries many large companies and trade associations deploy considerable resources to provide teaching aids: booklets, lecture notes, slides and filmstrips, wall charts, boxes of labelled specimens, sections of finished goods, and so on. The very fact that these are basic, rather than branded, products overcomes the sensitivity to any form of commercial pressure against which most educationists feel they must guard their charges.

Nevertheless, plenty of forward-looking commercial concerns ensure that their future customers are made aware of their goods by the legitimate means of offering to schools free, or almost free, publications and all forms of advice and assistance for teachers. That this is of practical value is shown by the fact that the National Union of Teachers publishes in *Treasure Chest for Teachers* a directory of commercial and non-commercial services available.

Direct communication to the community can take many forms. The conducted tour of the plant may be for housewives to see for themselves how a food product is hygienically prepared, or for engineering students to view a process from start to finish; it may be for members of the river board to see how the company controls the release of effluents, or for careers masters to learn enough to be able to advise school-leavers about potential jobs.

An open day may be seen as mainly for the benefit of employees and their families, but each one of them is a member of the community and is in some form or another a communicator to others.

If a new plant is to be built in an area with little experience of industry, an open meeting, organized with the help of the local authority, offers an opportunity to meet the people, present a case, and attempt to answer questions and allay fears.

Whatever aspect of the organization's activities needs to be understood, the communications techniques of public relations can be brought to bear—provided, of course, that the attitudes of the audience and the suitability of the method of communication are taken into account.

The second common denominator, regardless of the type of organization and the nature of its social surroundings, is the desirability of direct participation in the life of the community. Again, this may take any number of forms, but it is essential for participation to be active rather than passive. Mere donations to charitable causes do not constitute playing an active role in local life. Indeed, to try to buy one's way into a community by easy generosity is usually an expensive failure: it leads to the company being regarded as a 'soft touch', an outsider with more money than sense rather than an insider willing to help.

Charitable generosity must be selective. It should be controlled: in a big way by a small committee to decide on the disbursement of an agreed sum each year, or in a small way by establishing a short list of worthy causes and sticking to it, with a modest contingency fund for special occasions.

Cash donations do not necessarily help very much to establish the company as a good corporate citizen. A name in the small-print list of sponsors at the local sports, for example, is less likely to gain a good impression than the free provision of the public address equipment and the electricians to operate it. To help is fine, but to be known to want to help is better when reputation is at stake.

The forms of participation are endless, dependent upon the nature of the community and its institutions, and of the talents and time of those who are willing to help. In some ways it is as well to allow the contribution to local affairs to grow naturally, to let those with the enthusiasm or desire to do so lead the youth groups, take over the secretaryship of the film society, become Red Cross instructors or whatever it may be. Still, it is reasonable to encourage this genuine desire to help and make it part of the company's approach to the community.

Men and women who wish to take part in local affairs, and local government in particular, can be given time off for their duties. If a foreman takes over a scout troop, the firm's sports pavilion might be put at his disposal. A local debating society may find a programme organizer among the office staff, but could they use the office duplicator occasionally?

The plant manager will probably find it useful to belong to Rotary or the Chamber of Commerce, and senior executives to branches of their professional institutions, but beyond this it can be made known that the company is prepared to encourage participation by other employees in productivity associations, voluntary fire services, the special constabulary, savings groups, and so on.

It helps to know what it going on in the community, particularly for newcomers. Established local information points, like the librarian, the newspaper editor or someone in the town hall, can help build a list of organizations and activities. Equally, it helps to know what skills and interests exist within the company: who might want to start a bee-keeping club or a children's theatre, who runs a pop group in his spare time or gives up his weekends to entertaining the sick.

Needs and talents, opportunities and inclinations can often be matched. This is a matter for subtle human judgment and the thoughtful assessment of whether an idea is workable as well as superficially attractive. A blatant attempt to foist company people or facilities on to local organizations would be as disastrous outside as a bald suggestion that all employees should take part in community affairs would be within.

The impression that a company is trying to muscle in could easily result from an over-eager attempt to take part in too many activities too soon, however well intentioned. Just as a new resident in a village is not immediately accepted but has to earn his place, so a firm new to a community must take its time getting to know and be known. Even an existing organization that has previously kept to itself cannot expect to change its reputation overnight by starting a bold community relations programme.

A contribution or a form of local participation that arises naturally from the company's own affairs is automatically more acceptable than a contrived endeavour to join in. A printer can do charitable work for nothing. A fruit packer can give to hospitals and old people at Christmas. A builder can repair a church, and a timber yard can give materials. A coach hire firm can provide transport for an orphan's outing. A waste merchant can help schoolchildren dispose of scrap materials collected for some good cause.

The company's experts can give their services, and maybe the company can contribute facilities to help them. Plumbers, painters, and carpenters can refurbish a failing youth club, but it may also need an accountant to straighten out its finances.

If the company's activities and skills do not lend themselvs directly to the aiding of local activities, direct cash contribution is not the only alternative. Sponsorship by industry and commerce has a role to play, partly replacing the patronage once given by the wealthy to the arts and to education.

A scholarship in a technical subject for a local college may appeal to one firm as much as becoming the patron of a local choral society may to another. Cultural leadership is not necessarily expensive; the gift of stereophonic equipment to a music group may well be more welcome than the endowing of an art gallery. It depends entirely on the local situation.

The position in large cities is difficult as, generally speaking, only the largest concerns can make a noticeable contribution to community life there. Education and the arts again offer openings for named awards, anything from a scholarship in metal-working to an annual piano contest for teenagers. Some activity crystallizing local or regional outlook, a bi-annual arts festival or sponsoring the revival of some ancient ceremony or sporting event, might be appropriate.

In many large towns the majority of companies can remain quietly anonymous unless they actively wish to participate in community affairs, but for a major organization with many branches and a reputation for civic responsibility, the problem for the management in an urban area is delicate.

It all comes back to deciding how a firm wishes to be thought of in its surrounding community. To be a good employer and to make a sound product will earn in time a reputation of one kind, in many ways the best kind. But to be known as a good corporate citizen, a thoughtful neighbour, and a discriminating supporter of good causes with money, facilities, and human effort may be of incalculable value, too.

The choice of what to do, how and when can only be made with a full understanding of local circumstances and attitudes. It is not beyond the bounds of possibility that a friendly letter of explanation and apology to nearby residents for noisy night working on a new plant extension could do more for a company's reputation than the gift of £1,000 by covenant to a national charity. Size and expense are not the criteria of value in community relations.

7.3 CUSTOMER RELATIONS

Human relationships are always complex and for the public relations man there are few times when this is more clear than in the dealings between a seller and a buyer .

At one end of any commercial transaction is a buyer, or customer. He may buy directly across a counter, or through the mail, or indirectly via a third party. In direct buying an immediate relationship is created between the seller, who may be a manufacturer or a distributor or a service company, and the buyer. In indirect buying, the buyer will have two relationships: one with the manufacturer whose goods he buys, and the other with the agent who actually sells them to him. In extreme circumstances, he may dislike the agent (for instance, a particular retailer) but want the goods so much that he suppresses the dislike.

In the pattern of commerce, wholesalers and retailers are, of course, also customers. Mostly, the customer is taken to mean the person who buys over the counter or by mail order and personally uses the product or enjoys the service. In the most easily recognized form, that person is the housewife purchasing the week's groceries, the football fan, the couple buying furniture in a department store or the man ordering garden tools from a mail order catalogue. However, there are many other kinds of customer whose attitudes must engage the study of a public relations man. The motor manufacturer who buys accessories and equipment from other manufacturers is just as much a customer as the woman buying groceries. The industrial organization building a new factory is a customer for materials, air-conditioning installations, machine tools, and a host of other items.

The differences between individuals and organizations are really only a matter of size. The seller makes a series of promises through his promotional and selling activities: his products are good and will thus give satisfaction; his deliveries are prompt and his after-sales service is first-class; his handling of queries is impeccable and friendly.

For as long as the promises are fulfilled, the relationship with the customer will be good. At any point at which they are broken, the relationship will be strained. If they continue to be broken, the relationship will end. But always the state of the relationship will be helped along by a degree of understanding of each other's problems. This is the area where an efficient public relations man can make a solid contribution.

It is at the moment when a complaint is made that the greatest problems arise, often because people who have not been involved in the original selling–buying transaction are drawn into the argument.

There are two kinds of complainant: the genuine one and the 'professional'. For the public relations man no distinction can really be drawn. When there has been an error or there is a fault in the product, it is the manufacturer's or supplier's duty to repair it or replace it, and in so doing to err on the side of generosity to the customer. The professional complainant banks on this, since it is sometimes difficult for the manufacturer to be certain whether he is in the right or not. The professional can hardly lose. He will happily distort the facts to suit himself. In the end, it is usually easier and cheaper to replace the goods.

However, when a customer feels a complaint coming on, it is not unusual for appeal to be made to the highest possible authority. This can be the managing director, or the sales director, or even a public personality who is known to be associated with the company. The appeal is made to them partly to flatter the ego of the complainant, partly in the belief that the higher the complaint goes, the quicker will be the action. The receiver of the complaint feels in honour bound to take action or to look as if he has taken action personally. Since he has almost certainly not been involved in the transaction beforehand, he must institute a chain of enquiries, which takes a certain amount of time.

There is, therefore, one rule which must be observed strictly. All complaints, genuine or not, must be acknowledged promptly, preferably on the day they are received. The acknowledgment should, if possible, indicate how long it will be before the matter can be resolved finally. Inevitably there are points along the lines of investigation when people will be trying to justify themselves or their actions. It is sometimes extremely difficult for the truth to be extracted. Meanwhile, the customer is sitting and fuming, and if he is a professional he will be gossiping to his acquaintances and telling them how badly he is being treated.

It almost goes without saying that prompt acknowledgment must go hand in hand with prompt attention. It must not be seen as an excuse for procrastination. In all circumstances, the customer must have the feeling that the complaint is being handled with the priority he feels it deserves.

Selling, in this context, is a business in which reputation is a paramount consideration. Reputation is created and maintained as a result of many seen and unseen influences. It can be earned over years and lost in minutes. It may be justified or unjustified. For the public relations man, it is entirely vital that he lays his groundwork properly. He must advise his management or client on their policy towards complaints, service, replacement, and the dozen-and-one other aspects of customer relations. When he has obtained management's agreement to the policy, he must see that it is made clear to all levels of staff. He should try to define it in a few straightforward phrases which will apply to all personnel, including directors, however infrequently any of them may come into contact with customers. He should add extra explanations on steps to be taken by specific departments, for example, counter staffs, service engineers, outside representatives, and so on. He must aim at simplicity, so that both the policy and its implementation are equally easy to understand and follow.

Many people bemoan the passing of the 'shop on the corner' where many minor things—cigarettes, papers, candles, groceries, and the like—could be bought at almost any time any day of the week. What they liked about it was partly the convenience, but more importantly the friendliness (real or imagined) of the shopkeeper. In many ways this was an archetypal public relations situation. The shopkeeper depended enormously for his business on the relationship he built up with his customers.

In contemporary society the 'little man' has largely disappeared because the economics of production and distribution are forcing him out. Vestiges of his assets remain in the voluntary group chains (especially in grocery) which try to achieve the economies of scale while continuing to focus the customer's attention on one easily identifiable shopkeeper.

The stores, supermarkets, and chains that are taking the place of the small man are most anxious to create and then preserve this same relationship with their customers. The ways in which they do it are necessarily different. He dealt with a few people, knew most of them by name, and often ran his shop in a haphazard fashion. They deal with hundreds of customers, most of whom remain anonymous, and they are extremely cost and profit conscious.

The size of the operation and the anonymity of the customers should, in theory, increase the importance of the products, since it is the products themselves and their quality which create the loyalty of the customer. But this fact cannot allow a diminution in the effort to be friendly and helpful on the part of managers or counter staffs. However, since much of the buying in, for example, grocers' shops is done on impulse a great deal of sales promotion—the art of pushing the customer towards the product—is needed. Special offers, window displays, leaflet promotion, local advertising, all these are common features of the store business. Their prime purpose is to increase store traffic, that is, the number of people who enter and walk through. Behind the purpose is the certain knowledge that once inside they will buy something, and often something more than they had intended to buy.

One of the most important aspects of the customer relations job is staff education. It is one in which the public relations man may well overlap with other executives: staff or personnel officers, floor or departmental managers, welfare officers and so on. The best displays, the most enticing products, and attractive prices can all be nullified by surly or ill-informed assistants. It is not easy, of course, for a shop assistant to maintain a cheerful appearance or manner especially in stores or departments which require the staff to be on their feet most of the day. It is also true that turnover in staff is usually high, whatever the pay and conditions are like. Enthusiasm is difficult to create and must be consciously fostered.

On engagement, any shop assistant should receive a booklet telling him or her something about the store. The information it contains should cover the products sold, the arrangement of departments and layout of the building, working conditions, holidays, time off, late night working, benefits, social amenities, and the like. It must tell newcomers something about the company that owns the store and whether there are other branches. If the store does any advertising, examples should be shown. The booklet should be produced by the public relations man, working closely with the personnel or training officer and any other relevant executives. The design should allow for additional material, whether new or amendments, to be inserted.

In ideal conditions, one of the best ways of introducing a new assistant to the right and wrong ways of serving is by a film. Indeed, such a film could be used in refresher courses for more experienced assistants. It could be made in a humorous vein. It should be remembered that every assistant is also a customer at other shops and should be able to relate mistakes made by shop assistants to his or her own experience. The film should not lecture, but should try to do its job by implication. An alternative which may work effectively is a filmstrip, or even a slide presentation, based on colour pictures and produced with a commentary on tape.

Training courses, both on arrival and as refreshers, must also exist for managerial staff. It is largely their responsibility to keep their staff, and to act as a buffer against which the occasional irate customer can vent his spleen. In certain circumstances, managers (as in banks) must do much more than this by becoming leaders in their communities. They must join local societies, or become identified with their aims, and should become involved in community problems and topics. However, when they do this, it must be with a proper sense of service and not in any cynical or hypocritical manner. In the context of customer relations, involvement like this can be important. It allows customers (and, better still, potential customers) to personalize the store in their minds. In a small way, it can help to avoid the anonymity that goes with large units.

Within a large store especially, there is much that can be done to simplify life for the customer. An enquiry desk near each entrance makes good sense. Signposting is vital, as are easily identifiable assistants (in many stores, staff look like customers). Simple procedures are needed for wrapping purchases, handling deliveries, and arranging hire-purchase terms. Strictly speaking these are not the duty of the public relations man, but he needs to run his own private checks from time to time to see that they are indeed working properly and being remembered as part of a deliberate customer relations policy.

Apart from the direct contact with the customer, there is indirect contact, through the issue of monthly accounts, catalogues, special offers and so on. All of these contribute to the attitude the customer acquires towards an organization with which he is doing business. Often they will be the direct job of the advertising department, but the public relations man should keep an eye on their format.

He may find possibilities for conducting research and attitude surveys through this regular material. For example, checking the response to special offers can indicate customers' feelings. Any openings for surveying customer attitudes should be explored.

Customer relations in operations where the buyer does not come into a building but buys through the mail present special problems. A mail order company must establish and then maintain a reputation for fast and efficient handling of orders. Secure packing is vital and replacement procedures are most important. If the buying is handled through local agents, their role in helping to promote the company needs to be carefully spelled out. This can suggest a monthly magazine or newsletter, or regular meetings with groups of agents. It can be the job of the public relations man to organize these activities.

In fact, the differences between one kind of customer relations and another are only matters of emphasis. The housewife in a shop, the company buying from another company, and the mail order buyer have one thing in common. They want satisfaction, and they expect the seller to provide it. They can deal remotely or closely with the seller, they can become heavily involved in activities like owner-drivers' clubs, co-operative movements, or even the collection of trading stamps, and they can be regular customers or occasional customers.

The exact ways in which a manufacturer, distributor or service company handles its customers can only be dictated by its particular circumstances. If a company does not sell its products or its service it goes out of business. If its customers or prospective customers think ill of it, they will go elsewhere. They are therefore of immense importance to the public relations man, and he should make constant efforts to see that they are treated as the key public they are.

7.4 DEALER RELATIONS

A manufacturer can be vitally affected by the distributors of his products, whether they are wholesalers or retailers. Assessing and influencing their attitudes is thus of prime importance in a public relations campaign. This is valid whether a company is making products to be sold over the counter, or supplying parts for other manufacturers.

There are many instances when the goodwill of the dealer can make the difference between success and failure for a manufacturer. Sometimes the dealer pushes the product towards the eventual customer, as in a supermarket handling manufacturer's branded lines. At others, the customer comes to the dealer and asks for the product, as in the mail order selling of nationally advertised lines.

Whether the dealer pushes, or the customer asks, the effect on the transaction of the manufacturer's reputation is a key factor. If the manufacturer enjoys a reputation for turning out good products at fair prices, the rate of acceptance of a new product, even one unconnected with what he normally makes, is likely to be higher. At the same time, the dealer's view of that reputation is crucial.

Broadly speaking, the dealer builds up an attitude towards a manufacturer as a result of various pressures. They include: what he reads about the manufacturer in the press, whether national, trade or local; how he is treated or served by the manufacturer's representatives; how simple or difficult are the procedures through which he has to go to re-order or get service; how his own customers view the manufacturer; how much promotional backing (directly with point-of-sale material or indirectly by advertising) he gets from the manufacturer; what discount rates or other preferential treatment he receives; and how many complaints he makes or his customers make.

The order of priority of these varies in each trade. It is the first duty of the public relations man, once he has discovered his employer's or client's distribution patterns and problems, to sort out that order. This is a situation in which some form of research may be necessary. It is a common failing among manufacturers to believe that they know what dealers think of them. They often fall into the error of complacency. Apart from professional research, a personal study can often be rewarding. Going on the road with a manufacturer's representative, or just going and calling on dealers can be highly revealing.

This is a public relations area on which it is worth spending a good deal of effort. Much activity on advertising, sales promotion, general editorial publicity, packaging, and the like can be wasted if the wrong relationships exist at the point of sale. The retailer who says to a customer: 'Don't have that product, madam, they've got trouble at the factory' can ruin the work of months in a moment.

At the same time, finding the reason why he made the remark can be either complicated or easy. His last order may have been late in arriving and he may have thus lost sales. He may have been badly handled by a representative. A sales promotion drive may have meant too much work for him to do. Or he may have been building up a resentment towards the manufacturer for many months. The smaller the distribution point—the corner grocer's shop is a good example—the more difficult it is to maintain good relationships.

The public relation man's job is threefold: firstly he must find out the distribution method and study it; secondly he must look at the whole trade in which he is involved, learn the history of distribution in it, and see how his company or client compares; and thirdly he must evolve the particular mixture of communications methods he needs to use to achieve his public relations objectives.

The communications methods present no special difficulties and have no special mysteries, but their application does call for constant study. This more true when the point of sales is a store or bar counter, if only because competition is more keen and account needs to be taken of the intangible but constant pressure of public attitudes and demands.

A traditional method of keeping in touch is a dealer publication. They come in various forms. Some are cheaply produced, some are expensive. The expensive method is not necessarily better than the cheap. It must be conditioned by the type of recipient, by budget, and possibly by the quantities involved. The format can be either that of a simple bulletin, a newspaper or a magazine.

If there is relatively little information to pass on but a need to pass it on frequently then the bulletin might be the best method. This can be duplicated or printed. If it is to be duplicated then some consideration should be given not only to the method (stencil duplicating machine or small offset-litho machine) but also the the paper used. It is usually wise to use the best quality paper to give the bulletin a clean appearance. If it is to be printed, perhaps with illustrations and colour on a coated paper, time will have to be spent on layout. This needs a professional's touch.

Producing a dealer publication as a newspaper or magazine inevitably means the services of an experienced editor. The decision of which format to use will be made after working out the frequency needed; the ease (or difficulty) with which information becomes available for dissemination; the type of information being disseminated; its urgency; the need for quality of illustration; the level of intelligence, awareness, or perception of the readers; and the quantity of the publication needed.

If the written material comes over better with high-quality illustration, a magazine format may be better. Despite the attempts of many people, a newspaper format only really succeeds on newsprint. At the same time, of course, merely using newsprint will not turn a bad layout and advertising-type headlines into a good newspaper. It is arguable that a dealer publication should not pretend to be a newspaper.

A commercial publication appears regularly at traditional intervals: daily, weekly, monthly, quarterly or whatever. A sponsored publication need not follow this pattern. There is no reason why a magazine should not appear only three times a year, or eight times a year—both of them slightly curious frequencies. There are times of the year in all industries when the dealers are frantically busy; at such moments they will probably not be anxious to read more than is absolutely essential. This should emerge from the initial study of the distribution pattern in an industry. However, if it is decided to establish an unorthodox publishing frequency it is wise to say so at the outset. It is in any event necessary to publish on time.

A magazine format has certain advantages. For one thing, it allows for depth or feature treatment which in some circumstances is the most effective way of putting over a point. The high-quality picture reproduction which is possible may be essential in telling the company's story. The one major disadvantage is that more time must be spent in reading a magazine and if the dealers involved are busy they may well not want to put in that time. Careful attention to design can, of course, help the dealer to read the paper quickly yet absorb its content.

Even after the method has been decided, there still remain several questions and further decisions. There is the policy of the publication. Is it to be a communication from the company to distributors, telling them what is happening in the company, the company's attitude to trade issues, giving news of new products, processes or services? Or is it to be a publication which tells dealers what other dealers are doing and carries only occasional company notices? Should it carry advertisements, whether from the company itself or from non-competing outside companies? Should it be hard-sell or soft-sell? Light-hearted or serious? Should it contain regular or occasional pull-outs or display pages that a dealer can put up on his wall? Should it aim to inform the dealer, or educate him, or amuse him, or enthuse him? Should it include material that is nothing to do with the company? These questions must be studied and talked out before a publication is launched.

There should be a periodic check on the acceptance of the publication. It is possible to do this through sales representatives, but it is almost certainly better to hand it over to a research organization. A sales force can take round a questionnaire, or it can be included, with a reply-paid envelope or label, in the paper itself. The danger of this method is that those few readers who take the trouble to reply are almost bound to provide the answers they think are wanted and the survey results will thus be biased. However, budget may come into this decision. A properly conducted survey which gives statistically correct and truly impartial answers is fairly expensive, since it takes time to carry out and time to evaluate.

Readers should always be encouraged to write letters to the editor and their opinions on new features should always be solicited, but do not expect too much.

In many ways the most important decisions are the twins of writing and editing. There is a fairly powerful case to be made out in certain types of dealer publication for copy written in an advertising style, with brash headlines and hard over-selling. The more logical style of a journalist may fail to impart the manufacturer's message.

The editor must also remember to demonstrate to the reader the value and desirability of the publication. Even commercial publications—which one must presume are bought because people actively want to read them—find it necessary to boast about themselves (their advertisement pulling power, or their editorial scoops) from time to time. A dealer publication usually comes free. In a sense it is thus suspect since it is obviously pleading a special case. To reduce its possible credibility gap, it is wise to take space occasionally to remind the dealers that they may miss some commercial advantage by not reading it.

In any event, the editing—in the sense of implementing policy, deciding on contributors, rewriting copy, writing headlines, handling layout, and so on—is a professional job.

The second major method of establishing and maintaining a relationship with dealers is the face-to-face meeting, conference, seminar or exhibition. In this area, it is the task of the public relations man to recommend whether one or more of these is right or wrong. It is then his task to set them up. The key point to remember is that dealers will ask certain kinds of questions and have certain kinds of attitudes, neither of them to be compared with the questions and attitudes adopted by eventual customers. Whoever from the company or client is on duty at a meeting, large or small, it is absolutely essential that they are properly briefed and have done their homework. Dealers cannot be fobbed off with half-answers or promises to get the information later.

Dealer meetings often have to be arranged in the evenings,

since the people are working by day. They must therefore be made interesting—the promise of value from a visit must be kept—or dealers will leave with a feeling of anger at having given up their spare time. It is seldom necessary to be lavish with hospitality, but even if the food and wine does flow it must be supported with useful information.

It is not, of course, an inviolable rule that meetings with dealers have to be in the evening. If the only way of showing dealers the story is to do it during the day, then that is the way that must be used. And it is wise to remember that dealers often have staffs of their own who may be involved in meeting or handling the final customer.

Travel agents, for instance, sell tours, airline services, shipping services, and so on. The producers of the tours, as well as the airlines and the shipping companies, rely to a large degree on the selling done by counter clerks. They, therefore, must not only inform the owners of the travel agencies, but also their staffs. In this particular industry, much time and effort is devoted to educational trips which mean staff being away from their offices for several days. No other method is equally effective.

Conferences or seminars for dealers are subject to the same basic rules as those for any other group. One difference, of course, is that a dealer will not usually be expected to pay to attend a conference arranged by a company. Any expenses he incurs must be paid to him. And since it is an unavoidable truth about human nature that people are often less interested in something they get for nothing than in something for which they pay, it is vital that the organization and administration of a dealer meeting are first-class.

The public relations man may find that the professional or trade body of his dealers is arranging a conference. This can present a possibility: a special minor event set up alongside the main conference. This could be a reception, a lunch, an exhibition or a film show, to name a few examples. Only one useful generalization can be made on this: the professional or trade body acting as main sponsor must give its approval—tacit or declared—to anything an individual company does. Not to ask them or inform them is not just discourteous, it is bad public relations. Further, to go ahead with any private plan in the face of their disapproval is to court disaster.

audience will be able to comprehend. The language of chairmen and financial experts is not often the language of the small shareholder and usually the skill (or at least the influence) of the public relations man needs to be brought to bear in support of clarity, simplicity, and avoidance of jargon.

There are many editorial and graphic design units capable of advising on and handling the production of annual reports. Company secretaries can sometimes be stimulated to consider a fresh visual approach by a study of the entries for the annual award sponsored by *The Accountant* for the best presentation of accounts.

The annual meeting, at which the shareholders are entitled to ask questions about the report and accounts and generally express their opinions, is often no more than a formality. In a great many companies, the meeting is regarded as an unavoidable nuisance and if more than a handful of shareholders appear the board is surprised. If a company is doing well or just proceeding on a steady course, it is understandable that a small shareholder in Cheltenahm should not take the trouble to visit London for a meeting which may only last for a few minutes.

If the company is in trouble of some sort, the shareholders are more likely to turn out in force, but large meetings are the exception, apart from those relatively few organizations which deliberately set out to attract shareholders to them. The company meeting, if the trouble is taken to gear it to the information needs of the concern, may be a potent means of dissipating the ivory tower feeling that the small shareholder may have about the directors.

In the first place, a meeting that is only a formality will never attract many shareholders, even if food and drink is offered. It is necessary to generate some interest that will bring them from a distance. This may be done by livening up the meeting or by taking the meeting to somewhere more interesting than a hotel room.

For a company with a wide public shareholding, an exhibition of products, particularly new ones, can be an attraction, especially if they are consumer goods. (Incidentally, the value of the mass of shareholders as potential consumers of the company's own products and as amateur sales promoters is too often overlooked.)

A display of photographs of impressive new production facilities or a film about a great overseas investment can also offer an enlivening interest. A large and diverse company could make an annual newsreel of activities and achievements.

None of these ideas need to be an expense solely set against shareholder relations, for they have an obvious potential for informing customers and employees as well.

Something to take away should always be provided at a major shareholder event, whether it is an attractive booklet to remind the audience of the main facts or a collection of samples of consumer goods to show to their neighbours.

When a new plant or laboratory has been built it is worth considering holding the annual meeting on the spot. If a layout or a process is involved which would make it dangerous or uncomfortable for visitors, some of whom may be elderly or infirm, to walk round, closed-circuit television might be the answer.

The sense of involvement with the company in one of its own locations is not the only value, as there may also be an opportunity for the shareholders to meet or at least be seen by the employees. The thought that the ordinary shareholder is no different from the ordinary employee can still be new to a man brought up with a black-and-white concept of capital and labour.

A company which has slowly developed—and it is a slow process—an interest among shareholders in its annual meeting as an event not to be missed, will find that it has created a major administration and budget item if it enters into visits to locations. Hiring of trains, ships, and aircraft is not unknown and large-scale disruption of production may have to be accepted. But even the smaller concern with a likely attendance numbered in tens rather than hundreds of shareholders can gain a great deal of appreciation of what it is doing by the use of the open day, not necessarily associated with the annual meeting.

Whatever the occasion, from a mass visit to a formal meeting, the policy should be to meet the shareholders as people in as friendly a manner as possible. And that does not only mean the public relations man and the secretary shaking hands with them at the door. It means the chairman, the managing director, the chief engineer, and the production director available for a chat over a cup of coffee or a drink. It is never less than worthwhile to prove to a few more active shareholders, even if their holdings are not significant, that the company, as represented by its top executives, cares about the folk who have entrusted their money to it. When a time of crisis comes, the faith of the ordinary shareholder may be critical.

The organization which relies heavily upon popular investment and its reputation in the market is likely to need to do more than make the most of the annual report and the annual meeting. Brief, attractive quarterly reports mailed to the shareholders can help to sustain interest and to indicate the trends of business. Mailing again can be useful, particularly in consumer goods companies, to introduce new products and services, but even basic industries can use direct communication to inform shareholders of major developments. An occasional shareholder news-sheet is worth considering in large and varied organizations.

As in so many other cases, the press is the most effective indirect means of telling shareholders and the financial community what is going on. The financial press and the City pages of the newspapers have changed in character in the past fifteen years or so from being solely concerned with share prices and company results to a wide-ranging coverage of industry and economics. This is partly a reflection of the need to foster greater understanding of industry and commerce, and partly a contribution to the greater participation of ordinary people in the capital structure of British industry. Many of these people are employees of the companies whose shares they hold, either from individual initiative or as the result of enlightened organizations' own share ownership schemes. They therefore have a dual interest in knowing about progress and problems, success and failure.

They all read papers of some sort and an essential ingredient of any shareholder information programme is to ensure that financial journalists are fully informed, kept up to date and aware that their questions will be readily answered. Their friendship and understanding can be invaluable, notably in the interpretation of short-term poor results or in the assessment of the merits of a take-over bid. The shareholders will have their own view, but they will also be influenced by what they read.

Who answers the questions when a shareholder telephones the

head office and says to the switchboard girl: 'I am a shareholder in your company and I want to know about so-and-so'? Perhaps it should be the public relations department, but there must always be a designated individual available to cope. It may be the company secretary himself in a small firm, or one of his staff in a larger concern. However it is handled, the shareholder should receive even more courtesy and help than any other caller. He feels that he is involved with the company; he should, therefore, never be made to feel that he is less than welcome, however eccentric or irrelevant his enquiry.

This sense of participation and identification can be enhanced in various ways. If a company has a firm visual design policy and its advertising, vehicles, packaging, and so on, are all immediately recognizable because of a symbol or a chosen type style, then that visual identity should be emphatically used in every form of communication with the shareholder. At the other end of the scale, if the company has a prestige or promotional magazine it may be worth including shareholders in the mailing list, or sending personal prints to every shareholder photographed during a meeting or visit.

The ways of creating links with shareholders are endless and many will be peculiar to individual companies, because of their structure. Some have an intimate relationship growing from a small shareholding concentrated geographically; others have to face the fact that their identity to their shareholders is blurred because the company is part of a larger group.

The company secretary is often the key man in deciding what is needed, for it is he who has the legal responsibility and the executive duty to carry out both the requirements of the law and the wishes of the board in matters of shareholder relations. A sound understanding of one another's position and of the varying skills of the jobs is vital if the company secretary and the public relations man are to work together to inform this special audience which, unlike most others, has a right to be told.

7.6 FUND RAISING

The basic purpose of fund raising is to finance a project of one kind or another, be it long-term or short-term. The subject is normally associated with voluntary, charitable or non-commercial operations, where people are asked to give money for the sake of the project itself, rather than for the sake of a financial or other return. Many examples spring readily to mind, such as restoring an ancient church, providing for the dependents of people who have fallen on bad times, building a new repertory theatre in a provincial town, succouring famine-stricken children. The list is endless.

As the pace of society becomes faster and faster the competition becomes fiercer and fiercer and the weak are left by the wayside. As modernity grips our cities, our links with tradition in the shape of historic monuments become weaker. One part of the world gets richer; the rest remains impoverished. When natural disasters overwhelm poor people, the rich give up a portion of their wealth to help. Causes are embraced as people seek ways of either keeping their individuality, repaying their good fortune, or buying their immortality.

Most good causes—or, to use another word, charities—are good. The place of most is readily recognizable and recognized. They may be international, national or local in scope. Yet to succeed they must promote themselves. They must create in the minds of both donors and possible donors an awareness of the good they do, and how they do it. All voluntary activities need finance. To get that finance they must approach their needs by the same rules as a commercial company. They must advertise. They must attempt to obtain editorial comment on their activities. They must send direct mail shots to subscribers, actual and potential. All these activities will maintain a flow of money and make it easier to raise new money to keep the activity going.

There is a line of distinction between professional fund raisers and public relations people. There is an overlap between their qualifications and duties. For the purposes of this chapter it is assumed that the two are synonymous. However, there *is* a difference between the two. It is the function of a fund raiser to raise money. It is the function of the public relations practitioner to create the conditions in which that money is raised more easily. It is the duty of the public relations man to report on attitudes towards the organization for which the funds have been raised, and to report how the money raised is being spent.

In the same way as advertising is used directly to sell goods, so professional fund raisers use their techniques to achieve their objectives. The normal techniques of the public relations man do not have their effect quickly enough to bring money in for deserving causes.

The two can, and should, work together. Each should recognize the place of the other and not try to supplant him or replace him.

To a degree the raising of money for charitable purposes relies on moral blackmail. It is often a deliberate policy, even if by implication only, to try to inculcate feelings of guilt in potential donors. The effect desired is: 'I have done well. I have some spare money. I should give it to others who are less lucky or are under-privileged'. This is the strategy that lies behind much of the copy in direct-mail shots or advertising for charities. It is certainly the motivation for the use of horror pictures of starving children.

The recognition of this element in charity appeals does not mean that it is wrong or evil. If the objects of the appeal are unquestionably to benefit people—for instance, to relieve famine—then it is arguable that the ends justify the means. If the only way to raise enough money to ameliorate suffering is to show pictures of children dying of starvation, then there is no reason why the pictures should not be shown.

To raise money costs money. One particular charity in Britain used to spend about £8,000 a year on what it called propaganda. Its total income was about £350,000 and its relief work was limited to what could be achieved on that sum. Five years later it was spending £100,000 and raising almost £2,000,000. The proportion of its revenue spent on fund raising had obviously risen more steeply than the amount it raised. But the key point was that on the total it was raising it was able to do far more good.

Another point the public relations man needs to remember is that charities are staffed and served by a mixture of professional paid staffs and volunteers. There are often clashes between the two. The public relations man has to stay between them, serving both, and in the process must watch his own relationships with them.

The public relations methods used in fund raising are dictated by the scope of the charitable operations being promoted. If its objective is to help the blind throughout the world the net can be thrown wide. On the other hand, if its objective is to restore a village war memorial the sources of money are strictly limited.

Thus, as in all public relations campaigns, the first job of the practitioner is to identify his publics and place them in an order of priority. One of two examples will illustrate the process.

Starving children are a regrettable phenomenon of the modern world. Everybody—almost without exception—likes small children and wants to help them. This desire goes as far as not caring about where the children are starving, their nationality or colour. Thus in a charity appealing for funds to feed starving children, all people are a public. This is an extreme example.

Restoring a village war memorial appeals to few people. At the same time, the appeal can be stronger since the few may well be more closely identified with it. The residents of the village: relatives of those who are commemorated by it; members of the regiments in which they served; people who used to live in the village—all these are first publics.

It is seldom difficult when preparing a list to pick out the groups at whom to aim an appeal. It is also much better to make the list as wide as possible, since it is a peculiar fact of fund raising for voluntary purposes that the most unexpected sources produce money.

Given a list, the public relations man must now face his second problem: how much money is needed. If the charity is permanent —as might be the case for starving children—it may be sufficient to say that 'as much as possible' is the total. A short-term appeal will have a limit.

With his list and target for the money needed, the public relations man must now decide his method of approach. This must always be governed by another rule of fund raising. Most of the total raised for a national appeal will come from a relatively few major donations, but the publicity created to attract hundreds of small donations will make the large ones possible. This is not an inviolable rule but it almost always happens.

Direct mail, editorial publicity, advertising, personal effort, and personal contact are the generally accepted methods used in fund raising. Their importance varies in each type of appeal, and it is dangerous to generalize.

The direct mail will take the form of letters and leaflets. The letters may be individually typed or produced with matched-in addresses (in which the letters look as though they have been individually typed). It is, of course, possible to produce a simple stencilled appeal which is broadcast as widely as possible, but this is seldom advisable. Remember the elements of blackmail and identification. The recipients of letters must react favourably, or with interest. A stencilled and generalized appeal is unlikely to make them do either.

Who signs the letter again depends on the circumstances. It may be signed by the patron, or president, or chairman, or by a notable personality, such as a television star. The signature may be from somebody completely unknown. This decision will be taken in relation to the recipients. For instance, an appeal to housewives might produce a better reaction if it were signed by a famous film star, but the same appeal sent to the managing directors of major industrial companies might produce nothing. An appeal for a football charity would evoke immediate interest if it appeared to come from Bobby Charlton, but his name would carry little weight in an appeal for a new piece of scientific apparatus for a university. The signature should be relevant and logical; it should not look forced or out of character.

The use of leaflets produces another set of specific decisions. There are dangers in producing a lavish, well-illustrated brochure, since it carries the implication that money is being spent rashly. On the other hand if it is possible to obtain the services of a designer, typographer, writer, and printer without charge and this is made clear on the leaflet, then the quality approach may be the best method.

Whatever the leaflet looks like, it must at all costs be informative and emotional. It must say clearly what are the objectives of the appeal, and as far as possible show how the money is to be spent, but it must do so in emotional terms. Remember again that the donations being solicited are spare money, that is, money which could be spent on other things. There is no financial return to the donor involved. Thus—put crudely—the leaflet must pull at his heart-strings or stir his memories. Genuine emotion will do this and its use is justified.

Editorial publicity plays a key role in all fund raising. Of itself, editorial publicity seldom raises large sums of money, but it creates the conditions for direct mail, advertising, and the other methods to work effectively.

Naturally, this applies less in situations of natural disaster. An earthquake which devastates a town obtains vast editorial coverage. The statements from the voluntary organizations which immediately swing into action appear immediately or within a day or so. This publicity attracts donations by return (which is partly why the statements of action are made).

In moments of lower drama, the purpose of editorial publicity is to keep attention focused on the charity. Obtaining it calls for constant vigilance on the part of the public relations man, so that he can exploit any work of the charity by bringing it to the attention of journalists. It also calls for considerable initiative in creating events which will merit editorial reporting. There is nothing immoral in deliberately building stories to keep the charity in the public eye. It is all a part of the public relations man's armoury.

The amount and type of advertising that can be involved again depends on the charity itself and its targets. A national charity for starving children will look to national paper advertising; an appeal for a permanent home for aged accountants would concentrate on business and trade papers. Whatever the media schedule, the advertising must follow certain rules. It must have a dramatic headline that instantly catches the eye. It is almost always better that this is supported by an equally dramatic picture. A photograph is better than a drawing. The copy must be explicit. It should demonstrate what the charity is trying to do, what it has done up to now, and what it wants to do in the future.

Above all it must make it possible for the reader to take action by including a coupon. If the combination of the headline, picture, and copy has done its job—that is, produced an emotional response in the reader—it must immediately capitalize on that success by providing the means for the reader to send a donation, or enter into a convenant, or (at worst) request more information. One purpose of this is obvious. The advertisement is inserted to raise money. If it fails to do that its cost is wasted.

The second purpose is slightly less obvious, but almost as important. It provides the charity with its own mailing list. Some charities use this to issue regular reminders to previous donors. The reminders can be specific appeals, or copies of a magazine, or the annual report.

The regular magazine has a certain value, but it should not be produced unless the public relations man is clear about its objectives and its contribution to fund raising. There is a tendency to keep people on a mailing list of this type for too long. The list should be compared with donations so that people who have not responded for some time are removed from it.

Any national charity relies heavily on the keenness, enthusiasm, and efforts of local honorary groups. An early job for the public relations man is to draw up a paper to guide these local groups on how to obtain money. This must detail how newspapers work, what sort of information they want to receive, the days and times at which it is best for them to receive it, how to invite them to functions, how to rewrite nationally issued press releases to give them a local slant, and so on. This move is absolutely essential and should be taken right at the start.

This guide should go further than dealings with the press. It should show local enthusiasts how to set up a group in their district, and how to keep it going. It should also cover local methods of maintaining interest in the charity, such as coffee mornings, bring-and-buy sales, and the like.

It is most difficult to maintain the enthusiasm of local groups. To do so means that the public relations man must keep feeding them with ideas and with reports on what the charity is doing. They must be made to feel closely involved. Equally, of course, they should never feel that the money spent on keeping them informed is being wasted in expensive-looking brochures. The secret lies more in the frequency with which they are told than the method.

The amount of personal contact needed in fund raising varies with each charity. Many charities have a list of patrons, vice-presidents, or honorary advisers. It is often the function of these people to set up individual or collective events at which the work of the charity can be explained face-to-face. Exactly how this is done is a matter for individual decision.

A growing feature of fund raising is the production of Christmas cards. This has an obvious value in that it allows people to do something which they would do anyway while also incorporating a donation to the charity through the profits it takes from the sale of the cards. These still represent a small proportion of the total number of Christmas cards sold, but it is growing apace. A number of printers now handle the design, printing, and bulk distribution of cards. Here again the question for the public relations man to ponder is the relevance of Christmas cards to his particular appeal. They entail a good deal of work, especially if the buyer can order individual overprinting of his own name and address. They are probably only worthwhile on a large scale. In any event they must be planned ahead. Planning usually starts not less than eighteen months before the Christmas for which they are needed. It is impossible to do the job properly in a shorter time.

Public relations work for a charity is satisfying since it is clearly directed to a socially good purpose. At the same time it poses problems for the public relations man, who has to exercise a more constant flow of initiative and skill over a broader front of activity than most of his commercial counterparts.

7.7 INTERNATIONAL PUBLIC RELATIONS

The role that a public relations man can play in handling or supervising campaigns overseas can be crucial. The proper support for overseas offices or representatives, whether gained by full-scale programmes of activity, or whether by simple press relations, can do a great deal in helping a company to maintain its overseas business or to penetrate new markets.

Language apart, many snares and obstacles face the public relations man who starts to operate outside his own country. Most of them can be overcome by a simple, if probably expensive expedient. There is no real substitute for local knowledge, whether it is supplied by a man who joins the staff or one who acts as a consultant.

If the campaign is to be continous it will almost certainly pay dividends to have a full-time local operator or the services of a local consultancy. Clearly this is costly and can only be entertained as a working method by the largest of companies. If it does arise, it is probably sensible for the overseas man or consultant to have a period of familiarization with head office. Equally, it will be necessary for the public relations man to pay regular visits to the country concerned to discuss progress and review the programme of activity, even if the visits take place only twice a year.

Of course, standards and methods vary in all countries. While it is reasonable to expect that the developed countries of the world will share many standards and methods, experience will show shades of variation that can be critical. It is wrong to try arbitrarily to impose the exact pattern of operation in one country on to another.

The public relations man will learn to look for results and not be too diverted by the way in which they are achieved. This does not imply any underhand practices. It merely recognizes that countries differ and the people in them differ, too. A journalist may be the same throughout the world in wanting a good story, but the way in which he gets it and reports it cannot be the same everywhere. Advertising-editorial links are much more common than in Britain. Business methods—such as the notorious 'tomorrow will do' philosophy in many Latin countries—may be intensely irritating to an executive accustomed to tight schedules and instant decisions, but he must learn to accept them and work within them.

How far the public relations man needs to take his involvement —even to the extent of learning the language of the country— must be controlled by how much he wants or needs to achieve. For most people international work often means no more than publicizing a visit by a sales director, or an important order, or participation in an international exhibition.

From the moment that a need or an opportunity arises, the public relations man has two courses open to him. He can follow either or both.

One of them is issuing information from this country to other countries; the other is contact on the spot with journalists or businessmen or whatever.

Issuing press material to overseas publications and agencies is a relatively simple task. The press attaché of the relevant embassy or legation can supply a list of publications, or will allow the public relations man to go in and consult a reference book. This is on the assumption that the material is to be issued direct. If it is, it must be translated into the language concerned.

Translation is full of pitfalls. It should always be done by nationals of the country. There are within easy reach agencies which handle translations, but it is sensible to check their staffing and methods beforehand. The Institute of Translators can advise.

Technical subjects should be dealt with by technical experts. The importance of having the translation handled by a national lies in the knowledge of idiom that only a national can have, although not if he has been out of his native country for many years and is thus out of touch with current idiomatic phrases.

Over the years, press releases, leaflets, and other literature in foreign languages have been littered with mistakes. Some of them will merely raise loud laughs, but there is always the danger that they will either cause offence or (perhaps worse) be inaccurate. It can be wise to send the original copy to an overseas branch office or representative for translation, especially if the material is technical. It all takes time, but it is always time well spent.

If the written material has to be accompanied by charts or drawings, captions and any labels on the charts must also be translated. The name and address of both the issuing source (staff public relations man or consultancy) and a local representative or agent should be included to facilitate press enquiries. Obviously, copies should be sent to the representative or agent. A possible variation is to mail copies in bulk to the local man with a press list and allow him to send the release himself. It is usually not a good course to allow him to make copies and issue them; doing this lessens the public relations man's control over the story.

An alternative, when the story is for lay newspapers rather than for trade publications, is to issue it—in English—to the London representatives of the country's press. Major countries' newspapers have representation in Britain. The names and addresses can be found in the list of members of the Foreign Press Association. When this is done, it should be made clear that it is being sent to them and not also direct to their head offices. Obviously, if the story is tied to a date, such as a visit by an important businessman, they must be allowed time to cable or write to their offices.

There are a number of international news agencies which will handle material for overseas. They apply the same rule as any domestic news agency: the story must be good enough to merit them spending the money it costs to issue it.

An effective organization is EIBIS (Engineering in Britain Information Service) based in London. This commercial agency prepares, translates, and issues material to specialist publications throughout the world. A subscriber may also pay a small fee for an item to be included in regular press bulletins on various technical subjects.

BBC overseas services cover almost every country in the world. Material can be sent to individual producers, or channelled through the BBC Future Events Unit, who normally take six copies (more if necessary) and circulate them to any producers likely to be interested.

There are export and other periodicals published which circulate overseas and which may sometimes afford a good opportunity, particularly for feature material.

Lastly, and perhaps best known, there is the Central Office of Information. The COI is a government organization operating through divisions which each specialize in providing a particular service and are all designed to help promote Britain and British interests throughout the world. The range of activities includes material for press, television, and radio; films; printed matter of all kinds; exhibitions; display material; and reference material.

The overseas press services division each year sends abroad more than 6,500,000 words of export news items and feature articles. The industrial section concentrates on a service of specialized press matter on industrial subjects. Each day it issues *British Industrial and Trade News* in English, French, Spanish, and Italian, with extra translations into other languages handled locally.

The photographic division will handle approximately 250,000 prints and 60,000 plastic printing blocks a year. The radio division is responsible for more than 4,000 recorded programmes a year. The films and television divisions cover more than 1,000 industrial stories a year and include them in the regular television and newsreel services they provide.

The exhibition division has the task of designing, producing, and managing all official exhibitions overseas. The reference division produces a documentation service primarily for use and distribution by British Information Services offices abroad.

The public relations man who wants to place stories overseas thus has many ways of doing it. By and large, of course, the ways detailed above are applicable mainly to the man who has the occasional story to issue. Provided it is a good piece of news he should have no difficulty in placing it.

Taking part in an exhibition, trade fair, conference or convention overseas—which is becoming more and more common as selling becomes more international—presents a different situation. To achieve success, both in public relations and publicity terms, requires a good deal of planning, hard work, and visits to the location. The first visit should be made well in advance. The public relations man should see the site as soon as possible. He will then be able to decide whether he can provide what is needed by making a series of visits and handling the job himself, or whether he should enlist the help of a local public relations consultant. The decision will usually rest on the scope of the event as well as his resources and his other commitments.

If he needs a local consultant he will find the national public relations association or society helpful in giving him a list of names. He can check it against the membership list of the International Public Relations Association, which includes biographical notes and the experience of most of the members.

However, even if he does use a local man this does not absolve him from the duty of being on the spot at least twice beforehand and for the preview and opening. The local consultant may be efficient, and he will have the added value of understanding local conditions and methods, but he cannot be expected to understand all the public relations problems of the client, especially when he is involved for only a comparatively short time. He needs guidance, and it is the duty of the public relations man to provide it.

The major problems encountered in publicity and public relations work of this type are mostly connected with the language. The public relations man will therefore find it sensible to retain the services of an interpreter who can be with him as he travels about. Alongside this there are problems of the handling of material. In some countries, for instance, printed matter can be held up for several weeks before it is cleared by customs. The purpose of the advance visits is to find out as early as possible what mechanical and procedural snags have to be overcome, and thus what planning must take place from head office.

In any event, close liaison should be maintained with organizations like the Board of Trade, British National Export Council, Confederation of British Industry, and specialized bodies for particular industries, such as the British Agricultural Export Council. Their services can be helpful over stand design and whether it can be carried out in Britain or whether it should be handed over to a local contractor. There are many points to watch. For instance, the use of some form of visual presentation to overcome language difficulties may have merit, but not unless it is made for the market concerned. A re-hash of existing material is seldom good enough.

The object of taking part in an overseas trade show may be simply to sell more goods. It may then be found that local laws or attitudes are a stumbling block in front of those hoped-for greater sales. This will then turn the public relations man's job away from simple publicity operations and into other aspects of public relations. He may find it necessary to mount a continuing press campaign, make and distribute films, conduct a series of conferences, or enter into negotiations with government departments. If that turns out to be the case, it is then the duty of the public relations man to make recommendations designed to solve the problems. It is for his management to decide whether the effort and expense are worthwhile. It will certainly involve retaining the best local services available.

Any overseas trip should include a visit to the British embassy or consulate. There, both the commercial attaché and press attaché are usually knowledgeable and helpful.

Even if the reason for going abroad is to seek publicity in the country visited, the public relations man must not neglect the opportunity it presents for publicity in his own country.

A successful selling tour in, say Zambia may produce good publicity in Zambia. It is also a publicity opportunity in Britain. Methods by which material can be funnelled back here should be established; a trade press news conference can be arranged for the day of the salesman's return; stories and pictures should appear in the organization's external or internal magazine.

Equally possible is arranging a visit to an overseas exhibition for trade journalists from Britain who are interested in the subject and may not otherwise have the opportunity to go. For an important exhibition in which they may only be interested in a small part (such as Expo 70) the investment should be amply repaid by the goodwill it creates for the future.

Overseas operations are not confined to press relations. In certain circumstances the public relations man may find that direct mail can play a useful part. He must then study the postal regulations and see that his material conforms to them.

The basic rule to remember is that when a public regulations man goes to another country it is he who is the foreigner. He must therefore adapt himself to the ways of his hosts. The least he can do is to spend some time studying facts about the country he is to visit; often a visit to the Stationery Office and a discussion with officials of the country's embassy or legation will provide enough background for him.

7.8 POLITICS AND GOVERNMENT

Political public relations, that is promotional and informational work on behalf of political parties and pressure groups, is an area of the business in which relatively few people are employed. Naturally, these tend to be individuals whose personal beliefs accord with the causes they are pleading. On the other hand, the average staff or consultancy public relations man, whatever his political views, is likely from time to time to handle issues which will involve the need to work with government departments and to inform Members of Parliament and other representatives of political parties. To tackle this aspect of public relations successfully, it is necessary to learn how the machinery of government works, to appreciate the attitudes of civil servants and politicians, and, most important, to understand the rules which must not be infringed.

The structure of the civil service departments dealing with various aspects of national and international affairs is set out in an official list (available from the Stationery Office) and in standard reference books. It is not immutable and reorganizations for political or practical reasons take place as the government of the day requires.

Responsible for each department or ministry is a minister

supported by the ministers of state, parliamentary secretaries and under-secretaries (all loosely known as junior ministers), the precise titles, posts, and numbers varying according to the size and complexity of the department. Ministers and their subordinates are almost all Members of Parliament, although a few may be members of the House of Lords. Some ministers will be members of the Cabinet, itself a variable body, and others will not.

Ministers come and go as the government reshuffles its talents and manpower. So do representatives of what is popularly known as the Shadow Cabinet. This is the Opposition group of potential ministers who study the activities and ideas of their opposite numbers in the government and speak on their chosen subjects in debates. Thus, in both Houses, there are recognized non-government speakers on particular topics, such as pensions, or Welsh affairs, or defence.

The ministries are run by civil servants. Most departments are headed by a permanent secretary, who does not change with internal government moves nor with alterations in the party in power. Beneath the permanent secretary is a staff of under-secretaries, assistants, principals, and officers in a complex structure that varies according to the needs of the department. Some ministries are much larger than others. All have their specialists, knowledgeable in the financial or technical aspects of trade, industry, and agriculture, the trends in overseas affairs, the requirements of the armed forces, or whatever may be applicable.

Most of the major departments that the public relations man is likely to deal with—Board of Trade, Ministry of Technology, Ministry of Power, Department of Employment and Productivity, Ministry of Agriculture and Fisheries, Ministry of Housing and Local Government, Ministry of Public Building and Works, to name the principal ones—have offices in provincial centres. The Welsh Office in Cardiff and, to a far greater extent, the Scottish Office in Edinburgh have a degree of autonomy and handle the functions of some of the specialist ministries. The Government of Northern Ireland, in Belfast, is much more autonomous and is a special case.

When faced with the need to obtain information from a government department, or to offer information about a project, the public relations man has both ethical and practical problems. The civil servants with whom he may have to deal will be working within the broad policies laid down by the government and within the precise terms of the legislation governing the activities for which their department is responsible. Yet the senior officials still exercise a considerable degree of personal discretion in their judgments and recommendations. They must preserve an absolute impartiality and it is an offensive error of judgment, to say the least, to endeavour to mislead them or persuade them beyond the presentation of facts, figures, and logical argument.

To take an example, if a company has to close a factory, it is necessary to inform the regional officials of the Board of Trade and the Department of Employment and Productivity. The effects of the company's action may, for instance, lead to questions in the House of Commons upon which the departments will be called to advise their ministers. More positively, prior notice of the situation to these departments would enable them to offer advice on the best way to go about it and to take action to cushion the effects on labour and industry in the area. Consultation and presentation of the situation in a frank and factual form is what is needed. It would be a grievous error to attempt to minimize the adverse effects of the closure by, say, trying to deceive ministry officials about the number of employees the company proposed to absorb elsewhere.

The practical problem for the public relations man is that sometimes he simply does not know where to start or whom to ask. Often the simplest answer to this is to seek the guidance of his colleagues in the public relations, press or information department of the ministry concerned. All ministries and government offices have information staffs who are prepared to help public relations people in industry and commerce find the answers to questions or to direct their approaches to the right officials.

In the more specialized departments, like those dealing with power, technology, and agriculture, for instance, there are experts who need to be kept up to date in their own subjects in order to be able to do their jobs properly. They may welcome the provision of information, whether in the form of literature or the opportunity to see films or take part in facility visits, but they are interested only in facts and not in persuasion. It is as well, therefore, to make individual contact (or, quite likely, establish a contact between the ministry man and a relevant expert in the client's or employer's organization) before offering material. Casual and unthinking mailing of sales material and invitations is useless to busy civil servants.

There is an attitude of helpfulness and willingness to learn in government departments that is entirely the opposite of what an outsider might suppose from the cartoonist's or playwright's version of the typical civil servant. The public relations man must discover how he and his client or employer can help and be helped and then respect the civil service tradition of impartiality, discretion, and confidentiality.

There is a great deal of misunderstanding about the relationship of public relations people and Members of Parliament. This stems partly from the abuse by some PR men of their freedom to communicate with MPs in the hope of persuading them of the rightness or value of some project, and partly from an excessive suspicion on the parts of some Members of any endeavour to inform them on topics in which they might, or perhaps should, be interested.

The duty of an MP is to represent his constituents and to support his party's policies. Many Members also have specific interests in subjects, possibly stemming from their own backgrounds or the geographical region they represent. A number of specialist subjects—such as television, transport, and the film industry—are discussed in party committees, the members of which often develop detailed knowledge.

On the government side, these committees are composed of backbenchers, since ministers' responsibilities preclude them from taking part, but the Opposition committees also include front bench members. These committees each have a chairman and sometimes a vice-chairman and secretary, and these are the Members to be contacted. The two major party offices, the Conservative Central Office and Transport House, should be able to supply the names of committee officers.

The interest of MPs in receiving information and its acceptability to them when received both depend on a discriminating approach to what is sent to whom. For example, a member of the film industry committee would probably be glad to have a copy of a market survey on cinema attendances. All Scottish MPs might conceivably be interested in a pamphlet proposing a new approach to rail transport north of the Border. Members who began their careers as journalists might be expected to be approachable on the subject of control of newspaper mergers. But a Member who is a farmer and represents a constituency in North Wales is most unlikely to be interested in any of these.

It might impress an unsophisticated management to say that the company's annual report has been mailed to all Members of Parliament, but it is not likely to do any good. All MPs, and most Peers, receive such a weight of mail that only the most relevant material has any hope of being studied.

The quickest way to learn about MPs, and Peers for that matter, is to buy Vacher's *Parliamentary Companion,* a pocket-sized book published six times a year which lists all members of both Houses of Parliament, party affiliations, MPs' constituencies, and frequently private addresses. It also lists the ministers and officers of the House, and outlines the departments of the government and the more important officials in each. *Whitaker's Almanack* and the list of Members published by *The Times* at each general election are also valuable reference material.

If a company has factories employing many people, the MPs in whose constituencies they are situated might be interested from time to time in being kept in touch with events. It depends on how large a factor the company is in the life of the community and, therefore, in the life of the MP. The major employer in a town may well rate a slice of the MP's over-filled time. A visit once a year, a copy of the annual report, even copies of the magazine if it is not too parochial, and certainly an invitation (which he will probably not be able to accept) to the dinner for the fiftieth anniversary—these are worthwhile. Putting the poor man on the mailing list for everything the company issues would be ludicrous and would be rightly resented.

If a major development is proposed, whether positive like starting a new plant in a development area or negative like making many employees redundant, it is helpful to inform the Member in advance. His ability to speak from knowledge on subjects raised in the House may be more than useful, especially on emotional issues. His ability to speak privately to ministers may have a beneficial effect. His ability to deal authoritatively with the queries and worries of his constituents on the basis of accurate information may be a cardinal point in the company's favour.

If he knows something of the background of the organization and its philosophy, he will be able to make his own judgment and speak his mind publicly and privately. But he must be left to make his own judgment. Members rightly guard their independence and the public relations man who tries to sway an MP's interpretation of a situation is courting disaster. There is great integrity in the House of Commons and the Member who is less than honest, or thought to be over-susceptible to persuasion, will have no useful influence on issues.

The rules of the Parliamentary game have to be played straight. The public relations man must learn those rules—most of which are unwritten. There are books describing the procedures of the House of Commons, the functions of the Lords, the duties of the various Parliamentary officials, the way in which Bills are drafted, debated, and become Acts, and all the time-hallowed paraphernalia of Parliament. These will help, but a reading of the debates in *Hansard* and the entertaining reports of the parliamentary sketch writers in the serious dailies can do more to establish an appreciation of the atmosphere of the House and the ways in which it thinks. The PR man should also attend and listen to debates and question time.

Indeed, of all the activities of the House of Commons, it is question time that may prove to be of the greatest interest to the PR man. During this period at the start of the day's proceedings, Members put questions verbally to ministers. The period is limited and those questions which are are not reached may be answered in writing. Non-urgent or non-contentious questions are also put in writing for written answers. Both are recorded in *Hansard*.

By custom, various ministers answer questions on specified days. The Member who has put down a question, and others who are interested, may ask supplementary questions and the ensuing exchange may produce more information than the responsible minister originally proposed to give or may serve as an opportunity for a Member to express a point of view. Question time is the liveliest part of the proceedings on most days.

Every MP is entitled to put down any question he likes,

although he may not get an answer that satisfies him or even an answer at all. He may wish to seek information; he may be prodding a government department about some action he thinks should be taken; or he may be using the form of a question to air a topic in which he is interested.

There is nothing wrong in asking a Member if he would care to put a question on a specific issue. For example, the PR man for a trade association might approach a Member known to be interested in that trade and suggest that he might put a question on some current problem. Whether the MP agrees to do so and, if he does, in what form he puts the question is a matter entirely for his discretion. The desirability and manner of making the suggestion is a matter of discretion on the part of the public relations man; he should be sure of his facts and the propriety of the situation before he acts.

The PR man's interest may be reversed if the organization for which he is working is the subject of a question. The commonest instances in recent years have been questions about government contracts and about proposed mergers. In such situations, forethought should have led to ensuring that both the appropriate government departments and the Members likely to be interested will have been informed of the facts as fully as possible.

The parliamentary service of the Press Association will provide advance notice of questions that have been put down by Members.

There is no better guide through the thorny paths of Parliamentary procedure and the sensitivities of Members than a Member himself. Contact with a sympathetic MP, or one who is particularly interested in the subject with which the public relations man is concerned, can lead to contact with other Members, some of whom are almost certain to have an opposing outlook. A Member can also be the host at receptions and dinner parties in private rooms in the Palace of Westminster. He can arrange, for example, for film shows for Members. He can bring Members and non-Members together more or less formally in committee rooms and informally in the public rooms. He can explain the complexities of what is and is not allowed in dealings with MPs: how a petition is presented, for example, or how bulk delivery of letters for hand distribution for MPs is not permitted (they must all be mailed individually).

There is no single book which explains exactly what is permitted and what is not, what might be acceptable, and what would probably be resented. Taking the advice of a Member or of someone fully experienced in the ways of the House is the only safe course. The sensitivity to outside pressures is such that all actions, particularly those like private parties or expenses-paid tours for MPs, should be examined most critically before the point of decision and handled with tact and discretion if it is found proper to go ahead.

In local issues, there is not only the sitting Member to consider. The Opposition party, and perhaps the Liberals and other parties, such as the Scottish National Party, will almost certainly have nominated candidates ready to fight the seat at the next election. Frequently it is worthwhile for an organization, or its local manager, to be in touch with these candidates, their agents (the parties' paid organizers) and the chairmen of the constituency parties. Often, in any case, these people are significant members of the community in their own right.

Above all, in this sphere of public relations, it is necessary to learn the structure of government, to try to understand the attitudes of those involved in politics and in the civil service, to take advice rather than to rush ahead in ignorance (which may well be seen as arrogance), and to preserve the strictest ethical standards.

7.9 EMPLOYEE COMMUNICATION

In any organization too large for every employee to be known by name to the top man there is bound to be a problem of communication. Conveying a message ceases to be a straightforward process. In concerns of any size there may be as many as four channels of communication: the normal management chain of command, the established relationship with a trade union or staff association, the joint works council or other consultative body, and the grapevine. Management cannot control these means of conveying information and attitudes to employees.

The managers and supervisors may not be good and conscientious communicators, their relationship with those under their command may be sour, or they may be lacking in clear guidance from the top on what to communicate and how.

Communication to members of unions and staff associations lies with the shop stewards or other elected representatives. They may not be skilled at this, however well they represent their members' interests, or they may be troubled by having to face a sharply divided membership, or they may not believe what the management has told them.

Even those consultative groups that have progressed beyond discussion of the price of tea in the canteen and the lack of soap in the washrooms are liable to cease to be effective at the point at which further communication by the employees' representatives becomes necessary. The good committee man is not automatically able to pass on clearly and interestingly the decisions of the works council and the reasons behind them. Quite likely the management does nothing to help him do so.

The grapevine is totally uncontrollable. Sometimes it carries a true story, usually a distorted one, often a wholly inaccurate one. Anything can start a rumour going, from newspaper speculation about a take-over bid to a messenger misunderstanding a half-seen memo on a secretary's desk. Natural curiosity, the desire to be first with the news, concern about job security, fear of change— all these help the grapevine to flourish.

There is no simple answer to the multifarious problems of communication within an organization, but a studied programme of employee relations based on a carefully thought out management attitude can help.

Essentially the objective should be to ensure that management policies and actions are defined and explained to employees so that they understand what needs to be done. If they understand, they are more likely to respond sympathetically to management initiatives and to perform their tasks well.

Employee relations is a loosely used term that often covers a wide range of activities spreading beyond the normal remit of the public relations man. It is usually taken to exclude labour relations —the area of wages and working conditions—but it can include virtually every other topic that is of common concern to management and employees. The precise meaning of the phrase can only be determined within the context of a particular organization; similarly, the role of the PR man in employee relations will vary widely from one organization to another.

It is possible, however, to make two generalizations. In most instances, the public relations function is concerned primarily with the communication problems of employee relations. And it is the company PR executive, with his more intimate knowledge of people and operations, who is likely to be deeply involved in employee affairs rather than the agency or consultancy executive. This is not to say that the outside view on what needs to be done is not sometimes clearer.

Just as the meaning of employee relations is open to definition afresh in every organization, so the relationship of the public relations man and his personnel colleagues will differ. In a large and enlightened firm the personnel department may have the staff, the budget, and the skills to handle the internal magazine or newspaper, write and publish factory handbooks, produce safety and suggestion scheme posters, sponsor films, and tackle all the other techniques of direct employee communication. But in many companies the personnel manager is likely to look to his PR colleague to suggest the means and provide the techniques to put across the messages that they will discuss together.

There can be no clear dividing line. Consultation and co-operation between the specialist functions of personnel and public relations is the only sensible way to meet the employee communication needs of an organization. However the two functions may be defined by management, together they share a responsibility for the communications link and for emphasizing the need for a policy of planned communication.

The basic principle of knowing one's audience and appreciating its capacity to accept a message applies in employee relations as in any other form of communication. A complicating factor is that a relationship will already exist that may hinder rather than help communication. For example, the chairman may be regarded by employees as so remote from any understanding of their way of life that a message from him is liable to be rejected as irrelevant. Or a factory manager may be looked upon as weak because he condones indiscipline and his genuine attempts to communicate may therefore be derided. Or a warning of hard times ahead from a manager who has previously painted a false rosy picture to employees to try to keep them happy may either not be believed or lead to disillusion.

Problems of this kind, which can only be recognized and understood after careful investigation, add to the initial difficulties of communicating in the right way. For instance, if it is necessary to communicate some basic change to all employees, then the *Daily Mirror* language that might be effective for the bulk of shop-floor people is likely to be looked upon as condescending by the graduates in the laboratory. As another example, an explanation for employees of why the company has made a loss needs not only to be spelled out so that all can understand it, but to be put before them at the same time as they read the City editors' strictures. When the house magazine comes out a month later the damage has been done.

Even if the public relations man, with the help of the personnel man, can thoroughly appreciate the attitudes of those to whom the message must be passed and can devise a way of putting it clearly and at the right time, there are still further difficulties. Perhaps the largest of these is the failure of top management to accept the difficulties the PR man is facing; this is particularly so with long-term senior managers who sincerely believe that they know the organization and its people inside out and cannot conceive that they are out of touch.

Another problem is that the audience reaction inside one company cannot be relied upon to be the same in every place and at every time. What goes over well in the Welsh valleys will not necessarily be acceptable on Tyneside and what succeeds in the Home Counties may well fail in Cornwall. Likewise, news of a redundancy danger will be even worse received if given just before Christmas, and an announcement of a drastic reorganization will be even less welcome immediately after a pay claim has failed.

There can be no substitute for knowing the management and the employees, the locations and the histories, the attitudes and the relationships when planning employee communication. There can be no blueprint for success; the problems are never the same in any two companies or in any two factories or offices. The techniques used to try to solve the problems may be common to them all, but only study and experience will show the right way to apply them.

In the face of all this, is it worth attempting to communicate to employees? The answer is that neglect of communciation is a management failure, allowing false ideas and distorted concepts to form and gain currency by default. Lack of communication, or inability to communicate clearly, is at the heart of a great deal of industrial unrest, job dissatisfaction, and operational inefficiency. Good communication can contribute to more harmonious working relationships, understanding of commercial conditions, the acceptance of change, and the improvement of productivity. It is not a panacea, but it is a vital part of good management.

Employee communication can, of course, have a general or a specific aim. The need may be to create a sense of belonging to a worthwhile organization or to explain the working of a new pension scheme; to improve safety standards throughout twenty factories or to revive a suggestion scheme in one. The choice of techniques, apart from deciding upon the most suitable for the subject and the audience, will depend upon the money, time, and skilled staff available. Often these are scarce commodities, for many managements still place a low priority on their personnel work, and upon their internal public relations activities, as opposed to the external publicity which appears to offer more tangible results.

While the choice is almost unlimited, certain means of communication have proved themselves effective in employee relations. Of these, the internal magazine or newspaper is both the most common and the most misunderstood. At its best, a successful internal publication can help employees to feel that they know how the company is doing, that there are others like themselves in different locations, and that the organization is being run by competent people who are human too.

At its worst, it can be a medium for numerous pictures of the chairman, for senior executives to pontificate about their holidays and their hobbies, and for exhortations to 'the workers' to pull together for the good of the shareholders, particularly at Christmas.

Where internal publications succeed it is usually as a result of management's genuine desire to communicate, as opposed to the lip service to the concept of communication which is paid by those who say, 'Of course, nowadays you have to tell them,' while thinking, 'Why can't they just do as they're told?'

It is frequently easy to gain acceptance for the idea that an employee publication should aim to bring employees news of the organization and an understanding of its affairs that they will not obtain from other sources. It is not usually so simple to establish that for this to be done adequately the editor needs to be fully informed. And those two words do not mean the kind of information that comes in an occasional memo from top management telling the editor about an action that has already been taken. An editor must be in constant and free contact with all levels of management and given advance knowledge of policy and action decisions.

It is a mistake to think that an efficient news-gathering system that brings the editor information from all parts of the organization is enough. It is vital to ensure that there is a flow of information downwards from the top as well, if he is to interpret and present the organization successfully to the people who make it run.

Many employee publications are started for the sole reason that it seems a popular idea. In fact, there are many practical questions to be asked before a sound beginning can be made. Format and frequency will depend upon a number of factors: the nature of the readership, the budget available, the time and skill of the staff, the character of the organization and therefore of the flow of information that can be expected.

To take an extreme example, there is little point in deciding to have a monthly tabloid newspaper for an organization with only a few hundred employees where major news stories occur infrequently and only the part-time services of an amateur editor are available. If the best story for an issue is yet another clutch of gold watch presentations, it is patently absurd to attempt to give it front page splash treatment.

Not every organization can be expected to provide enough suitable copy and pictures for a tabloid newspaper once a month, however desirable this form of publication may be because of its acceptability to most readers and its ability to imbue stories with impact and immediacy. The smaller and less eventful concern might do better to consider a two-monthly magazine, where more mundane material can be made attractive through skilled editorial presentation.

Newspaper writing, sub-editing, and layout is a job for the professional. Magazine editing can, if necessary, be tackled at a less skilled editorial level, since graphic design can be given to an outside expert. The relationship of content and visual presentation in a magazine is less close and less demanding than in a newspaper, where copy and layout go hand in hand.

The magazine approach also offers easy means to group minor items into collective features, to balance content evenly without the newspaper's demand for a story or picture to dominate each page, and to establish a pattern for the presentation of regular items.

The employees of any organization form a community of sorts; they have in common at least the fact that they all earn their living from the same source. They have many other things in common, too, such as an interest in the births, marriages, and deaths, the retirements and anniversaries, the sporting achievements, and the social events of the community within which they work. However much an employee publication acts as a means of management communication and information, the parochial news of each location is as important a part of its content as it is in every local newspaper in the land.

People want to read about people. The paper which is all management pill unsugared by stories about the readers themselves will fail even quicker than the magazine which is mainly head office news with little from the factories.

From the extreme of the multi-edition tabloids of the nationalized industries to the simple duplicated news-sheet serving one location, the need for a combination of management information and employee news is more or less the same. Also the same is the pattern of news-gathering, which must rely not only upon what the editor finds out for himself and learns from management sources, but upon a network of contacts around the factory, or correspondents in every store in the chain, or whatever is applicable.

The duplicated news-sheet, if well written and neatly laid out, should not be despised. In small organizations, or in separate locations where it can fill the gap between issues of a company publication, it can serve a useful purpose.

Reliability of publication is another cardinal factor. Readers are used to commercial publications appearing on time, so the employee paper that is persistently late or misses an issue because the editor is busy on something else damages its acceptability and depreciates the value of its content. If there is genuinely not enough material to fill a monthly magazine, then it should be a two-monthly or even a quarterly. If a quarterly cannot be sustained, then the publication should be forgotten and the money and effort applied to some other means of communication.

Whatever the type and frequency of an employee publication, the first qualification for an editor is enthusiasm. The second is often thought to be a comprehensive knowledge of the organization, but this is by no means correct. If the publication is to be lively, vital, interest-rousing, attractive, and able to compete successfully for readers' attention, then a professional editor is more likely to succeed than a long-term employee lacking in journalistic skills. One of the attributes of a journalist is that he can rapidly get under the skin of a community and discover what makes it tick. For the competent journalist, tackling a house journal is no different from moving from a local weekly to a specialist magazine.

An industrial editor should ideally be able to handle every aspect of news-gathering, feature writing, sub-editing, design and production—and often photography too—and also to be capable of interpreting and sustaining a clear editorial policy. Without a firm policy no employee publication can hope to succeed, but what that policy will be depends entirely upon the communication needs of the organization. This is a matter for study and decision by the management.

When a publication has been running for some time, it is feasible to seek reader reactions to what they are being given, but a readership survey of any size and complexity is an occasion for seeking professional research advice. Experience has shown that it is pointless just asking employees what they would like: worthwhile answers cannot be expected from people with no concept of what is involved in creating a paper.

The best employee publication possible will fail in its endeavours if satisfactory methods are not devised to get it to its readers. The decision on whether it should be distributed free to every employee or have some value put upon it by making a small charge (possibly for a company charity, like the pensioners' outing or the children's Christmas party) is not one to be taken lightly. The way in which each issue is sold or handed out needs careful consideration and endless policing; it is no use having the printers send a parcel to each location unless it is established that it is someone's duty to handle distribution and that adequate means are at his disposal.

There is always a temptation to try to extend the use of an employee publication by sending it to an outside audience. There is some merit in considering distribution of a few copies selectively in the community surrounding a factory, or to trade union officials, or to the relevant specialist press, but no attempt should be made to use a publication with a strictly internal content for sales promotion purposes by sending it to customers. They may be interested in the company, but they are not likely to care much about its employees.

If there is a demand for a sales promotion or prestige magazine, then this should be handled separately. Here, as elsewhere in communication, it is a mistake to try to make one medium carry more than one message to more than one audience.

In recent years industrial editing has become recognized as a highly specialized branch of journalism and of management, largely due to the efforts of the British Association of Industrial Editors. Its education courses provide detailed instruction in every facet of this area of employee communication and there are also several sound British books on the subject.

The periodical employee publication may be the centre-piece of an organization's communication programme, but it cannot be expected to do everything by itself. There are always instances where a message needs to be conveyed more urgently and there are many long-term forms of communication for which a news-paper or magazine is not the most suitable medium.

Immediacy of communication can of course, most readily be achieved through the spoken word, but there are two problems about calling general meetings of employees to pass on informa-tion and answer questions. Firstly, work has to cease, or the meeting has to be called out of working hours when people may not want to stay; also with shift working it is difficult to get everyone together at once. Secondly, mass meetings will be seen as a means of by-passing the established union machinery or works council unless this is sorted out first with the officials concerned and explained to employees at the meeting itself.

In general, a meeting called by the management to explain something should be reserved for emergencies, like an impending merger, and even then a carefully planned programme of informing senior staff, supervisors, and union officials in advance needs to be worked out.

The public address system is theoretically a means of communication, but one better forgotten for general use. For fire and ambulance calls, paging of individuals, and 'wallpaper' music it may be acceptable. As a method of conveying anything more complex it is too impersonal and usually too inaudible.

Closed-circuit television is a valuable aid for special occasions. If there is a royal personage touring the plant, monitor sets in the departments not being visited can bring every employee into the event. If the company has contributed something vital to a new ocean liner, a landline link could involve every employee in the launching when only a few official representatives could attend in person. This is expensive but worth considering for its beneficial effect on morale.

A quarterly bulletin sent from the managing director to all senior management with confidential information on how the company is doing; a monthly report in concise, pungent form from the plant manager to all foremen; a twice-yearly open letter from the top man to everyone in the company, written informally and with a facsimile signature—these simple forms of direct communication, if skilfully written and presented, can help solve problems both of short-term and long-term communication.

If the company wins an export award or gains a massive order or is taking over a competitor, there is cause to consider explaining the facts through an open letter for urgent issue to everyone. Otherwise they will get the story—late, incomplete or inaccurate —from the press, from superiors only half aware of it themselves, or from the rumour mill.

Because of expense, films can seldom be made solely for internal communication purposes, except in the largest organizations. Sometimes they can share a use, as for example a yearly newsreel of company activities which could be shown to shareholders at the annual meeting, sent to overseas agents, and also distributed to every location for employees to see. Many general and sales films also have sufficient interest to be shown to employees who generally like to know what the organization is doing.

If a company appears in the newspapers, there is usually interest in press-cutting displays to demonstrate that the world outside knows and, apparently, cares about what has been achieved. The local press itself is an indirect means of communication with employees: they like to see evidence that the company is notable as part of the community and that its people and affairs are worth publication. One or two companies, deeply identified with their own communities, have even organized their own columns in the local press, although this is a somewhat artificial approach.

There is usually an interest, too, in seeing what the company does or what customers make from its products. If the factory makes the gearbox for a new motor scooter, then a local dealer will probably be willing to arrange an exhibition and demonstration of the machine and perhaps offer special purchase terms. If a company has both raw material and manufacturing plants, the employees in the former will like to see what the others make from their output; conversely, those in the manufacturing works may like to learn how the raw material is produced.

Expensively, but effectively, some companies provide touring shows of their products, either by display caravans or by display cases at each location with an exhibit changed monthly. With consumer goods, it is only commonsense to make the most of enthusing the internal audience for the products, but with any type of business there is value in showing—in addition to telling—employees what happens and how.

Within any office, shop or factory, there are a variety of items of information to be conveyed, some of them statutory, such as fire and health regulations. This is information which must be given to employees. There is also information which a management feels employees should have: the social club programme, the price of safety shoes, National Savings campaigns, the availability of mass X-ray facilities, and so on.

Usually these extremely variable pieces of information appear on a noticeboard, the most neglected means of communication in any organization. Torn posters for last autumn's cricket club dance, unread and voluminous minutes of the safety committee, a fire drill notice that is so faded it is unreadable, an ill-worded and badly duplicated announcement about the summer outing— these and similar failures to communicate moulder uselessly together.

Organization, control, and the hand of the professional communicator can, with not a little trouble, convert a nasty mess into a modestly effective way of keeping the wheels of information turning.

Firstly, it is vital to establish responsibility for the design, maintenance, and siting of noticeboards. Secondly, it is necessary to establish control over authorization to use the boards to display items, the size and nature of those items, and the length of time they remain. These are the tasks of the public relations man, with the assistance of whatever allies he can find in the personnel department, among the maintenance staff and the trade union or staff association officers.

The potential content of a noticeboard is vast, so it is as well to try to define the various relevant categories and divide boards into sections. These might include union branch; works council; sports and social; safety and welfare; suggestion scheme; official; publicity (cuttings, extracts from press releases, photographs, and advertisement proofs); sales and wants, if personal use of the boards is allowed; and so on.

Design is a matter of taste and of suiting the information requirements of the situation. The rule for display is to be sure that everything is neat and bright, that all lettering is large enough to be read easily, and that the total effect is attention-getting. Commonsense and imagination should do the rest.

Messages to be read by people passing by should not contain more than a few words. A press release about an export order might run to 300 words; fifty words would be the right length for the noticeboard. The full minutes of the works council are too long to go on the noticeboard, and a digest of the main decisions should be all that is posted (or, better still, circulated to all employees).

Constant change keeps attention alive and prevents material from ageing visibly. Permanent notices should be covered by glass or plastic to preserve them. The basic principle remains to convey information briefly and quickly. If the notices fail to meet this criterion, they should be altered, or the information conveyed in some other way.

A wall newspaper has a different function. As its name implies, it is set in type and laid out like a newspaper, although one to be read by people standing before it at a distance of several feet.

This limits its uses, as the number of occasions on which people will stop to read something in which they have no inherent interest are relatively few. However, with skilful adaption of newspaper writing and layout techniques, using bold headlines, big pictures, short, crisp stories set in readily legible tyefaces, and predominantly dateless material, it is possible to create an eye-catching sheet which will cause some passers-by to stop and read.

The wall newspaper has been used effectively as a poster, too, by charities, religious bodies, and political organizations whose public audience could be expected to pass by only once. In an office or factory, the audience can be relied upon to pass by several times during the life of each issue and it may therefore be hoped that different items may be read on different occasions.

In most organizations there is a need to put information into the hands of employees in some more permanent form, perhaps for reference or training. There may be a welcome booklet as part of the induction course, or a factory handbook containing a variety of facts and figures of value in the working day, or a book of guidance on office procedure for secretaries and clerks, or a safety manual, or a leaflet expounding the suggestion scheme and encouraging employees to participate, or a booklet issued to each man as he becomes eligible for the pension fund.

Responsibility for such material will probably lie with the personnel department, either at head office or in each location, but the public relations executive has a contribution to make. He is likely to have, or know how to obtain, the creative skills to make such publications more effective, Lively writing, clarity of explanation, bright illustrations, and attractive cover designs help to get the necessary messages across and are vital when it is remembered that personnel publications have to be intelligible to the lowest common denominator among employees.

As in so many areas of employee communication, this is a

matter for consultation and co-operation with the personnel staff. In fact, they share not only the duty of trying to communicate effectively and to make the importance of good communication understood through all levels of management, but also the difficult task of trying to make communication a two-way affair.

Management needs to communicate to get work done and ought to communicate to ensure that employees understand what must be achieved, how and why. But employees can communicate too, not only through the official channels of the unions and joint consultative machinery, but directly as individuals through their immediate superiors and indirectly through formalized means such as suggestion schemes.

An atmosphere in which upward communication is fostered can only arise in an organization in which there is a genuine desire on the part of the management to hear as well as to speak. The personnel manager and the public relations man are listening posts; they are almost invariably the sort of people to whom others talk and their duties mean that they have contacts in every part of an organization and at every level. They need to retain their objectivity—no 'organization man' can ever be expected to present an unbiased view of the organization he works for—and to be able to face up to the difficult task of telling top management what employees think about them and the organization.

Their subjective judgment can from time to time be reinforced by scientific investigation and measurement of employees' attitudes and reactions. To persuade a management to undertake the expensive and troublesome task of endeavouring to determine employees' attitudes is not easy but the result can be rewarding, particularly in organizations with labour difficulties, poor productivity, heavy absenteeism or similar troubles. Such research is a subject for expert advice and execution.

The scope for employee relations activities is almost limitless. The problems of all organizations have certain elements in common—particularly inadequate communication—but no two are exactly the same, so the priorities and the methods to be used can only be decided after study of an individual situation and the character and atmosphere of a concern.

The public relations man could do worse, however, than keep the subject constantly alive in the mind of management by sharing with them his nightmares brought on by bad communication. Most managers have their own chamber of horrors on this subject, like the case of the thousands of workers at a Midlands car factory who first learned of their impending redundancy from the local evening paper as they came out of the gates! Unbelievably, this was in the second half of the twentieth century.

The task for the public relations man, and his personnel colleagues, is vast.

7.10 CONFERENCES

All public relations people at one time or another become involved in the organization of conferences, symposia, congresses, dinners and dances, public meetings, and other assemblies of varying size, duration, and purpose. The key to success lies in a combination of meticulous planning and administration and a commonsense application of the basic principles of communication. This applies whether the event is a parents' protest meeting about a school closure or a formal reception and dinner for 500 overseas visitors with a top policitian as guest speaker.

As with most forms of communication, the first two questions to be asked are: 'What is the object to be achieved and what is the message to be conveyed?' Given the answers to these two queries, the vital third question is: 'Would any other medium of communication convey this message to this audience better than by gathering individuals together in one place for a specified time?'

The answer to the third question depends upon a clear-sighted interpretation of the situation. The annual lunch of a trade association may be an established event and perhaps it is social interchange among members that provides its true value, rather than the opportunity for the president to communicate to those present. An international convention for welding technologists held in a different country every five years may seem to have no other purpose than the exchange of up-to-date technical information. A sales conference for the field representatives of a consumer goods manufacturer may purport to introduce them to the new season's lines, but in fact may be no more than a morale-booster or an excuse for the boys to enjoy themselves.

Each of these three examples may or may not involve a valid reason for holding an event. If the president of a trade association wishes to communicate with the members as a whole he would do better to visit the branches; or he can communicate with them through the trade press. The information the welding technologists want to exchange might be better given to a wider audience through a technical publication. The consumer goods sales force might be told all they need to know by samples and a brochure describing the new products and the promotional plans for them, and given their morale-booster by a cash incentive scheme.

Assuming that the worth of an event is agreed, its shape and nature will depend upon a firm understanding of its purpose. With this understood by all concerned, it is possible to determine the physical arrangements best suited to achieve the purpose and to begin the process of planning and organization that is vital to every type of occasion from a private dinner party to a mass political rally.

It helps to treat the organization of an event like a military operation, with each individual in the team given his own responsibilities and timetable, one person in command, and a written plan of operation that includes every point that needs attention. A preliminary planning meeting to establish objectives and define areas of responsibility is vital. If the team consists solely of the public relations man and his secretary, a quiet session thinking out every step in the operation, timing it, and putting it on paper is still essential.

The purpose of the event and the character of the audience will determine the main lines of approach. For example, does a symposium have so much potentially valuable content that it requires more than one day, and if so should it be held away from London to keep down costs or in London so that overseas delegates can fly in and out more easily? Or is the prize presentation for a competition so uninteresting that it needs to be made more attractive by holding it in a thoroughly novel location? Or again, will executives at a management conference welcome the quiet of a university setting for their deliberations or should they be given the four-star hotel treatment to which they may be accustomed?

Decisions on locations, timing, type of accommodation,

transport, and similar basic physical factors can be taken in the light of the answers to questions such as these. Then the work really begins. The first step is to settle a budget. Whether or not the event is one involving payment by those participating, it is necessary to establish from the outset the sum that may be spent and to prepare estimates for the various ways in which that sum will be used. The budget can be planned in relation to the main organizational requirements of the occasion. Obviously, these vary greatly according to the nature of the event, but the major constituents are likely to be: accommodation, catering, transport, fees, printing, display material, visual aids, publicity, and entertainment.

Major items such as these form the subjects of the checklists which it is essential to prepare. Within each list should be enumerated everything that needs to be done or to be provided, with a timetable of target dates. The variety and content of these checklists is endless, but, as an example, here is one that might be applicable to a public lecture in a hotel room:

> Examine room personally
> Confirm booking in writing
> Confirm by telephone numbers expected
> See manager about:
>> arrangement of chairs
>> flowers
>> dais
>> top table
>> lectern and gavel
>> speaker's microphone
>> roving microphones
>> projector, screen, and projectionist
>> timing of coffee service and clearance
>> signposting
>> reserved cloakroom accommodation
>> ventilation
>> curtains and light controls
>> ashtrays
> Check acoustics and sight lines
> Secure table for ticket collection

Instal publications rack
Arrange cash box, float, and deposit
Instal display panels (power points for lighting needed?)
Check danger of noise from outside
Have public address system turned off in room
Arrange press table
Prepare press copies of speech
Note press attendance and deliver speech to papers not
   represented
Reserve seats at rear for latecomers
Prepare chairman's notes and timetable
Organize 'planted' questions to start discussion
Organize proposer for vote of thanks.

This is not exhaustive, but it gives an indication of how many points there are to be borne in mind for even a simple, straightforward event of a couple of hours' duration. For a major occasion there may be anything from chartering aircraft and seeking police assistance with traffic control to engaging cabaret artistes and advising the chairman on diplomatic protocol. Whatever the extent of the detail, checklists and timetables must be built up with care and thought.

For an event of any size and complexity, outside contributions become part of the organiser's problem. He may be dealing with a first-class hotel where conference organization is well understood or with a resort where the local authority has a conference officer to help. He may just as likely be dealing with an academic authority whose principal preoccupation seems to be to get the whole thing over with as little disruption as possible.

Whether the public relations man has no more to arrange than finding an electrician to adjust the lighting and a carpenter to fix a squeaking board in the platform, or has to face up to driving display contractors to complete an exhibition in time and rehearsing entertainers in a sales-orientated sketch, he dare leave nothing to chance. It will *not* be all right on the night unless he has planned for every contingency, timed the routine to the minute, ensured that every form of outside assistance is reliably available, and checked that all his helpers and participants are playing their parts properly.

Yet with clear planning and firm control, it is still possible for conferences and similar events to fail, because there are two other elements necessary for their success: commonsense and showmanship.

Opportunities for the application of plain commonsense are so many that it is almost impossible to suggest examples. However, it is commonsense not to face delegates with a heavy statistical lecture after a lavish lunch preceded by an hour's cocktail session. If they go to sleep it is not their fault; it is the organizer's. It is commonsense not to leave delegates' wives with nothing to do during business sessions and equally sensible not to fill their programme so full that they have no time for shopping and sight-seeing. It is commonsense not to expect delegates to turn out promptly at 9 a.m. for a tough debate if most of them have been up until 2 a.m. at the official dinner-dance.

It is commonsense to restrict a speaker at a business lunch to thirty or forty minutes if his audience has to hurry back to work. It is commonsense to brief speakers at a symposium thoroughly to avoid the danger of overlapping and contradiction. It is commonsense not to hold a party for 200 old-age pensioners in a fifth-floor banqueting hall when the lift will carry only six at a time. It is commonsense to offer soft drinks as well as tea and coffee if children as well as adults are to be present. And so on *ad infinitum*.

If the public relations man has sufficient mental discipline the process of working step by step through his plan for an event and asking at each stage 'will it work and, if so, how?' should be enough to prevent the worst gaffes. If he cannot do this he should not be in public relations.

Showmanship is not altogether the mystique that show business folk would have one believe. It is a combination of a straightforward appraisal of the needs of a presentation and the ability to imbue it with imagination and drama to attract and retain attention, enhance interest, and increase the impact of the message.

It also involves meticulous attention to detail. It does not by any means necessarily involve any element of entertainment: showgirls carrying sandwich boards may suit a car dealers' convention and live music may encourage a warm atmosphere at a charity reception, but a conference for investment analysts or medical missionaries needs different thinking.

There is showmanship in presenting a subject with two speakers on either side of the rostrum and a cinema screen between them, rather than in sitting one lecturer at the traditional green-baize-covered table with a musty decanter and glass and a pointer to rap for the next slide. There is showmanship in touching the hearts of these coming in to a charity event with a vast blown-up photograph immediately inside the door. There is even showmanship in arranging the chairs in a semi-circle, rather than in straight rows, and adjusting the distance of the front row from the speaker so that the sense of division, of him and us, is avoided.

There is showmanship, too, in ensuring that everything runs smoothly and that everyone knows his cues for action as in a stage production: no pleas of 'May we have the lights out now,' no slides upside-down, no hunting for the head waiter to announce that lunch is served.

The beginner can help himself to learn by making a practice of studying every event he attends and working out in his own mind how it operates, how it might be improved and how—as a participant or member of the audience—he would prefer to have been treated. It is possible to learn from anything from a church service to a protest demonstration if an analytical approach is applied.

With practical experience in the organization, planning, and administration of events of all kinds, the innumerable variations and nuances that are possible will gradually come to be understood. To take the simplest example, an invitation card may be enough to attract members of an organization to a social event, but an invitation card rarely contains enough information for journalists to form an opinion on whether or not the event might be worth covering.

The hazards of the pointless and frugal civic reception that bores delegates stiff, the dangers of hotel rooms that are suffocating with the windows closed and deafening with them open, the horror of the chairman who lets the questioning die an agonizing death, the panic that starts when the star speaker has not arrived and the delegates are already seated—all these are likely to be experienced. The PR man must learn how to avoid recurrence.

Another essential item is the post-mortem examination of every event: where it succeeded and where it went wrong, where the plan broke down and where outside agencies failed in their responsibilities.

Time and experience will show the public relations man those he can rely upon. When he finds an outside caterer, a hotel manager, a film projection outfit, even a florist who show that they understand the needs of the organizers of events and that they can get on with their jobs without excessive supervision, he should use them to the fullest. He will have more than enough to do himself without having to do other people's work for them.

8

Advertising

PUBLIC RELATIONS is concerned with the relationships that exist, for whatever reasons, between groups of people. To maintain, improve, or otherwise affect those relationships, it is necessary to communicate from one to the other and back again. The public relations man is normally concerned with certain methods of communication, and has probably been particularly trained in a few of them. The advertising practitioner is concerned with other methods. There are many instances when their training, or the ways in which they conduct their job, overlap. The overlap may be extensive. Both may be trying to reach the same objective.

Advertising has existed in one form or another for thousands of years. In its present organization—at least in societies like those of Britain, Continental Europe, or the United States—it has existed since the late nineteenth century. Equally, the practice of public relations has existed for thousands of years, but has only developed to its present state of organization since the 1920s.

Put simply, if crudely, advertising consists of shouting your wares. Success will come to him who shouts loudly enough or cleverly enough. If a need is fulfilled by the product, people will buy it, even if they do not like the seller. They may even buy it without trusting him. The point of departure is ability to sell. It does not necessarily depend on the level of understanding by the customer.

The reasons for this are not difficult to find. There are now more and more products competing for their share of the market. The world has become more complex and society more complicated. Profit margins are lower. Success is ever more essential. Small-time operations must reach the big-time if the return on the capital invested is to be worthwhile. The differences between products become harder and harder to see.

Clearly this is an extremely simple explanation. It ignores many aspects of human nature and society, the study of which does not belong in this book. It can all be put another way.

If a manufacturer believes he makes the best product in the market, that is his opinion and he is entitled to express it. There is no reason why he should not clothe his expression of his opinion in the most flamboyant language and in the most dramatic ways, and put it before as many people as possible. This is the job of the advertising man.

An understanding of advertising, its methods, its rules, its scope, its advantages, and its drawbacks, is essential to a public relations man. The understanding need go no further than knowing when to hand over a problem to advertising men, or how to support a campaign involving advertising. But without that understanding there is an irreplaceable gap in the public relations man's armoury.

The basic purpose of advertising is pointed communication, the point being to sell a product, a service or an idea. Its most common form is the purchase of space in newspapers or magazines or on billboards. This has grown into the purchase of time in cinemas, on commercial radio or on television. From its fairly simple beginnings it has developed into a national industry employing thousands of people and handling more than £500 million of business a year in Britain alone.

One of the greatest problems faced by advertising is confusion. Because a consumer group, Member of Parliament, or professional do-gooder objects to the shocking maltreatment of the English language in an advertising campaign, all advertising is therefore condemned. Because the advertising of a luxury product is brash, indeed almost hysterical, there is a tendency to forget that serious social subjects can sometimes be aired only by advertising. Since there are constant undertones and overtones of sex in much advertising, it is charged with promoting the more permissive society that has grown around us. Many of the allegations are true and many are not. Much of advertising is non-sensical, childish or repellent. The worst advocates of advertising are in the business itself. But none of this entirely invalidates the fact that advertising is a proved method of communication which is a powerful instrument for putting over an idea or promoting the sales of a product.

A great deal of money is spent on advertising and perhaps for this reason alone it is subject to constant public scrutiny. Since it involves large sums of money, many companies have in their own organization an advertising manager or department.

For the purpose of creating advertising campaigns and implementing them, the business is organized in advertising agencies. There are approximately 650 agencies in Britain, but of those only about 100 are of any size. The largest agencies in the country are responsible for handling appropriations (the name given to the amount allocated to advertising by a company) running into millions of pounds.

The staffs of agencies range from more than 700 down to a handful of people. There are agencies which specialize in certain types of business and agencies which will handle anything. Some are marketing-based and others are creative 'think boxes'. There are agencies controlled by accountants, and agencies controlled by artists or copywriters. One way and another, there is no advertising problem which cannot be tackled.

Many big companies place advertising for different products through three, four or more agencies. At the same time, few agencies will agree to handle competing clients.

The easiest way to explain the method of working is to illustrate a hypothetical example: Product X.

A director is nominated as leader of the agency team in its work on Product X. His job is to see that the agreed campaign is implemented. In a growing number of agencies the directors are a partnership whose combined ideas will create the campaign. However, one man (or woman) will be the face that the directors and advertising manager of the company making Product X will deal with most often.

The director will be responsible for a number of accounts (clients), and will probably also have responsibility for some other facets of the agency's operation, such as training, media buying (the purchase of advertising space or time), management of the office, and so on. He will have alongside him a number of group heads, or supervisors, who will be his first line of action. If he is responsible for the direction of a dozen accounts, he will perhaps have three group heads, each handling four of those accounts. In their turn, the group heads are surrounded by account executives, each handling, say, two or three accounts. Account executives may report back to more than one group head. On a large account in a large agency there will also be assistant executives, who have varying titles such as detail service men or progress chasers.

At first sight this may look like an enormous number of people or like a variation on the old verse about 'great fleas have little fleas and lesser fleas to bite 'em'. It would be unfair to make this charge. At any time an advertising agency may be handling more than 100 different items for a client, from national television advertising to the production of the client's Christmas card. There are often half-a-dozen different elements within each assignment. Equally, there is the need for long-term planning and this cannot be done by people who are loaded down with detail jobs.

As the next circle around the contact personnel there are the creative services of the agency, headed by a creative director. It is their job to create campaigns in visual terms, to illustrate advertisements, posters, leaflets, and the rest, and to write copy for television commercials, press advertisements, printed material, and the like. Approximating to the group heads are group art directors and copy chiefs, who may be all-rounders or specialists. The agency will have a number of writers, and will also call on outside free-lance copy men. Its artists will include specialists in figure drawing, lettering, and many other forms of commercial art. In a large agency the creative staff may top 100, though there has been a tendency in recent years to reduce the numbers of staff and buy more services from outside.

Since advertising costs a great deal of money it is important that it should not be wasted. There are therefore media specialists, who decide where advertisements should appear. It is they who will recommend whether the best return can be obtained by advertising on television, or in the press, or by posters. It is their job to analyse the costs involved in advertising in any of these, and other, media, and show what results it should produce.

At one time, media departments were fairly passive, being merely the bookers of space. In recent years, their importance has grown and their range of activities has extended. They now devote more attention to planning for the future and researching possible developments in television and publishing. They have made notable contributions to the services offered by publications to advertisers, particularly in the analysis of circulation and readership. They have also made considerable contributions to analysing the effectiveness of advertising, reaching into the computer world in so doing.

Leading advertising agencies all have market and opinion research facilities, either as departments or as wholly-owned subsidiary companies.

Advertising has, like all trades and professions, a jargon of its own. Thus advertising men talk of the division in a budget (appropriation) as above-the-line and below-the-line. This arbitrary line is drawn to distinguish between the part of the appropriation spent in television or press advertising and that part spent on items such as print (including window material, showcards, point-of-sale material), premium offers (like steak knives with soap powders, and so on), participation in exhibitions, sales letters, and a host of other things.

Print is a steady item in all advertising, whether it means making blocks of advertisements or printing catalogues, and agencies have always had departments which looked after this side of their business. The design and merchandising of point-of-sale material, to name but one example, has grown so enormously in the last few years that it has led agencies to establish either subsidiary companies or departments to deal solely with this aspect of their business. Even more striking has been the establishment of design departments, concerned not just with elementary functions (like letterhead design) but with major tasks like a company's corporate identity programme, or its exhibition policy, or the design of the packaging for its products.

Certain agencies have other specialist units, the setting-up of which is either a reflection of their clients' needs or a reflection of the type of clients the agency wishes to attract. Among these is a home economics department (more easily described as a test kitchen) used by agencies which are heavily involved in food or domestic appliance products. A handful of the really big agencies have taken their involvement even further by running shops or self-service stores of their own. Latest in the long line of additions to the basic service offered by advertising agencies is what are called new product workshops, where ideas are tried out for new products which could be manufactured by existing clients.

It will be clear from all this that the advertising agency business is constantly evolving and growing from its original function of producing advertisements for newspapers. Some of the development has been forced upon it; some has been created in an effort to do for itself what it is trying to do for its clients; give an agency a recognizable difference from its competitors.

There has, however, been a marked change in recent years with the remarkable growth in the number of small, creatively dominated agencies. They concentrate on the production of ideas and their visual interpretation, buying other services from outside.

Equally, the type of recruit to advertising is changing. As in journalism, more and more university graduates or men and women with high professional qualifications are coming into the business. Media men, for instance, were once the kind who could pick newspapers from a list, add up their space rates, and make up a rough-and-ready schedule. Today, media departments are controlled by men and women with degrees in economics or sociology. The qualification for an account director or executive was once the ability to consume enormous quantities of gin with the client and stay coherent. Today's account director needs considerable and obvious ability in the techniques of marketing. Advertising exists to help business on the road to success; it thus needs businessmen in its agencies.

Big agencies have large subsidiaries handling public relations work, often trading under a different name from the parent agency. Others keep the PR operation as an agency department. Publications—notably national newspapers—reacted violently years ago and refused to accept editorial copy emanating from advertising agencies. This attitude has disappeared and copy is judged on its merit, whatever its source. And while it is true that many agencies ran their PR departments or subsidiary companies at a loss as a service to advertising clients, fewer and fewer of these now remain.

From the point of view of an advertiser there can be several advantages in dealing with his agency's PR facility. He may feel that both sides are closer together in outlook than separate companies might be. He may find it easier to brief the advertising and PR sides of his agency together. Much more relevantly, his PR needs may be best satisfied by a campaign closely related to and supporting his advertising. There is no simple or acceptable generalization on this question. It must always depend on a proper definition of the PR needs of the company concerned.

It is true that the public relations man, especially the junior, is subject to certain unwelcome pressures in an advertising agency. It is also true that the PR men and advertising men in agencies do not always work happily together, tending to think in different ways. This is a temporary phase and a relatively minor problem. It disappears when the PR man ensures that he can maintain his professional independence, and when his standards of work are unremittingly high.

Advertising is governed by many more rules—nationally and legally created, or imposed on the industry by itself—than public relations. Newspapers, for instance, have the right to refuse to accept advertising in the same way that they can refuse to accept editorial material. They exercise the right more often than the general public is aware. Television advertising is strictly controlled. Poster campaigns have to conform to planning regulations.

The various sides of advertising work quite closely together, through bodies such as the Institute of Practitioners in Advertising (the agencies' own professional organization, with both corporate and individual membership, the latter normally only available by examination), the Incorporated Society of British Advertisers, the Advertising Association, the Independent Television Companies' Association, and so on.

The young public relations man or woman can usually learn a good deal from his opposite numbers in advertising. Since the agency business has been organized for longer than public relations, its training methods are equally more organized and its structure is more codified. Each person's job is more closely defined and in order to make progress the young advertising man has to fight harder, learn quicker, and ensure his efficiency.

Although it is probably hardly worthwhile for an entrant into public relations to sit an advertising examination, it is certainly worth his while to make strenuous efforts to learn advertising's rules and to understand what it contributes to society. There are still many public relations objectives which can only be achieved by good advertising.

9

The Future of Communication

THE INTENSITY of communication will continue to increase. That is probably the safest forecast that can be made in a business where crystal-gazing is notoriously hazardous. The pace and variety and pressure of communication today are vastly greater than even ten years ago. There is on the one hand a frenzy of sales promotion and on the other a growing recognition of the need to provide information and stimulate discussion in order to motivate people. This applies as much to employees and customers as it does to members of political parties and enthusiasts subscribing to recondite societies.

The media of communication will continue to change, too, as technology progresses. Colour television is a fact. Satellite links around the world—and from space—in vision and sound have become commonplace. Computer-operated photocomposition for web-offset newspapers is at hand. Decentralized production of national morning papers is technically possible and the economic and labour problems involved are being tackled. Techniques are constantly changing in every medium.

Instant national and international news is presented on radio and television; almost immediate pictorial coverage is available. Detailed background and expert assessment are provided by all the media within hours, often within minutes, of any major occurrence.

Instant information, instant opinion, instant comprehension— these are the apparent needs of a society in a hurry. While the accuracy of the first is usually astonishingly high, the real value of the second is often questionable, and the very existence of the third frequently doubtful.

The public relations man needs to study trends in communication, to understand the significance of technical developments in the media, and to try to keep in touch with the changing attitudes of the many audiences which form his public.

Yet he need not worry overmuch about science fiction predictions of an electronic news-sheet produced in every home from a slot in a three-dimensional TV set. What if books are reproduced on miniaturized tapes so that one can "read' a story from a transistor plugged into the ear while riding on a motorway in a car controlled by a master computer? Even if advances (if that is what they are) such as these come to pass in a few years' time, the basic principles of communication outlined in this book will remain unchanged.

Of course, the PR man of the future will need to appreciate the requirements of new and changed media and know how to use them to convey information to chosen audiences. But the essential requirements of the professional communicator will still be an understanding of the nature of defined segments of the public and their ability to comprehend, plus the skills to identify the essential elements in a message and to present them clearly and attractively.

This will apply in spite of the increasing specialization in all forms of commercial and industrial activity which creates problems of the intelligibility of highly complex subjects and the jargon with which they are surrounded. The greater general literacy promised by the educators makes little contribution to any man's ability to understand either his neighbour's job or the attitudes of other sections of society.

It will still remain the task of the public relations man of tomorrow to use whatever techniques of communication science and commerce make available to him to convey information to general and specialized publics with the aim of increasing understanding.

IO

Working in Public Relations

10.1 ENTRY AND TRAINING

ABOVE ALL, a public relations man needs judgment, initiative, and perseverance. He cannot possibly succeed in his career without these personal qualities, partly born in him but mostly created by diligence and experience. He must add qualifications, which he can acquire by constant reading, constant writing, constant practice, and study and examinations.

The tools with which a public relations man works are words and pictures. The words may be written or spoken and the pictures may be still or moving. It is not possible to communicate in a sophisticated society without words and pictures. He needs judgment to know when to use words and pictures and in what way. He needs initiative to create new uses of them. He needs perseverance because he spends many years of his life using them and his energies must not flag. He needs qualifications to know how to use the words and pictures. He must always be striving to achieve understanding through communication. There is a widespread misconception that it is only press officers who are concerned with words and pictures. This is entirely wrong. In whatever aspect of public relations activity a man is engaged he will find the same need. Whether he is communicating to shareholders in an annual report, to employees with an exhibition in a canteen, to politicians with a leaflet, or to overseas buyers with a film he must choose and use words and pictures with care and precision.

The need for these qualities is not unique to public relations. The make-up of successful people in other crafts is much the same, but that does not in any way diminish the importance of understanding that effective public relations men do not just happen. They become effective because they work at it.

A student in public relations should spend a great deal of time reading, watching, and listening. He must read newspapers, books, annual reports, government publications—almost anything on which he can lay his hands. He should watch television. He should listen to speeches and to the radio. He should practise writing and have the courage to be objectively critical of his own writing. There is no mystery about writing: it comes from reading good writing and practising it incessantly.

A public relations man may be faced in one day with the need to write a brief news release for local weekly papers in the Highlands; to draft a feature article for a monthly trade paper; to prepare a speech for a social occasion; and to summarize a complicated legislative issue in such a way that a board of directors can decide their attitude to it in the minimum time. If he does not know how to put words together he will be unable to undertake these tasks. This remains true even when he has progressed professionally to the point where he has other people doing the writing for him. He must still know whether they are good or bad and be able to show them how to improve.

Journalists are obvious candidates for jobs in public relations because they are trained in the use of words and to have an enquiring attitude of mind. However not all journalists happily accept the disciplines of public relations, which are different from their own. For instance, they plan both their days and their years in different ways, and often find the transition from one method to the other difficult to achieve. In some ways, the best journalistic training for public relations work is free-lancing. A successful free-lance can see several ways of presenting the same story, and thus make it interesting to a range of publications. A public relations man is usually telling the same basic story (X is a company making good products which it sells at fair prices and it treats its shareholders and employees well). He can find it professionally profitable to think like a free-lance journalist.

Given the three basic qualities mentioned earlier (and the desire to channel them effectively by acquiring qualifications) a public relations man can enter the business from almost any background, although experience elsewhere in the communication business is obviously valuable. He will find that he needs to be able to adapt quickly to new situations (or quickly enough to recognize old situations in new disguises), to have an enquiring mind and catholic interests, and certainly the ability to handle people. Many would-be public relations men list as one of their assets the fact that they like meeting people. This is irrelevant. Meeting people is an agreeable social habit, but the practice of public relations is too serious to depend on a facility to make entertaining conversation over a drink.

Public relations is a demanding pursuit. It does not go with clock-watching or dilettante amateurism. It is a rewarding calling for people who are prepared to work hard, people who remember that they can go on learning for as long as they are working, and people who recognize that there is always more to be done.

Looking to the future, it seems clear that public relations is a growth industry. While it will always need new entrants who are mature and widely experienced, it will increasingly offer career opportunities to young people possessing the characteristics already described. But they must also be willing to study.

Like all professional bodies, The Institute of Public Relations has membership qualifying examinations. The diploma in public relations consists of Part I and Part II.

Normally Part I will be taken at around 23 or 24 years of age and after one or two years' practical experience. Success in Part I enables the student to apply for associate membership. Part II, which includes a thesis, will normally be taken two or three years later. Success in Part II qualifies the student for full membership.

There are several routes to the diploma. Holders of a degree from a British university and holders of the Higher National Diploma in Business Studies may sit Part I after one year's experience in public relations.

To meet the needs of the many young people who go straight from A-levels into full-time jobs, the Department of Education and Science has recently approved public relations as an optional second-year subject for the Higher National Certificate in Business Studies. Candidates holding the HNC (PR option) are exempt from Part I, and provided they have not less than three years' experience in public relations, may proceed direct to Part II.

It should be noted that, although success in diploma Part II qualifies the student for full membership of the Institute, the minimum age at which this is granted is 28.

Students intending to work for the HNC (PR) qualification should register with the Institute as student members so that they can take advantage of the IPR student workshops and other helpful activities. They are also advised to find out, at the time of registration, which of the non-vocational subjects the Institute recommends for their first-year business studies programme.

Broadly speaking, the pre-diploma studies (of whichever type) are expected to train the student to think analytically in a wide variety of situations. The diploma, combined, as it must be, with minimum practical experience requirements, provides the specialized knowledge of public relations and training in the techniques of professional practice.

Public relations is rewarding because of its creative scope and because new challenges have constantly to be accepted and successfully met. And public relations is a business which offers a career to both men and women. Although there is still a tendency for men to command higher salaries, the gap is becoming narrower. Women with the right qualities can find jobs as easily as men and their future is as bright.

10.2 SOURCES OF INFORMATION

The public relations man is faced constantly with the need to find information: statistics, opinions, facts, background, dates, lists of left-handed schoolgirls, and so on. He needs only to remember two things: somebody somewhere has the information he needs, but finding them may take a great deal of persistence.

Some information is easy to discover. There are many organizations which exist to provide it. On the other hand, some information is not readily available, and finding it may mean going from one person to another. Some information comes from the most unlikely sources. Few people will refuse to give information, provided it is not confidential.

A public relations man should build up his own list of sources and contacts. This will include trade associations, trade papers (most are helpful, but they should not be pestered), trade or professional people relevant to his interests, and a host of others.

He will receive direct-mail shots from companies offering all kinds of services. He should keep the essential details. He will read about new services, equipment, organizations, and the like; he should make a note of them.

A contact book of this kind will answer many of his regular needs, but problems will still arise when he is required to find information unusual to him.

The *Daily Telegraph* Information Bureau is a first-class organization which will answer most questions or lead the enquirer to another source. It operates Mondays to Fridays between 10 a.m. and 5 p.m. The list of members of The Institute of Public Relations contains the names of many people who exist to provide information; it is surprising how often this obvious source is overlooked. The list is free to members, but can also be bought from the Institute, at 20–26 Lamb's Conduit Street, London W.C.1. The Board of Trade, Victoria Street, London S.W.1, can supply trade information and much useful guidance, as can all ministries and government organizations, such as the British National Export Council.

In this context, a valuable reference book is *Business Efficiency: An ABC of Advisory Services,* produced by the National Economic Development Office, and published by the Stationery Office (available either from NEDO, Millbank Tower, 21–41 Millbank, London S.W.1, or from HMSO, 49 High Holborn, London W.C.1). This book gives details of the information and services available from a wide list of organizations, including ministries, government-sponsored bodies, universities, trade and professional associations, and the like.

It is wise to sit and think for a minute before going out to seek information. Trade promotion bodies, the embassies of foreign governments, local authorities, social service organizations, the local reference library, even telephone directories, are all sources to consider before approaching any organization: the public relations man should make sure that he has taken the obvious steps. Nobody appreciates having their time wasted and if information is readily available in printed form in standard reference works the public relations man should be able to find it for himself.

Somebody somewhere has the information needed and is

prepared to impart it. Presented with the problem of finding out who it is, the public relations man does well to remember the old saw: 'If at first you don't succeed, try, try, try again'.

There are a number of organizations with whose aims, objects, and work the public relations man should be especially familiar, since they impinge on him closely. They include:

Advertising Standards Authority
5 Clements Inn, London, W.C.2

Advertising Association
1 Bell Yard, London, W.C.2

British Association of Industrial Editors
17 Church Road, London, S.W.13

British Federation of Master Printers
11 Bedford Row, London, W.C.1

British Institute of Management
Management House, Parker Street, London, W.C.2

British Standards Institution
2 Park Street, London, W1Y 4AA

Commonwealth Correspondents' Association
3 Salisbury Court, London, E.C.4

Commonwealth Press Union
154 Fleet Street, London, E.C.4

Confederation of British Industry
21 Tothill Street, London, S.W.1

Council of Industrial Design
28 Haymarket, London, S.W.1

Foreign Press Association
11 Carlton House Terrace, London, S.W.1

Guild of British Newspaper Editors
Whitefriars House, Carmelite Street, London, E.C.4

Incorporated Society of British Advertisers
45 Hertford Street, London, W1Y 8DJ

Independent Television Companies' Association Ltd
52 Mortimer Street, London, W1N 8AN

Industrial Society
  48 Bryanston Square, London, W1H 8AH

Institute of Directors
  10 Belgrave Square, London, S.W.1

Institute of Journalists
  2 Tudor Street, London, E.C.4

Institute of Personnel Management
  5 Winsley Street, London, W1N 7AQ

Institute of Practitioners in Advertising
  44 Belgrave Square, London, S.W.1

International Public Relations Association
  4 Syngrou Avenue, Athens 403, Greece

Management Consultants' Association
  23–24 Cromwell Place, London, S.W.7

Market Research Society
  39 Hertford Street, London, W1Y 8EP

National Union of Journalists
  Acorn House, 314 Grays Inn Road, London, W.C.1

Newspaper Publishers' Association
  8 Bouverie Street, London, E.C.4

Newspaper Society
  Whitefriars House, 6 Carmelite Street, London, E.C.4

Periodical Proprietors' Association
  Imperial House, Kingsway, London, W.C.2

Trades Union Congress
  23–28 Great Russell Street, London, W.C.1.

In addition, there is the European Centre of Public Relations, CERP—which acts as a platform where public relations people from eight European countries can discuss their profession. It is a grouping of national bodies, formed in 1959. Its aims are carried out by three working parties, CEDAN, CEDET, and CEDAP.

CEDAN is the European Conference of National Public Relations Associations, and is in charge of the co-ordination of the activities of the national bodies to reach agreement on professional principles, ethics, and practice.

CEDET is the European Study Group for Public Relations and Communications Techniques, and is a forum for the exchange of views between specialists who practise in various professions but are all interested in humanistic studies and information.

CEDAP is the European Committee for the Application and Development of Public Relations, and is composed exclusively of professionals in public relations in a personal capacity: senior advisers, directors, and associates of public relations agencies.

Information about CERP and its working parties is available from the General Secretary, M. Alfred de la Motte, 10 Quai Paul Doumier, 92 Courbevoie, France.

11

A Basic Library

MOST BIBLIOGRAPHIES are too long. The list that follows is not intended to be exhaustive. It is intended to give a basic library of books that every public relations man should own. Most of them contain their own lists of further reading so that deeper knowledge can be obtained of any one subject.

In addition to these, however, a public relations man should be familiar with standard reference books, most of which are listed in section 4.36 in this book dealing with the organization of a press office. The public relations man must also be familiar with the contents of his local reference library, where he can usually find a great deal of up-to-date information that will help him in his job and the pursuit of his career.

Advertising: A General Introduction, Robert S. Caplin (Business Publications, 1967).

The Complete Plain Words, Sir Ernest Gowers (HMSO, 1957).

Dangerous Estate, Francis Williams (Arrow Books, 1959).

Essential Law for Journalists, L. C. J. McNae (Staples Press, 1967).

The Handbook of Public Relations, edited by Nigel Ellis and Pat Bowman (Harrap, 1963).

Hidden Persuaders, Vance Packard (Penguin, 1960).

The Nature of Public Relations, John E. Marston (McGraw-Hill, 1963).

Newspaper Design, G. Allen Hutt (Oxford University Press, 1967).

The Practice of Journalism, edited by John Dodge and George Viner (Heinemann, 1963).

Public Relations in Business Management, James Derriman (University of London Press, 1964).

Doing It In Style, Leslie Sellers (Pergamon, 1968).

The Simple Subs Book, Leslie Sellers (Pergamon, 1968).

Headlines All My Life, Arthur Christiansen (Heinemann, 1961).

Publish and be Damned, Hugh Cudlipp (Dakers, 1953).

Practical Newspaper Reporting, Geoffrey Harris and David Spark (Heinemann, 1966).

The House of Commons at Work, Eric Taylor (Penguin, 1961).

Modern Market Research, Max K. Adler (Crosby Lockwood, 1956).

The Structure of Local Government in England and Wales, W. Eric Jackson (Longmans Green, 1949).

How the City Works, Sir Oscar Hobson (Dickens Press, 1966).

Company–Investor Relations, James Derriman (Oxford University Press, 1969).

Teach Yourself Public Relations, Herbert Lloyd (EUP, 1963).

Industrial Editing, Bernard W. Smith (Pitman, 1961).

House Journals and Company Publications, John Hazzlewood (Studio Vista, 1963).

Public Relations and Management, David Finn (Chapman and Hall, 1960).

Conference Planning and Administration, O. K. Skelley (Industrial Society, 1966).

Style for Print, R. A. Hewitt (Blandford, 1957).

ABC of Film and TV Working Terms, Oswald Skilbeck (Focal Press, 1960).

International Public Relations Encyclopaedia, Peter Biddlecombe (Grant Helm, 1968).

Fund-raising Techniques, E. Hereward Phillips (Business Book Centre, 1969).

Industrial Publicity Management, W. Paterson (Business Book Centre, 1968).

Appendix

THIS CODE defines and implements paragraph 3 (*a*) (ii) of the Memorandum of The Institute of Public Relations under the heading 'Objects', namely 'to encourage and foster the observance of high professional standards by its members and to establish and prescribe such standards'. Public relations is concerned with the effect of conduct on reputation. The following principles have been laid down to embody this concept and enhance relations between the Institute's members and the public to whom they are directly or indirectly responsible in the performance of their duties.

1. A member shall conduct his professional activities with respect for the public interest.
2. A member shall at all times deal fairly and honestly with his client or employers past and present, with his fellow members, and with the general public.
3. A member shall not intentionally disseminate false or misleading information, and shall use proper care to avoid doing so. He has a positive duty to maintain truth, accuracy, and good taste.
4. A member shall not engage in any practice which tends to corrupt the integrity of channels of public communication.
5. A member shall not create or make use of any organization purporting to serve some announced cause but actually promoting a special or private interest of a member or his client or his employer which is not apparent.
6. A member shall safeguard the confidences of both present and former clients or employers. He shall not disclose except upon the order of a court of competent jurisdiction any confidential information which he may have obtained in his official capacity without securing and making known the consent of the said client or employer.

7. A member shall not represent conflicting or competing interests without the express consent of those concerned given after full disclosure of the facts.

8. A member in performing services for a client or employer shall not accept fees, commissions or any other valuable consideration in connection with those services from anyone other than his client or employer unless such practice is acceptable to the client or employer.

9. A member shall not cause or allow to be done anything for the purpose of touting or advertising calculated to attract business unfairly.

10. A member shall not propose to a prospective client or employer that his fee or other compensation be contingent on the achievement of certain results; nor shall he enter into any fee agreement to the same effect.

11. A member shall not intentionally injure the professional reputation or practice of another member, but if such a member has evidence that another member has been guilty of unethical, illegal or unfair practices it shall be his duty to inform the Institute in accordance with the Memorandum and Articles.

12. A member shall not engage in or be connected with any occupation or business which, in the opinion of the Council, is not consistent with membership of the Institute.

13. A member shall not seek to supplant another member with his employer or client, nor shall he encroach upon the professional employment of another member unless both parties are assured that there is no conflict of interest involved, and are kept advised of the negotiations.

14. A member shall co-operate with fellow members in upholding and enforcing this Code.

Index

Public relations–*cont.*
  ethics of, 24–8
  fund-raising and, 218–25
  international, 225–31
  need for today, 6–10
  political and governmental, 231–8
  programmes, 33–8
  research, 38–44
  with the community, 191–9
  with the customer, 199–205
  with the dealer, 205–11
  with the employee, 252–8
  with the shareholder, 211–18
Public Relations News, 3
Public relations officer, 12
  advertising related to, 259–66
  community relations and, 193
  conferences and, 252–8
  consultant, 16
  costs and, 19
  'creative' and 'passive', 16–17
  customer relations and, 200–1, 203, 204
  dealer relations and, 206–7, 209, 210, 211
  dealing with journalists, 95–104
  direct mail and, 58–9
  employee relations and, 240, 241, 249, 251–2
  ethics and, 26–7
  exhibitions and, 156–65
  films and, 137–49
  fund-raising and, 219, 220, 221, 224, 225
  house style and, 166–74
  importance of objectivity to, 31–2, 33
  international, 225–31
  keeping a photo library, 135, 136
  photography and, 128–37
  place of, 14–15
  political and governmental PR and, 231–8
  preparing letters to the editor for, 92–3
  press relations and, 67–8, 69, 80, 81, 82, 91–2

print and design for, 115–27
promotions and, 183, 184, 185
qualities required by, 269
radio and, 175–82
relations with MPs, 234–8
shareholder relations and, 212–13
sponsored events and, 183, 185–90
television and, 149–56
work of, 13–14
writing PR material for the press, 82–95

RAC Handbook, 111
Radio, 175–82
  speech training for, 180–1
  See also British Broadcasting Corporation
Research, PR, 38–44
  costs of, 42
  language of, 42–3
  sampling, 40, 41
  surveys, 39
Reuters, 72
Robinson, Prof Edward J., 1, 4
Rotaprint machines, 122
Royal Institute of British Architects, 190

Sampling, 40, 41
Scottish Daily Express, 69
Scottish Office, 232
Shareholder relations, 211–18
  annual meeting and, 215–16
  annual report and, 214
  company secretary and, 213, 218
  courtesy and, 217–18
  rights of shareholders, 212, 213
  visits to company, 216–17
Shell company, 172
Smith, Paul I. Slee, 2
Society of Industrial Artists, 169
Sound Services Ltd, 147
Sponsored events, 183, 185–90
  costs of, 185–6, 187
  field of sponsorship, 189